The Official
Arsenal
Book of
Records

First published in 2013. Second edition 2015

Copyright © Carlton Books Limited 2013, 2015

A CIP catalogue record for this book is available from the British Library.

Carlton Books Limited, 20 Mortimer Street, London W1T 3JW

ISBN: 978-1-78097-668-6

Editor: Martin Corteel
Art Director: Luke Griffin
Designer: Darren Jordan
Picture Research: Paul Langan
Production: Rachel Burgess

Printed in Dubai

ABOVE & RIGHT: Emirates Stadium, which opened in 2006.

The Official
Arsenal
Book of
Records

SECOND EDITION

Iain Spragg

CARLTON
BOOKS

Contents

ALL PICTURES, FROM LEFT TO RIGHT: Patrick Vieira with the FA Cup in 2005; Arsene Wenger; celebrations after winning the 1994 European Cup Winners' Cup; Ted Drake in action in 1935; Thierry Henry during the 2005–06 season; David O'Leary with the Division One trophy in 1991; Tony Adams lifts the Premier League trophy.

Introduction

One of the most famous and successful sides in English football, Arsenal is a club with a proud and illustrious history. From embryonic days as Royal Arsenal in south-east London in the 1880s to the modern era and life at the magnificent Emirates, the Gunners have been synonymous with both style and silverware.

Founded by workers at the Royal Arsenal factory in Woolwich back in 1886, the Gunners turned professional five years later and in September 1893 the Club broke new ground when it played its first-ever game in the Football League, a 2–2 draw with Newcastle United at the Manor Ground in the old Second Division.

It was the beginning of a remarkable footballing story and, in the 120 years since the Club began its transformation from fledgling league newcomers to one of the biggest clubs in Europe, Arsenal have lifted trophies with a reassuring regularity.

The 1930 FA Cup was the first to grace the Highbury trophy cabinet and 12 months later they were crowned Division One champions for the first time. Since then the Gunners have amassed 27 more major honours, including a record three League and FA Cup doubles, to underline the Club's pedigree as an undisputed thoroughbred of the English game.

Many of football's most legendary players and managers have forged their reputations with Arsenal and from the early days of Herbert Chapman and Cliff Bastin in the 1930s, Bertie Mee and Frank McLintock in the 1970s, through George Graham and Tony Adams in the 1980s and 1990s and Arsene Wenger and the Invincibles in the Premier League era, the Gunners have always been a major force.

This book charts the collective and individual achievements of those who have pulled on the famous red and white shirt since 1893, and is the most comprehensive guide available to the Club's player and team records and managerial milestones.

The book also celebrates the most iconic players and coaches to have been associated with the Gunners over more than a century of domestic and European titles and triumphs, providing a definitive and invaluable guide to the rise of one of football's greatest and most popular teams.

RIGHT: Arsene Wenger celebrates winning the 2003–04 Premier League title on the pitch at Highbury.

PART 1
Team Records

Over the years the Gunners have boasted countless outstanding individual players but football remains a team game and this opening chapter is all about the greatest collective achievements in the Club's long and glorious history.

Including matches played in the Premier League, the Football League, FA and League Cups and Europe, the section details the Club's all-time team records from 1893 to the present day.

From their dazzling 26–1 demolition of a hapless Paris XI side in a friendly early in the 20th century to their biggest-ever success in the League Cup in 1979, Arsenal have regularly raised the bar in front of goal and all their biggest wins are included in the pages that follow.

This chapter also focuses on the side's longest unbeaten sequences in all competitions, their fantastic winning streaks, highest points totals in a single season and the team's best defensive campaigns as the Gunners have emerged as a powerhouse in English football.

Triumph, however, cannot come without the occasional tear – so there are also details of Arsenal's worst-ever defeats in both league and cup competition, as well as the side's longest runs without tasting victory and the Gunners' worst campaigns in terms of goals conceded and points amassed.

ABOVE: Bertie Mee in 1971 with the Division One trophy and FA Cup – the famous double.

RIGHT: Frank McLintock captained the Gunners to the double in 1970–71.

OPPOSITE: The Arsenal team parade the FA Cup and Division One trophy through the streets of Islington.

All-Time Records

In this section the focus is on the Gunners' most comprehensive wins and defeats in the Football League, FA Cup and League Cup, as well as the side's friendly fixtures. The Club's longest victorious streaks, losing sequences and most prolonged series of draws are also included.

BELOW: Michael Thomas (right) scores in injury time at Anfield to win the 1988–89 Division One title.

All-Time Records – Biggest Wins

PARISIANS HUMBLED

Arsenal's recent French connection – since Arsene Wenger's arrival in London in 1996 – is well documented. But more than a century ago there was a distinct lack of Anglo-French camaraderie when the Gunners faced a Paris XI at the Manor Ground in Plumstead.

The 1904 match was no more than a friendly, with the Gunners fielding a team bolstered by reserve players. But the Parisians clearly didn't travel well and Arsenal romped to a stunning 26–1 triumph, the most comprehensive victory in the Club's history.

Arsenal were 8–1 to the good at half-time but really cut loose in the second 45 minutes with 18 more strikes – and legend has it that the French side's only goal came when Gunners goalkeeper Jimmy Ashcroft took pity on the hapless visitors, kicked the ball to the opposition and allowed them to score.

Inside-forward Robert Watson was top scorer with seven, but his exploits were not enough to secure a long-term future with the Club. In July the following year he was sold to Leeds United after making just 10 competitive appearances for the Gunners.

ASHFORD ANNIHILATED

The FA Cup has proved a happy hunting ground for Arsenal over the years and back in October 1893 the competition pitted the Gunners against Ashford United in the first qualifying round.

To describe the contest as one-sided would be an understatement. When the final whistle sounded – much to the delight of the beleaguered Ashford players – Arsenal had found the back of the net a dozen times for a record-breaking 12–0 victory.

The game produced two hat-trick heroes with Scottish inside-forward James Henderson and English inside-left Arthur Elliott each recording a treble.

ABOVE: Striker Alan Sunderland scored 92 goals in 281 appearances for the Gunners.

LEFT: Jack Lambert was a major part of Arsenal's record win against Grimsby Town in the 1930–31 season.

◀ GRIMSBY TOWN DEMOLISHED

The old First Division was the pinnacle of English league football before the birth of the Premier League, and Arsenal's record triumph in the division came in the 1930–31 campaign when Grimsby Town were the visitors to Highbury.

Record signing David Jack did the damage with a superb four-goal salvo, while Jack Lambert scored a hat-trick and at full-time the Gunners were 9–1 winners.

▲ SEVENTH HEAVEN

The Gunners may not have lifted the League Cup in 1979–80 but it was the season in which they posted their biggest-ever win in the competition – a resounding 7–0 victory over Leeds United in September 1979.

A week earlier the first leg of the second-round tie at Elland Road had finished 1–1 but the 35,133 supporters who packed Highbury seven days later for the return match did not have to endure any second-leg nerves as the home side ran riot.

Striker Alan Sunderland led the way with a hat-trick while Liam Brady twice scored from the penalty spot and Terry Neill's team marched effortlessly into the next round.

LOUGHBOROUGH ROUT

The advent of the 20th century saw Arsenal playing in the old Second Division and in March 1900 they entertained Loughborough Town in the capital in a clash that would see the Gunners rewrite the record books.

Loughborough were in the midst of a financial crisis so severe that most of their first team had already been sold to try to balance the books. Arsenal even had to help the club with their travel costs to get to London.

The Gunners' generosity, however, did not extend to the pitch. Harry Bradshaw's side mercilessly put Loughborough to the sword, running out 12–0 winners to register the Club's biggest-ever victory in league football.

Yorkshireman Ralph Gaudie helped himself to a hat-trick, a haul that saw the prolific centre-forward finish as Arsenal's top scorer that season, with 15 goals in 25 league appearances.

► DRAKE DOMINANT IN BIRMINGHAM

Home advantage can often prove decisive but Arsenal made a mockery of that theory in December 1935 when they played Aston Villa at Villa Park, racing to a 7–1 success and the Club's largest-ever league victory on the road courtesy of seven goals from Gunners legend Ted Drake.

RIGHT: Ted Drake made history with his superb seven-goal salvo against Aston Villa.

▲ GUNNERS AT THE LANE

The Second World War played havoc with the football calendar, but despite the widespread disruption there were still some friendly games on offer to distract people from the hostilities.

One such match saw Arsenal play Clapton Orient. Bizarrely, the game took place at White Hart Lane, but the unfamiliar surroundings obviously didn't unsettle the Gunners players and they stormed to a 15–2 win.

The undisputed Man of the Match was Leslie Compton, who was a centre-half by trade but, pressed into emergency service as a centre-forward on the day, scored 10 of the 15 goals.

Sadly, as the game was not classed a competitive fixture, his remarkable tally could not be included in his official career statistics and when he left Arsenal in 1952, his record amounted to a rather more modest six goals in 273 appearances.

ABOVE: Leslie Compton reached double figures in a friendly against Clapton Orient in a match played at White Hart Lane during the Second World War.

ARSENAL'S FOOTBALL LEAGUE RECORD 1893–1913

Division Two

	P	W	D	L	F	A	PTS	POS
1893–94	28	12	4	12	52	55	28	9th
1894–95	30	14	6	10	75	58	34	8th
1895–96	30	14	4	12	59	42	32	7th
1896–97	30	13	4	13	68	70	30	10th
1897–98	30	16	5	9	69	49	37	5th
1898–99	34	18	5	11	72	41	41	7th
1899–1900	34	16	4	14	61	43	36	8th
1900–01	34	15	6	13	39	35	36	7th
1901–02	34	18	6	10	50	26	42	4th
1902–03	34	20	8	6	66	30	48	3rd
1903–04	34	21	7	6	91	22	49	2nd

Division One

	P	W	D	L	F	A	PTS	POS
1904–05	34	12	9	13	36	40	33	10th
1905–06	38	15	7	16	62	64	37	12th
1906–07	38	20	4	14	66	59	44	7th
1907–08	38	12	12	14	51	63	36	15th
1908–09	38	14	10	14	52	49	38	6th
1909–10	38	11	9	18	37	67	31	18th
1910–11	38	13	12	13	41	49	38	10th
1911–12	38	15	8	15	55	59	38	10th
1912–13	38	3	12	23	26	74	18	20th

All-Time Records – Biggest Defeats

AGONY AT THE ATHLETIC GROUND

The Gunners may have enjoyed their record Football League victory against Loughborough Town in March 1900 – a 12–0 success – but it was against the same opposition nearly four years earlier that the Club also suffered its most humbling league defeat.

The old Second Division clash in December 1896 was held at the home side's Athletic Ground and it was to prove a truly miserable 90 minutes for the visitors as Loughborough scored eight times without reply. The final 8–0 scoreline, however, could have been even worse for Arsenal were it not for the referee disallowing two further goals for the home side.

"The Arsenal never gave up," read the match report in the local Loughborough newspaper, "the forwards exerting themselves to the end. Their half-backs were pretty good and so were the forwards,

but the backs were weak and the custodian had scarcely any chance with the shots that scored."

The most dejected of the Gunners XI must surely have been the custodian in question – Arthur Talbot, who was playing only his second league game for the Club. Three more league appearances followed but, with memories still fresh from the eight-goal demolition, Talbot was released at the end of the season.

At least the travelling Arsenal support had reason to be more cheerful, however, when it was announced the Club would refund the cost of their match tickets as a gesture of apology for the team's performance.

SIX-GOAL MISERY

Arsenal's exploits in the FA Cup have provided many golden moments in the Club's history but on three separate occasions the team has fallen to record 6–0 defeats in the game's oldest knockout competition.

The first came in the third round in January 1893 when they were ambushed by Sunderland at Newcastle Road. They succumbed to the same scoreline six years later at the same stage of the tournament at home against Derby County.

The Club's most recent 6–0 FA Cup reverse was also in the third round when West Ham United proved too strong at Upton Park in January 1946.

▶ CUP MAULING

Arsene Wenger is renowned for fielding experimental sides in the League Cup but his decision to name what was effectively a reserve team for a fourth-round meeting with Chelsea at Highbury in 1998 was not his finest hour.

The visitors had established a slender 1–0 advantage at the break courtesy of a Frank Leboeuf penalty, but the Gunners' second-half fightback failed to materialize as Chelsea took complete control with a brace from Gianluca Vialli, a Nelson Vivas own goal and a fifth from Gus Poyet to inflict Arsenal's heaviest-ever defeat in the competition.

RIGHT: The Gunners suffered a shock 5–0 defeat against Chelsea in the 1998–99 League Cup.

LIVERPOOL VICTORIOUS

Arsenal and Liverpool have produced some epic encounters over the decades but the Division Two clash between the two in October 1893 was one to forget, from the Gunners' perspective, with the game at the Manor Ground finishing 5–0 to the Merseysiders. It remains Arsenal's joint worst league defeat at home.

ABOVE: Arsenal take on Liverpool during the 1905–06 season.

TERRIERS TRIUMPHANT

The Gunners were ever-present in the old First Division between 1919 and 1992 and while the Club's 73-year unbroken stay in the top-flight brought 10 title triumphs, there were also setbacks.

Perhaps the most sobering was when they faced defending champions Huddersfield Town at Highbury in February 1925 and found themselves on the wrong end of a 5–0 scoreline – the Club's worst top-flight defeat at home.

The Terriers went on to win the league that year for a second successive season, but Arsenal had their revenge at Highbury 14 months later in the shape of a 3–1 victory.

LEAKY DEFENCE

Arsenal are no strangers to scoring seven but they have also conceded seven away from home in the league four times in their history.

They suffered their first 7–0 reverse against Blackburn Rovers at Ewood Park in October 1909 and their defence was again breached seven times without reply at the Hawthorns against West Bromwich Albion in October 1922.

Newcastle United emerged 7–0 winners against the Gunners at St James' Park three years later while the Club's most recent seven-goal demolition came against West Ham United at the Boleyn Ground in March 1927.

ARSENAL'S FOOTBALL LEAGUE RECORD 1913–39

Division Two

	P	W	D	L	F	A	PTS	POS
1913–14	38	20	9	9	54	38	49	3rd
1914–15	38	19	5	14	69	41	43	5th

Division One

	P	W	D	L	F	A	PTS	POS
1919–20	42	15	12	15	56	58	42	10th
1920–21	42	15	14	13	59	63	44	9th
1921–22	42	15	7	20	47	56	37	17th
1922–23	42	16	10	16	61	62	42	11th
1923–24	42	12	9	21	40	63	33	19th
1924–25	42	14	5	23	46	58	33	20th
1925–26	42	22	8	12	87	63	52	2nd
1926–27	42	17	9	16	77	86	43	11th
1927–28	42	13	15	14	82	86	41	10th
1928–29	42	16	13	13	77	72	45	9th
1929–30	42	14	11	17	78	66	39	14th
1930–31	42	28	10	4	127	59	66	1st
1931–32	42	22	10	10	90	48	54	2nd
1932–33	42	25	8	9	118	61	58	1st
1933–34	42	25	9	8	75	47	59	1st
1934–35	42	23	12	7	115	46	58	1st
1935–36	42	15	15	12	78	48	45	6th
1936–37	42	18	16	8	80	49	52	3rd
1937–38	42	21	10	11	77	44	52	1st
1938–39	42	19	9	14	55	41	47	5th

All-Time Records – Winning Sequences

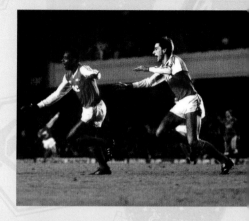

BELOW: Michael Thomas celebrates after scoring, this time against Everton, during the 1987–88 campaign.

▶ FOURTEEN VICTORIES

The ability to string together a sustained sequence of victories is the hallmark of a great side and during the 1987–88 season the Gunners proved their pedigree with 14 wins in succession to set a new Club record.

The incredible run began in mid-September when an Alan Smith goal gave Arsenal a 1–0 victory over Nottingham Forest at the City Ground in the old First Division. Wimbledon were despatched 3–0 at Highbury the following Saturday and, when Doncaster were defeated by the same scoreline in a second-round, first-leg League Cup clash at Belle Vue, George Graham's side were gathering momentum.

West Ham, Charlton, Doncaster and Oxford United were all beaten before Arsenal faced arch-rivals Tottenham at White Hart Lane in mid-October. There, courtesy of goals from Michael Thomas and David Rocastle, the Gunners came away with a priceless 2–1 victory and an eighth win in eight.

Defeats of Derby, Bournemouth in the League Cup, Newcastle, Chelsea and Norwich followed and the superb run climaxed with a fourth-round League Cup clash with Stoke at Highbury in November. Goals from David O'Leary, Rocastle and Kevin Richardson sealed the 3–0 triumph that set the new milestone.

The sequence featured 10 Division One wins and four in the early stages of the League Cup, also making it Arsenal's most successful series of Football League victories.

RIGHT: Aaron Ramsey was on target in a 2–1 victory at Swansea City in September 2013, the Gunners' record eighth successive away win.

◀ ON THE ROAD

A win away from home can be frustratingly hard to come by, but the Gunners were in prolific form away from the Emirates in 2013, recording nine conscutive victories on the road to set a new Club record for the most top-flight league wins on the bounce.

Arsenal's previous best run had come in 1977 in the First Division, with six successes, but they surpassed that milestone at the end of the 2012–13 and beginning of the 2013–14 campaigns. The magnificent sequence began in March 2013 with a 2–0 victory over Swansea. Victories over West Bromwich Albion, Fulham and QPR followed before Arsene Wenger's team ended their season with a 1–0 win at Newcastle.

The Gunners continued the superb run in 2013–14 with a 3–1 defeat of Fulham in August to make it six in succession. Sunderland and Swansea were subsequently beaten (3–1 and 2–1 respectively) to make it eight away wins from eight. The winning sequence finally came to an end when they drew 1–1 with West Bromwich Albion at the Hawthorns on 6 October 2013.

MARVELLOUS MANOR GROUND

Arsenal were in sensational form in 1903–04. As well as winning their first eight games, the side also registered 15 league wins on the bounce at home for the Club's most-successful-ever sequence in the Football League.

The first four wins came in the initial eight-match run and, although that came to an end, the Gunners remained indomitable at the old Manor Ground in Plumstead and reeled off 11 more victories between November 1903 and April 1904.

The all-conquering run saw Arsenal score 67 times and concede just four times. Of the 15 defeated sides, only Bradford (4–1), Stockport (5–2) and Glossop (2–1) were able to find the back of the Gunners' net.

BELOW: Malcolm Macdonald scored 57 times for the Gunners during his three-season spell with the Club.

ARSENAL'S FOOTBALL LEAGUE RECORD 1946–59
Division One

	P	W	D	L	F	A	PTS	POS
1946–47	42	16	9	17	72	70	41	13th
1947–48	42	23	13	6	81	32	59	1st
1948–49	42	18	13	11	74	44	49	5th
1949–50	42	19	11	12	79	55	49	6th
1950–51	42	19	9	14	73	56	47	5th
1951–52	42	21	11	10	80	61	53	3rd
1952–53	42	21	12	9	97	64	54	1st
1953–54	42	15	13	14	75	73	43	12th
1954–55	42	17	9	16	69	63	43	9th
1955–56	42	18	10	14	60	61	46	5th
1956–57	42	21	8	13	85	69	50	5th
1957–58	42	16	7	19	73	85	39	12th
1958–59	42	21	8	13	88	68	50	3rd

▼
RECORD START TO NEW SEASON

The 1903–04 season saw Arsenal finish as Division Two runners-up to Preston North End and earn promotion to the top-flight of English football for the first time. But manager Harry Bradshaw may have been disappointed not to have won the title after the sensational start his side made to their campaign.

The Gunners began the season with a 3–0 win over Blackpool at the Manor Ground in September thanks to a brace from the prolific Bill Gooing – and in their next four league games they beat Gainsborough, Burton United, Bristol City and Manchester United without conceding a goal.

In October the Arsenal defence was finally breached when they faced Glossop away from home but another brace from Gooing was enough to seal a 3–1 victory. The unbeaten run continued a fortnight later after a 3–2 win against Port Vale at the Athletic Ground.

The side made it eight from eight just 48 hours later when they demolished Leicester Fosse 8–0 in London courtesy of a hat-trick from Irish inside-forward Tommy Shanks. Although the run finally came to an end at the end of October when Barnsley ran out 2–1 winners at Oakwell, the sequence remains the Gunners' most successful start to a Football League season in terms of victories.

In total, Arsenal conceded just three goals and scored 35 during their irresistible spell with Gooing top-scoring with nine.

ABOVE: Arsenal's 1903–04 promotion winning team, who won their first eight games of the season, a Club record in terms of victories.

All-Time Records – Undefeated Records

▼ HOME SWEET HOME

Highbury was famous as a fortress for the Gunners but its predecessor – the Manor Ground in Plumstead – was also an intimidating venue for visiting teams. It was here that Arsenal set a Club record of 33 home games unbeaten in the Football League at the start of the 20th century.

The streak started in November 1902 when Manchester City were beaten 1–0 in the old Division Two and by the time Aston Villa lost 1–0 in Plumstead in October 1904, courtesy of a Bill Gooing goal, Arsenal had strung together a sensational 33 home league games without defeat. The Gunners completed the entire 1903–04 season without losing at the Manor Ground to earn promotion to the old First Division for the first time, but the step up in standard was to ultimately end the sequence when they faced Nottingham Forest and were 3–0 losers.

The run featured 28 wins in 33 fixtures and the side kept a total of 23 clean sheets. More remarkably, however, Arsenal scored a grand total of 105 goals in the process and only let in 11.

BRILLIANT BACK FOUR

By definition, a clean sheet means a team cannot lose, and unsurprisingly the Arsenal Club record in the Football League for not conceding at home was set during the side's 33-match unbeaten record.

Their first clean sheet was recorded in April of the 1902–03 campaign when Chesterfield were beaten 3–0. By the time the same opposition was demolished 6–0 at the same venue in November of the 1903–04 season, the Gunners had gone eight games at the Manor Ground without their defence being breached.

LEFT: The Arsenal team of 1903–04. They never lost at the Manor Ground that season.

BELOW: Sweden midfielder Anders Limpar was part of Arsenal's 13-game unbeaten away run.

▶ LUCKY THIRTEEN

The Gunners' unbeaten streak that spanned the 1989–90 and 1990–91 seasons also saw the side set a new Club record of 13 Football League games away from home without defeat.

The 2–2 stalemate with Norwich at Carrow Road in May 1990 was the catalyst, and over the next nine months Arsenal travelled 12 more times in the league and each time came home with at least a point.

The highlight of the run was a 1–0 victory over Manchester United at Old Trafford in October, thanks to an Anders Limpar goal, while the final game in the sequence saw the side held to a goalless draw by Spurs at White Hart Lane before a defeat by Chelsea at Stamford Bridge.

GRAHAM'S SIDE SPARKLE

George Graham's Arsenal were crowned Division One champions at the end of a dominant 1990–91 campaign and it was little surprise the Scot's team walked away with the silverware after a superb season in which they registered a Club-record 26-match unbeaten run in the Football League.

The sequence actually began in 1989–90 when the Gunners beat Millwall and Southampton and drew with Norwich in their final three fixtures of the campaign. They picked up where they had left off in August in 1990–91 with a convincing 3–0 victory over Wimbledon at Highbury. Arsenal were now firmly in their stride and in their next 13 matches they collected 31 from a possible 39 points to set the pace.

In early December, the team faced defending champions Liverpool at Highbury but any fears that the sequence might come to an abrupt end were dispelled with a resounding 3–0 win, the goals coming from Lee Dixon, Alan Smith and Paul Merson.

Three successive draws against Luton, Wimbledon and Aston Villa followed before the Gunners returned to winning ways – and when Everton were beaten in north London in January, courtesy of a Merson strike, the streak had reached an incredible 26 matches featuring 17 wins.

A 2–1 defeat in the London derby with Chelsea at Stamford Bridge a fortnight later was the end of the fairytale, but the sequence provided enough of a platform for Arsenal to dethrone Liverpool as champions by seven clear points.

ABOVE: Paul Merson scored 16 times for the Gunners in the 1990–91 campaign.

ABOVE: George Graham's 1990–91 side were unbeaten in 26 games.

CHAMPIONS ELECT

The Club's best-ever start to a Football League campaign in terms of unbeaten matches also came in the 1990–91 season as Arsenal posted a Club-record 23 games before they found themselves on the losing side.

It began with the 3–0 victory away to Wimbledon in August and climaxed with a 1–0 win at Highbury over Everton in January.

The streak featured three games in which the team hit four goals against the opposition. The first was the 4–1 mauling of Chelsea in September while a Smith brace and further goals from Merson and Limpar saw Southampton despatched 4–0 in November. In December Sheffield United were beaten at Highbury by the same scoreline, courtesy of another brace from Smith.

The Gunners won 15 of the 23 matches, scoring 42 goals and conceding just 10. They also kept 15 clean sheets, including six in a row from early October, and a 2–0 victory against Norwich, to mid-November and the side's demolition of Southampton.

ARSENAL'S FOOTBALL LEAGUE RECORD 1959–79
Division One

	P	W	D	L	F	A	PTS	POS
1959–60	42	15	9	18	68	80	39	13th
1960–61	42	15	11	16	77	85	41	11th
1961–62	42	16	11	15	71	72	43	10th
1962–63	42	18	10	14	86	77	46	7th
1963–64	42	17	11	14	90	82	45	8th
1964–65	42	17	7	18	69	75	41	13th
1965–66	42	12	13	17	62	75	37	14th
1966–67	42	16	14	12	58	47	46	7th
1967–68	42	17	10	15	60	56	44	9th
1968–69	42	22	12	8	56	27	56	4th
1969–70	42	12	18	12	51	49	42	12th
1970–71	42	29	7	6	71	29	65	1st
1971–72	42	22	8	12	58	40	52	5th
1972–73	42	23	11	8	57	43	57	2nd
1973–74	42	14	14	14	49	51	42	10th
1974–75	42	13	11	18	47	49	37	16th
1975–76	42	13	10	19	47	53	36	17th
1976–77	42	16	11	15	64	59	43	8th
1977–78	42	21	10	11	60	37	52	5th
1978–79	42	17	14	11	61	48	48	7th

All-Time Records – Miscellaneous

TWO-POINT MILESTONE

The three-points-for-a-win system was adopted by the Football League in 1981. But in the era of a modest two points for a victory, Arsenal set an enduring Club record in the 1930–31 season with an impressive tally of 66 from 42 games.

The Gunners won 28 times in the old First Division to claim the title for the first time and were beaten just four times, finishing with a goal difference of plus 68 and seven points clear of runners-up Aston Villa.

ABOVE: Arsenal were in prolific form in the 1930–31 season, registering well over a century of league goals – a record.

RECORD GOAL TALLY

The 1930–31 campaign was a remarkable season for Arsenal and, as well as registering a record 66-point haul, the team scored an incredible 127 league goals.

It's a milestone that is yet to be eclipsed and saw the Gunners average more than three goals per game en route to the silverware.

The highlights of the all-conquering season included a 7–1 thrashing of Blackpool, a 9–1 demolition of Grimsby courtesy of a four-goal salvo from David Jack, and a 5–0 victory against Bolton at Highbury on the final day of the season.

In total, the team scored 60 goals in their 21 away games that season – which is another record for the Club.

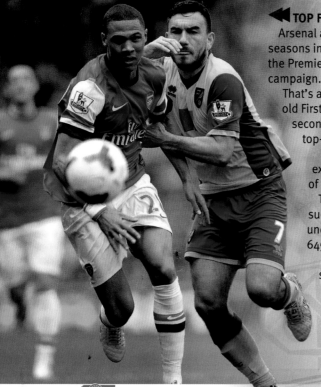

TOP FLIGHT MILESTONES

Arsenal are rapidly closing in on an unprecedented century of consecutive seasons in the highest division of the English game and their appearance in the Premier League in 2013–14 was the Club's 88th successive top-flight league campaign.

That's an ongoing record which began when they were promoted to the old First Division in 1919 and leaves the Gunners significantly ahead of the second best team, Everton, on the all-time list. The Toffees have played top-flight football for 60 consecutive seasons.

The 2013–14 campaign was also significant because it saw Arsenal extend their record for the most away wins in the league in the history of top-flight English football.

The 2012–13 campaign saw the Club overtake Liverpool as the most successful ever side on the road with 638 victories and their 11 wins under Arsene Wenger in 2013–14 meant that the Gunners had made it 649 in total.

The first of those 11 triumphs away from home came with a 3–1 success against Fulham at Craven Cottage in August and concluded with a 2–0 defeat of Norwich City at Carrow Road in May on the final day of the Premier League season

LEFT: Kieran Gibbs was part of the Arsenal XI which beat Norwich in May 2014, the Club's 649th top-flight league win on the road.

TWO THOUSAND AND COUNTING

When Arsenal beat Sunderland 2–0 in October 2014 at the Stadium of Light, the victory meant much more than simply collecting three points – it was the Gunners' 2,000th win in the club's long history of league football. The milestone triumph came courtesy of a brace from Alexis Sanchez.

It took the club 4,381 fixtures to reach the 2,000 victories following their maiden league game back in 1893, with 463 wins coming in the Premier League, 1,321 in the old Division One and 216 in Division Two. In those 4,381 games, the Gunners scored 7,344 goals and conceded 5,533. Arsenal's most prolific season in terms of victories came in 1970–71 when they won 29 times during the campaign.

Following their success at Sunderland, the team registered 19 more Premier League victories during the 2014–15 campaign to take the club's record to 2,019 league wins in 122 years, placing them third on the England football all-time list.

RIGHT: Alexis Sanchez scored both of the Gunners' goals in a 2–0 victory at Sunderland in October 2014; it was Arsenal's 2,000th win in league football.

FIRST LEAGUE SUCCESS

Arsenal may have been founded in 1886 but it was not until the 1893–94 season that the Gunners first sampled league football when the Club became the first southern side to play in the old Second Division.

The team began the historic campaign with a 2–2 draw against Newcastle United followed by a 3–2 defeat away to Notts County. But two days later – on 11 September 1893 – the Gunners despatched Walsall 4–0 courtesy of a hat-trick from Joseph Heath for the Club's first-ever league victory.

DREADFUL DEFENDING

Marshalled by the likes of Tony Adams, Lee Dixon and Nigel Winterburn, the Arsenal defence was famously miserly in the 1980s and 1990s but the same couldn't be said of the Gunners' back four in the 1926–27 Division One season when they conceded a record 86 times in 42 games.

The damage was done away from Highbury with 56 goals coming in their 21 matches on the road.

Arsenal, however, did not learn their lesson and in the 1927–28 campaign the side again let in 86 goals.

ABOVE: The Gunners side that played Cardiff in the 1927 FA Cup final with manager Herbert Chapman front right.

ARSENAL'S FOOTBALL LEAGUE RECORD 1979–92
Division One

	P	W	D	L	F	A	PTS	POS
1979–80	42	18	17	7	52	36	52	4th
1980–81	42	19	15	8	61	45	53	3rd
1981–82	42	20	11	11	48	37	71	5th
1982–83	42	16	10	16	58	56	58	10th
1983–84	42	18	9	15	74	60	63	6th
1984–85	42	19	9	14	60	47	66	7th
1985–86	42	20	9	13	49	47	69	7th
1986–87	42	20	10	12	58	35	70	4th
1987–88	40	18	12	10	58	39	66	6th
1988–89	38	22	10	6	73	36	76	1st
1989–90	38	18	8	12	54	38	62	4th
1990–91	38	24	13	1	74	18	83	1st
1991–92	42	19	15	8	81	46	72	4th

Premier League Records

The start of the Premier League in 1992–93 began a new chapter in Arsenal's history and this section details the Club's most significant records and feats in the competition, as well as reviewing the phenomenal performance of Arsene Wenger's fabled Invincibles side during the famous 2003–04 campaign.

ABOVE: Arsenal celebrate at Highbury after claiming the Premier League title for a third time in 2003–04.

Premier League Records – Biggest Wins

▼ TOFFEES TORN APART

Since the old First Division underwent a radical overhaul in the summer of 1992, re-emerging as the Premier League, Arsenal have continued their proud record as ever-present in the top-flight – and their biggest victory in the rebranded division came in May 2005 when Everton were spectacularly swept aside at Highbury.

The Gunners' record-setting 7–0 triumph was built on the genius of Dutch striker Dennis Bergkamp, whose sublime touch and vision set up goals for Robin van Persie and Robert Pires inside the opening 12 minutes in north London. Bergkamp was pivotal once again as Patrick Vieira scored the third on 37 minutes and at half-time the match was already over as a genuine contest.

Arsenal, however, were far from finished yet. A second from Pires and an Edu penalty compounded Everton's misery before Bergkamp helped himself to the goal his performance so richly deserved to make it six. Substitute Mathieu Flamini rubbed even more salt into the wound five minutes from time, and at the final whistle the Gunners were literally in seventh heaven.

It was an irresistible but not unique performance from Arsene Wenger's side and just eight months later they repeated the feat when Middlesbrough came to Highbury in January 2006.

Bergkamp had been Everton's tormentor-in-chief the previous season but this time it was Thierry Henry who stole the show with a

RIGHT: Edu celebrates after scoring from the spot in a 7–0 demolition of Everton at Highbury in 2005.

devastating hat-trick as Boro were hit for seven.

The prolific Frenchman opened his account with a stunning early volley, clinically broke clear for his second on the half-hour and completed his treble midway through the second half with another characteristically cool finish.

Philippe Senderos, Pires, Gilberto Silva and Alexander Hleb were the Gunners' other scorers but – with his third goal taking him to 150 in the league and in the process equalling Cliff Bastin's tally for the Club – the day undoubtedly belonged to Henry.

RIGHT: Ian Wright was the Gunners' top scorer in the 1992–93 season with 30 goals.

▲ WRIGHT ON TARGET

The first Premier League season of 1992–93 saw the Gunners average less than a goal per game but, despite their relatively modest haul in front of goal, the team did twice record 3–0 victories in that inaugural campaign – against Coventry City and Crystal Palace.

Arsenal hit three against the Sky Blues at Highbury in November through Ian Wright, Alan Smith and Kevin Campbell, and repeated the trick in May in north London against the Eagles with goals from Wright and Campbell again and a third from substitute Paul Dickov.

DERBY DELIGHT

The first north London league derby against Tottenham was played back in December 1909 – a 1–0 victory for Arsenal – and since the start of the Premier League the Gunners have scored five against their old rivals three separate times.

Their first five-star performance against Spurs was in November 2004 when a pulsating game at White Hart Lane was settled by a Robert Pires goal on 81 minutes as the visitors emerged 5–4 winners.

There were five more for the Emirates faithful to cheer in February 2012 when Arsene Wenger's side recovered from going 2–0 down to record a sensational 5–2 win. And in November the same year the Gunners again ran riot at home in another 5–2 triumph over their London neighbours.

HEAVYWEIGHT BATTLE

Arsenal and Manchester United are the two most successful sides in Premier League history in terms of overall victories. In 42 clashes with the Old Trafford side since 1992, the Gunners' most comprehensive win came in September 1998 when they despatched the Red Devils 3–0 at Highbury.

Arsene Wenger's side had already beaten United 3–0 in the Charity Shield at Wembley in August and they inflicted the same scoreline on the Manchester side a little over a month later with goals from Tony Adams, Nicolas Anelka and substitute Freddie Ljungberg.

ABOVE: Tomas Rosicky scores in the 5–2 romp against Tottenham at Emirates in February 2012. At one point the Gunners were 2–0 down before scoring five in a row.

RIGHT: Patrick Vieira was on target for the Gunners in the 6–1 victory over Middlesbrough at the Riverside.

ARSENAL'S PREMIER LEAGUE RECORD

	P	W	D	L	F	A	PTS	POS
1992–93	42	15	11	16	40	38	56	10th
1993–94	42	18	17	7	53	28	71	4th
1994–95	42	13	12	17	52	49	51	12th
1995–96	38	17	12	9	49	32	63	5th
1996–97	38	19	11	8	62	32	68	3rd
1997–98	38	23	9	6	68	33	78	1st
1998–99	38	22	12	4	59	17	78	2nd
1999–2000	38	22	7	9	73	43	73	2nd
2000–01	38	20	10	8	68	38	70	2nd
2001–02	38	26	9	3	79	36	87	1st
2002–03	38	23	9	6	85	42	78	2nd
2003–04	38	26	12	0	73	26	90	1st
2004–05	38	25	8	5	87	36	83	2nd
2005–06	38	25	7	8	57	25	82	3rd
2006–07	38	19	11	8	63	35	68	4th
2007–08	38	24	11	3	74	31	83	3rd
2008–09	38	20	12	6	68	37	72	4th
2009–10	38	23	6	9	83	41	75	3rd
2010–11	38	19	11	8	72	43	68	4th
2011–12	38	21	7	10	74	49	70	3rd
2012–13	38	21	10	7	72	37	73	4th
2013–14	38	24	7	7	68	41	79	4th
2014–15	38	22	9	7	71	36	75	3rd

◢ MIDDLESBROUGH MAULED

Arsenal's heaviest victory away from home in the Premier League dates back to April 1999 when they headed north to face Middlesbrough at the Riverside Stadium.

The tone of the match was set in the third minute when Nicolas Anelka was hauled down in the area and Marc Overmars converted the resulting penalty. Anelka himself added a second on 38 minutes, and when Man of the Match Kanu produced a sublime solo effort in first-half injury-time the Gunners were already out of sight.

Patrick Vieira made it 4–0 on the hour before Kanu and then Anelka helped themselves to a second apiece. Although Alun Armstrong scored a late goal for the home side, it was no more than a consolation effort as Arsenal recorded a 6–1 triumph – their biggest win on the road since 1935 and Boro's worst defeat at home in the 100 years since they turned professional.

Premier League Records – Biggest Defeats

SKY BLUES TAKE THREE POINTS

The opening day of a new season is a chance to set the tone for the rest of the year but Arsenal's 1993–94 campaign got off to the worst possible start when they were beaten 3–0 by Coventry City at Highbury.

A Micky Quinn hat-trick condemned the Gunners to their worst-ever first-day defeat in the Premier League – but it's worth noting that the side recovered from the shock result to finish the season with the division's most miserly defence, conceding just 28 goals in 42 games.

▼ END-OF-SEASON BLUES

Arsenal finished the 1999–2000 Premier League season as runners-up but as the campaign drew to a close in May, the Gunners were preoccupied with preparations for their UEFA Cup final showdown with Galatasaray rather than gathering league points.

The last league game against Newcastle United at St James' Park fell just three days before the final and an under-strength Gunners side proved no match for the Magpies on home soil, falling to a 4–2 defeat despite goals from Kanu and Stefan Malz.

It remains the Club's biggest last-day defeat in the Premier League.

RIGHT: The Gunners' 1999–2000 Premier League season ended in defeat at Newcastle.

▶ DERBY DEFEAT

The Premier League era has seen Arsenal dominate Tottenham in terms of results and the Lilywhites won just once at Highbury before the Gunners bid a fond farewell to the stadium in 2006.

That rare victory came in May 1993 in the final league game of the season and owed much to George Graham's decision to rest key players ahead of the FA Cup final against Sheffield Wednesday at Wembley just four days later.

Tottenham took a two-goal lead through Teddy Sheringham and John Hendry and although Paul Dickov reduced the arrears early in the second half, a second from Hendry was enough to give the visitors a 3–1 win and their biggest – and only – Premier League success at Highbury.

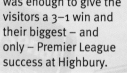

ABOVE: George Graham's Arsenal side faced Tottenham 11 times at Highbury during his managerial reign.

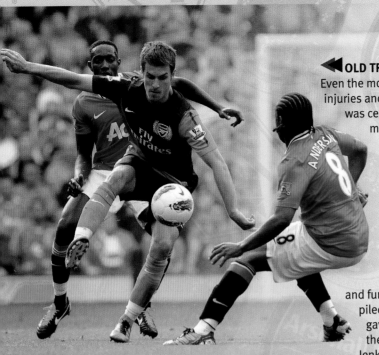

◀ OLD TRAFFORD NIGHTMARE

Even the most accomplished managers are powerless when injuries and suspensions ravage their squad and Arsene Wenger was certainly left stony-faced when he was forced to field a makeshift XI against Manchester United at Old Trafford in August 2011. The game ended in a sobering 8–2 defeat, Arsenal's record Premier League reverse and the Club's heaviest loss for 115 years.

Danny Welbeck opened the scoring for the home side on 22 minutes but the writing was on the wall for the Gunners when Robin van Persie's penalty was saved moments later. Theo Walcott did breach the home defence in first-half injury-time but at the break United were 3–1 ahead.

Wayne Rooney completed his hat-trick after the break and further goals from Ashley Young, Nani and Park Ji-Sung piled on the misery. Van Persie's 74th-minute effort briefly gave the travelling Arsenal fans something to celebrate but their temporary delight quickly turned to despair when Carl Jenkinson was sent off for a second bookable offence.

▶ FEELING BLUE

The Club's 8–2 loss to Manchester United in 2011 is Arsenal's heaviest ever defeat in the modern era in terms of goals conceded, but the Gunners have lost another Premier League fixture by six – in March 2014 against Chelsea at Stamford Bridge. The match was Arsene Wenger's 1000th in charge of the team and buoyed by victory over Spurs at White Hart Lane in the league the previous weekend, hopes were high that the Gunners could celebrate the manager's milestone with another major win on the road. Sadly, it was not to be and, after leaking two early goals, things went from bad to worse for Arsenal when Kieran Gibbs was wrongly shown a straight red card after Alex Oxlade-Chamberlain had handled in the box and the home side took full advantage of their numerical advantage to score four more.

The 6–0 result was Chelsea's biggest win over the Gunners and a day to forget for Wenger on his Arsenal anniversary.

ABOVE: Aaron Ramsey in action against Manchester United at Old Trafford, where Arsenal suffered their worst loss for 115 years.

ABOVE RIGHT: Full-back Kieran Gibbs saw red in Arsenal's heavy defeat at Stamford Bridge in March 2014.

ELLAND ROAD ROUT

The inaugural season of Premier League football was not a vintage one in Arsenal's history and the low point of the campaign came in November 1992 when they faced Leeds United at Elland Road.

The Gunners were unbeaten in their previous 15 meetings in all competitions against the Yorkshire side but, despite holding the reigning Division One champions to a goalless first-half, they were overrun after the break with goals from Chris Fairclough, Lee Chapman and Gary McAllister condemning the visitors to a 3–0 loss and their biggest defeat of the 1992–93 season.

ARSENAL PREMIER LEAGUE RECORDS

Most Individual Goals In A Season 30 – Robin van Persie (2011–12), Thierry Henry (2003–04)	
Most Team Goals In A Season 85 – 2002–03	
Fewest Goals Conceded In A Season 17 – 1998–99	
Most Goals Conceded In A Season 49 – 1994–95, 2011–12	
Highest Points Total 90 – 2003–04	
Lowest Points Total 56 – 1992–93	
Most Victories In A Season 26 – 2001–02, 2003–04	
Fewest Victories In A Season 13 – 1994–95	
Biggest Victory 7–0 v Everton (May 2005) 7–0 v Middlesbrough (January 2006)	
Biggest Defeat 8–2 v Manchester United (August 2011)	

Premier League Records –
The Invincibles

2003 — 2004

ABOVE: The Invincibles, under Arsene Wenger's expert guidance (right), are presented with the Premier League trophy after their magnificent unbeaten campaign, which lasted nearly 18 months.

▲ THE LONG RUN

The 7th of May 2003 was a special day in the history of Arsenal Football Club. The Gunners may have been licking their wounds after surrendering their Premier League crown to Manchester United just three days earlier, but the Highbury faithful were still in good voice as a Jermaine Pennant hat-trick inspired a 6–1 demolition of Southampton.

Little did Arsene Wenger or the 38,000-strong crowd that day realize that the result was the beginning of an unprecedented, undefeated Premier League run that would last 17-and-a-half unbelievable months, span 49 glorious games and comprehensively rewrite the record books.

No wonder the all-conquering side became known as "The Invincibles", such was their complete dominance.

The destruction of the Saints was Arsenal's penultimate league game of the 2002–03 campaign. They

followed it up with a 4–0 win over Sunderland on Wearside and, as the summer break beckoned – albeit not before the small matter of an FA Cup final triumph over Southampton at Wembley – thoughts turned to recapturing their Premier League title in the following season. They were to achieve their target in truly devastating style.

The new season in mid-August began with the visit of Everton to Highbury and goals from Thierry Henry and Robert Pires in a 2–1 success ensured the momentum of May's back-to-back victories did not evaporate. Three more wins and a draw followed but in late September the Gunners' embryonic record was nearly lost as the side headed north to face Manchester United in the "Battle of Old Trafford".

Controversies in previous meetings between the two sides ensured the match was another ill-tempered,

fractious affair. There were seven yellow cards in total and a red for Patrick Vieira in the 80th minute, but a goal looked a remote possibility until United were awarded a penalty in the final minute and Dutch striker Ruud van Nistelrooy stepped forward to take it. Unexpectedly, he crashed his effort against the crossbar and Arsenal's unbeaten sequence remained intact.

It was now eight games and counting. Buoyed by their escape at Old Trafford, the Gunners marched on. The 20th game in the run saw Wolves despatched 3–0 at Highbury, the 30th finished with a 2–0 victory over Bolton at the Reebok Stadium while the 36th ended with a 2–2 draw with Tottenham at White Hart Lane, a result which confirmed the Club were champions once again.

The final fixture of the Premier League season brought Leicester City to Highbury but the script did not feature the Foxes taking a first-half lead through former Gunner Paul Dickov. Wenger's side, however, were not to be denied and a goal from Henry – his 30th league strike in 37 appearances – plus a second from Vieira completed a 2–1 win and ensured the side completed the campaign with a phenomenal unbeaten record.

Arsenal became the first side since Preston in 1888–89 to win the league without suffering a single defeat. But while North End had played a modest 22 games over a century ago, the Gunners had remained unbeaten over the course of 38 fixtures, extending their overall streak to 40.

German goalkeeper Jens Lehmann was the only player to feature in all 38 matches while Henry and Kolo Toure (37 appearances), Pires (36) and Sol Campbell (35) were the other mainstays of perhaps the greatest side ever to grace Highbury.

There was of course more to come. The 2004–05 season kicked-off with a comprehensive 4–1 victory over Everton at Goodison and two-and-a-half weeks later the side broke yet another record when they demolished Blackburn at Highbury, in the process eclipsing Nottingham Forest's 26-year-old

record of 42 league games unbeaten.

Five more victories and a 2–2 stalemate with Bolton followed and the sequence was now an unparalleled 49 Premier League matches since Arsenal had last tasted defeat.

On Sunday 24 October 2004, the run came to an end. The side headed to Old Trafford once again but this time van Nistelrooy was on target from the penalty spot as Manchester United overcame the visitors 2–0 and the Gunners were finally beaten.

The statistics of the team's sensational sequence barely tell the full story of their achievement. The 49 games yielded 36 victories and 13 draws, they scored 112 goals and conceded just 35 and they claimed the 2003–04 Premier League title by 11 clear points from second-place Chelsea.

Many believe the amazing exploits of Wenger's "Invincibles" between May 2003 and October 2004 will never be surpassed. Whatever happens, the team's place in the history books is assured.

BELOW: Thierry Henry top scored for Arsenal with 30 goals in 37 Premier League appearances.

THE INVINCIBLES' RECORD RUN

2002/2003
1. Arsenal 6–1 Southampton (7 May, 2003)
2. Sunderland 0–4 Arsenal

2003/2004
3. Arsenal 2–1 Everton
4. Middlesbro 0–4 Arsenal
5. Arsenal 2–0 Aston Villa
6. Man City 1–2 Arsenal
7. Arsenal 1–1 Portsmouth
8. Man Utd 0–0 Arsenal
9. Arsenal 3–2 Newcastle
10. Liverpool 1–2 Arsenal
11. Arsenal 2–1 Chelsea
12. Charlton 1–1 Arsenal
13. Leeds 1–4 Arsenal
14. Arsenal 2–1 Tottenham
15. Birmingham 0–3 Arsenal
16. Arsenal 0–0 Fulham
17. Leicester 1–1 Arsenal
18. Arsenal 1–0 Blackburn
19. Bolton 1–1 Arsenal
20. Arsenal 3–0 Wolves
21. Southampton 0–1 Arsenal
22. Everton 1–1 Arsenal
23. Arsenal 4–1 Middlesbro
24. Aston Villa 0–2 Arsenal
25. Arsenal 2–1 Man City
26. Wolves 1–3 Arsenal
27. Arsenal 2–0 Southampton
28. Chelsea 1–2 Arsenal
29. Arsenal 2–1 Charlton
30. Blackburn 0–2 Arsenal
31. Arsenal 2–1 Bolton
32. Arsenal 1–1 Man Utd
33. Arsenal 4–2 Liverpool
34. Newcastle 0–0 Arsenal
35. Arsenal 5–0 Leeds
36. Tottenham 2–2 Arsenal
37. Arsenal 0–0 Birmingham
38. Portsmouth 1–1 Arsenal
39. Fulham 0–1 Arsenal
40. Arsenal 2–1 Leicester

2004/2005
41. Everton 1–4 Arsenal
42. Arsenal 5–3 Middlesbro
43. Arsenal 3–0 Blackburn
44. Norwich 1–4 Arsenal
45. Fulham 0–3 Arsenal
46. Arsenal 2–2 Bolton
47. Man City 0–1 Arsenal
48. Arsenal 4–0 Charlton
49. Arsenal 3–1 Aston Villa (16 September 2004)

Premier League Records – Other Undefeated Records

AWESOME AWAY FORM

Going away from home in the Premier League is a challenge for any side but in 1997 Arsenal left north London five times in succession without letting in a goal.

A goalless draw at Elland Road against Leeds in February was the catalyst for the sequence and the Gunners followed it up with a hard-fought 0–0 draw with old rivals Spurs at White Hart Lane. A 2–0 win over Everton at Goodison, a 2–0 triumph against Southampton at The Dell and a 3–0 mauling of Chelsea at Stamford Bridge followed, and it was not until Dion Dublin beat David Seaman at Highfield Road in April in a 1–1 draw that Arsenal allowed the home side to score.

ABOVE: David Seaman kept five consecutive clean sheets away from home in 1997.

STRONGEST START

Arsenal's best-ever start to a Premier League season in terms of not conceding a goal came in 2012–13 when the Gunners went a Club-record 315 minutes of play before the defence was finally breached.

The side began the campaign with a goalless draw against Sunderland at Emirates and kept another clean sheet in their second game after a scoreless draw with Stoke at the Britannia Stadium.

A 2–0 victory over Liverpool at Anfield a week later extended the run and it was not until Danny Fox beat Wojciech Szczesny on the stroke of half-time in the Gunners' 6–1 demolition of Southampton that the side allowed the opposition to score.

IMMACULATE ALMUNIA

Keeping clean sheets is a guaranteed way to avoid defeat and Arsenal went a record eight Premier League games unbeaten at Emirates in 2008–09 without conceding a single goal.

The impeccable run began on 28 December 2008 with a 1–0 victory over Portsmouth in London and through January, February and March, Bolton, West Ham, Sunderland, Fulham, Blackburn, Manchester City and Middlesbrough were all unable to find a way past the Arsenal defence.

Spanish goalkeeper Manuel Almunia was in goal for all eight matches but made way for Lukasz Fabianksi for the clash with Chelsea at Emirates in May, a game which the Gunners lost 4–1 to bring their impressive streak to an end.

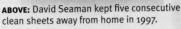

LEFT: Manuel Almunia was a hard man to beat during the 2008–09 campaign.

TITLE TRIUMPH

The Gunners were crowned Premier League champions for the first time in 1997–98, edging out Manchester United by a single point, and the success of the side was built on two superb but separate unbeaten sequences over the course of the season.

Arsenal's initial 12-match streak began on the opening day of the campaign with a 1–1 draw with Leeds United at Elland Road after an Ian Wright goal. It was to be 11 more games before Arsene Wenger's side were finally toppled, losing 3–0 at Derby County in early November.

The initial burst had confirmed Arsenal as genuine title contenders but it was the side's subsequent 18-match unbeaten streak that secured the silverware.

Their second sequence began on Boxing Day with a 2–1 win over Leicester City at Highbury and they went all the way through to May before tasting defeat again.

The highlight of the run came in March when the team travelled to Old Trafford to face Manchester United and came away with three crucial points courtesy of Marc Overmars' goal. Although a heavy 4–0 loss to Liverpool at Anfield brought things to an abrupt halt, the Gunners had already done enough to lift the Premier League trophy.

ABOVE: Ian Wright was on target 10 times in 24 Premier League games in 1997–98.

SEVEN-MATCH SEQUENCE

The inaugural 1992–93 Premier League season was far from Arsenal's best but the Gunners signalled that they would become a force to be reckoned with in the future with a seven-match unbeaten run in the new league.

It started in September with a goalless draw against Sheffield United at Bramall Lane and over the next two months Manchester City, Chelsea, Nottingham Forest, Everton, Crystal Palace and Coventry all failed to prevent the Gunners taking at least a point.

WENGER MASTERMINDS SUPERB STREAK

The record-breaking achievements of Arsene Wenger's "Invincibles" are well documented but the Arsenal side of 2007–08 and 2008–09 was almost as difficult to beat. Between April and December 2007, the team strung together an impressive 22-match unbeaten run.

A goalless draw with Newcastle at St James' Park was the start and in their final six fixtures of the 2007–08 campaign, the Gunners recorded three wins and three draws.

They continued their fine form at the start of 2008–09 with a 2–1 opening-day win over Fulham at Emirates, with goals from Robin van Persie from the spot and Alexander Hleb and extended the streak for another 14 games, culminating in a 1–1 draw with Newcastle in the north-east.

Middlesbrough's 2–1 win at the Riverside four days later stopped the superb sequence – but not before the Gunners had collected 50 points from a possible 66.

LEFT: Robin van Persie in action against Fulham at the start of the 2008–09 season.

LONGEST UNBEATEN SEQUENCES SEASON-BY-SEASON

1992–93	7 games
1993–94	19
1994–95	5
1995–96	7
1996–97	10
1997–98	18
1998–99	19
1999–2000	9
2000–01	12
2001–02	21
2002–03	12
2003–04	38
2004–05	12
2005–06	6
2006–07	7
2007–08	15
2008–09	21
2009–10	10
2010–11	16
2011–12	8
2012–13	10
2013–14	5
2014–15	10

Premier League Records – Miscellaneous

ABOVE: Freddie Ljungberg scored 72 times in 328 games for the Club.

◀ SCORING SEQUENCE

The aim of football is essentially simple – get the ball by any legal means into the back of the net. It's a message that hasn't fundamentally changed since the game was invented and Arsenal certainly took heed between May 2001 and November 2002 when they scored in an incredible 55 consecutive Premier League games, a milestone that has yet to be surpassed by any other club.

It was on 19 May in the final fixture of the 2000–01 season that the Gunners began their prolific streak, with goals from Ashley Cole and Freddie Ljungberg in their 3–2 defeat to Southampton in the final-ever league game at The Dell.

The summer break did not dampen the side's attacking instincts and they kicked off the 2001–02 campaign with a 4–0 demolition of Middlesbrough at the Riverside. The goals continued to flow and by the end of the season the remarkable run in front of goal stood at 39 games.

Another summer of inactivity again failed to stem the flood of goals. The opening-day fixture in 2002–03 saw Birmingham despatched 2–0 at Highbury with strikes from Sylvain Wiltord and Thierry Henry – and the side continued the amazing sequence through to the end of November when a brace from Henry and a third from Robert Pires sealed a 3–1 triumph over Aston Villa in north London.

Arsenal finally drew a blank in a 2–0 loss to Manchester United at Old Trafford in December but the loss took none of the sheen off the side's unprecedented, record-breaking 55-match run in which they netted 116 times and lost just eight times.

▶ TOO HOT TO HANDLE

The Gunners were in fine form throughout the 2014–15 campaign and between February and March registered eight consecutive victories in the Premier League, a record run for the competition that season.

It began with a 2–1 win over Leicester at the Emirates, courtesy of goals from Laurent Koscielny and Theo Walcott, and continued with league defeats of Crystal Palace, Everton, QPR, West Ham, Newcastle and Liverpool. The eighth success was a 1–0 victory over Burnley at Turf Moor thanks to an Aaron Ramsey strike.

The sequence was finally brought to an end in late April when Arsenal were held to a goalless draw by Chelsea in north London.

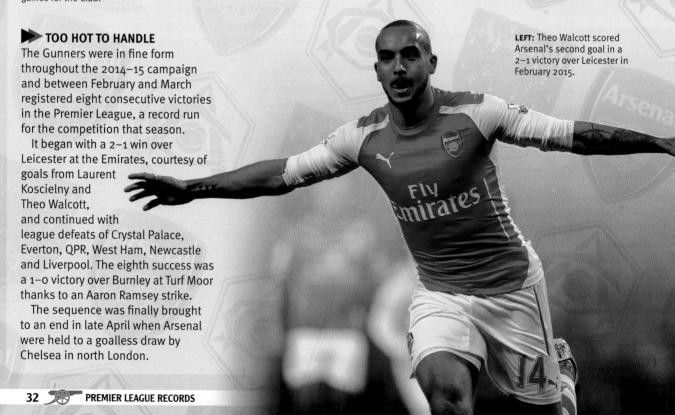

LEFT: Theo Walcott scored Arsenal's second goal in a 2–1 victory over Leicester in February 2015.

CLEAN SHEET RECORD

The Arsenal defence was incredibly miserly during the 1998–99 season. The Gunners may have missed out on the title by a single point, but the back four could certainly be proud of their collective efforts after conceding just 17 goals in 38 games.

Remarkably, only one side managed to score more than one goal in a league match against Arsene Wenger's team – Aston Villa in their 3–2 win at Villa Park in December – and in total the Gunners kept 23 clean sheets during the campaign.

To put the Club-record feat into context, champions Manchester United conceded 37 times that season while the next meanest defence belonged to Chelsea with 30 goals scored against the Blues.

EIGHT UP AT ASHBURTON

The 2014–15 campaign saw Arsene Wenger's side in fine form at the Emirates, and between December and April his side set a new Club record with nine Premier League victories on the bounce at the new stadium for the first time.

The sequence was sparked by a disappointing home defeat to Manchester United in November, but the Gunners recovered to beat Southampton 1–0 at the Emirates with an 89th-minute winner from Alexis Sanchez. Newcastle United and QPR were both despatched in north London before the turn of the year and, in their first home game of 2015, Arsenal comfortably beat Stoke to make it four in a row.

A 5–0 demolition of Aston Villa in February continued the run before Leicester and Everton both left the Emirates pointless, while seven wins became eight in March when goals from Olivier Giroud, Aaron Ramsey and Mathieu Flamini condemned West Ham to a 3–0 defeat. The brilliant sequence was further extended in April when the Gunners put Liverpool to the sword with a 4–1 triumph.

The next visitors to the Emirates were Chelsea three weeks later, but Wenger's side were unable to make it ten successive home wins after they were held to a goalless draw by their London rivals.

EMIRATES CENTURY

The Gunners' final home league match of the 2013–14 campaign saw the side despatch West Bromwich Albion 1–0 to record a 99th Premier League victory at the Emirates since 2006. Arsene Wenger's side, however, wasted little time in reaching a brilliant century of wins at Ashburton Grove, beating Crystal Palace 2–1 in their first game at the Emirates in the 2014–15 season courtesy of an Aaron Ramsey injury-time winner.

LEFT: Aaron Ramsey's vital late goal earned Arsenal victory over Crystal Palace in the opening game of the 2014–15 Premier League season.

FA Cup & League Cup Records

Arsenal have lifted the FA Cup 12 times since their first triumph at Wembley in 1930 and have won the League Cup twice – and the next 10 pages are packed with all the team's notable milestones in English football's two major domestic knockout competitions.

LEFT: Alan Sunderland celebrates his dramatic winning goal in the 1979 FA Cup final against Manchester United.

BELOW LEFT: Paul Merson races away after scoring against Sheffield Wednesday in the 1993 League Cup final.

BELOW: Patrick Vieira lifts the 2005 FA Cup after Arsenal overcame Manchester United.

RIGHT: Arsenal made it two FA Cup final victories in a row when they beat Aston Villa 4–0 in 2015.

FA Cup & League Cup Records – Winners

▶▶ GUNNERS MAKE CUP HISTORY

Following their triumph in the 2014 FA Cup final, Arsenal set their sights on becoming the most successful side in the competition's history, and it took Arsene Wenger's side just 12 months to achieve their goal.

Arsenal's 4–0 demolition of Aston Villa at Wembley in 2015, courtesy of goals from Theo Walcott, Alexis Sanchez, Per Mertesacker and Olivier Giroud, took their Cup haul to a remarkable 12, eclipsing Manchester's United total of 11 successes.

The Gunners' progress to the final also set two new outright FA Cup records. Their appearance in the semi-final against Reading in April was the 28th time the Club had made it through to the last four, a tournament

milestone, while their subsequent appearance in the final was the 19th time they had contested the showpiece game, beating Manchester United's 18 finals.

The comprehensive win over Aston Villa took the Club's overall record in the FA Cup to 253 victories in 459 matches with 105 defeats and 101 draws. The Gunners scored 836 goals and conceded 478 in the process.

The result was also Wenger's record-equalling sixth triumph in the competition, drawing him level with the haul of six FA Cups registered by George Ramsey at Aston Villa between 1897 and 1920 and one ahead of Manchester United's Sir Alex Ferguson (1990–2004) and Blackburn Rovers' Thomas Mitchell (1884–91).

ABOVE: Celebration time for Arsenal as they celebrate their 4–0 victory over Aston Villa in the 2015 FA Cup final.

▶▶ FIRST TROPHY TRIUMPH

The Gunners first sampled the unique atmosphere of an FA Cup final in 1927 when they were beaten 1–0 by Cardiff City in front of a crowd of 91,206 at Wembley. Three years later skipper Tom Parker, a survivor of the previous clash, was finally lifting the famous trophy after Arsenal beat Huddersfield.

After drawing a blank against Cardiff, Scottish inside-forward Alex James made history with his 16th-minute strike against the Terriers to become the first Arsenal player to score in an FA Cup final while Jack Lambert doubled the lead for Herbert Chapman's side two minutes from time to seal a milestone 2–0 victory.

The side's 2–0 triumph was also the Club's first-ever piece of major silverware, 39 years after the Gunners had turned professional.

RIGHT: The Gunners in action in the 1927 FA Cup final against Cardiff.

NICHOLAS' WEMBLEY HEROICS

George Graham won six major trophies during his nine-year reign as Arsenal manager. His first silverware at Highbury came in the shape of the 1987 League Cup after his side triumphed over Liverpool in front of a 96,000-strong crowd at Wembley.

Appointed to succeed Don Howe in May 1986, Graham made an immediate impact as Arsenal cruised effortlessly through the early rounds of the competition before drawing old rivals Tottenham in the semi-finals.

Spurs won the first leg at Highbury 1–0 thanks to a Clive Allen goal but the Gunners responded by winning the return leg at White Hart Lane 2–1 courtesy of strikes from Viv Anderson and Niall Quinn, to make the tie 2–2 on aggregate.

A replay was required as away goals did not count double. So a coin was tossed to decide the venue for the rematch and the two teams headed to White Hart Lane once again to settle the issue.

Another Allen goal gave the home side the early advantage but Arsenal were plotting a dramatic denouement and strikes from Ian Allinson and David Rocastle in the final eight minutes booked the Gunners' place at Wembley.

The final also saw Graham's side forced to stage a late fightback after Ian Rush opened the scoring for Liverpool in the 23rd minute. Charlie Nicholas equalized seven minutes later but the two teams were locked at 1–1 until late in the second half and injury-time beckoned.

Nicholas, however, had other ideas and his second goal, in the 83rd minute, gave Arsenal a famous 2–1 win. It was the Club's first League Cup triumph and went some way to erasing the painful memories of defeat in the finals of 1968 and 1969.

ABOVE: Charlie Nicholas was Arsenal's hero in the 1987 League Cup final.

BELOW: Marc Overmars celebrates after scoring the Gunners' first goal in the 2–0 defeat of Newcastle in the 1998 FA Cup final.

ARSENAL'S FA CUP RECORD 1889–1915

1889–90 – Fourth Qualifying Round (Lost 5–1, Swifts)
1890–91 – First Round (Lost 2–1, Derby County)
1891–92 – First Round (Lost 5–1, Small Heath)
1892–93 – First Round (Lost 1–0, Sunderland)
1893–94 – First Round (Lost 2–1, Sheffield Wednesday)
1894–95 – First Round (Lost 1–0, Bolton Wanderers)
1895–96 – First Round (Lost 6–1, Burnley)
1896–97 – Fifth Qualifying Round (Lost 4–2, Millwall)
1897–98 – First Round (Lost 3–1, Burnley)
1898–99 – First Round (Lost 6–0, Derby County)
1899–1900 – Third Qualifying Round (Lost 1–0, New Brompton)
1900–01 – Second Round (Lost 1–0, West Bromwich Albion)
1901–02 – First Round (Lost 2–0, Newcastle United)
1902–03 – First Round (Lost 3–1, Sheffield United)
1903–04 – Second Round (Lost 2–0, Manchester City)
1904–05 – First Round (Lost 1–0, Bristol City)
1905–06 – Semi-Finals (Lost 2–0, Newcastle United)
1906–07 – Semi-Finals (Lost 3–1, Sheffield Wednesday)
1907–08 – First Round (Lost 4–1, Hull City)
1908–09 – Second Round (Lost 1–0, Millwall)
1909–10 – Second Round (Lost 5–0, Everton)
1910–11 – Second Round (Lost 1–0, Swindon Town)
1911–12 – First Round (Lost 1–0, Bolton Wanderers)
1912–13 – Second Round (Lost 4–1 Liverpool)
1913–14 – First Round (Lost 2–0, Bradford Park Avenue)
1914–15 – Second Round (Lost 1–0, Chelsea)

DUTCH DELIGHT

Jensen paved the way for Arsenal's foreign legion in the FA Cup. Five years after his landmark appearance at Wembley, Marc Overmars picked up the baton when he became the first non-British or Irish player to score for the Club in a final.

The Dutch winger was on target midway through the first half in 1998 as the Gunners beat Newcastle United 2–0 to lift the trophy for a seventh time. Ironically, Arsenal's second goal came courtesy of French striker Nicolas Anelka, 46 minutes after Overmars' opener, but it was too late to earn a place in the record books.

The victory also saw the Gunners complete the fabled league and cup double for the second time, the first Club in the history of the English game to achieve the feat twice.

LEWIS'S RECORD DOUBLE

In total Arsenal have appeared in 17 FA Cup finals since first making it to Wembley in 1927. Including the 1993 replay against Sheffield Wednesday, the Gunners have scored 20 times in the showpiece game of the English domestic season.

There have been 14 different scorers for the Club but Reg Lewis remains the only player to have found the back of the net twice in the final.

His unique achievement came in 1950 when Arsenal faced Liverpool at Wembley and his 18th and 63rd-minute strikes ensured the Gunners were champions for a third time.

Ian Wright and Freddie Ljungberg both also boast two FA Cup final goals on their CVs but their efforts came in separate games.

SUCCESSFUL TROPHY DEFENCE

Only seven sides have recorded back-to-back triumphs in the FA Cup in the long and illustrious history of the competition, and Arsenal joined the exclusive club in May 2003 when they overcame Southampton at the Millennium Stadium.

The game was settled by a solitary Robert Pires goal in the first half in Cardiff to secure the trophy for a ninth time and in the process lift the Gunners to second outright in the all-time winners' list above Tottenham.

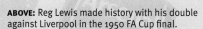
ABOVE: Reg Lewis made history with his double against Liverpool in the 1950 FA Cup final.

LJUNGBERG ON TARGET AGAIN

The 2002 FA Cup pitted the Gunners against Chelsea in an all-London final and history was made when Freddie Ljungberg found the back of the net in Arsenal's 2–0 victory at Wembley.

The Swedish midfielder was on target in the 2001 final defeat to Liverpool and when he scored in the 80th minute against Chelsea, following up Ray Parlour's 70th-minute strike, he became the first player to score in successive finals since Tottenham's Bobby Smith 40 years earlier.

Days later the Gunners beat Manchester United 1–0 at Old Trafford courtesy of a Sylvain Wiltord goal to win the Premier League title and in the process draw level with Manchester United on three league and cup doubles.

LEFT: Robert Pires' goal proved pivotal against Southampton at the Millennium Stadium in 2003.

▶ MORROW DENIES OWLS

The Gunners' second success in the League Cup came in 1993 when Graham steered his side to the final for a second time in five years, lining up against Sheffield Wednesday at Wembley in April.

As they had in 1987, Arsenal went behind in the match when John Harkes beat David Seaman after only eight minutes, but the revival began when Man of the Match Paul Merson was on target 12 minutes later.

The two teams went in at the break level but it was Graham's team who were to emerge 2–1 winners at the final whistle thanks to a rare Steve Morrow goal in the second half.

Captain Tony Adams proudly climbed the famous Wembley steps to collect the trophy and, while the silverware was handled with due care and attention, he was less careful when he hoisted Morrow above his shoulders in the post-match celebrations, dropping his team-mate and breaking his arm.

PENALTY SHOOTOUT

Arsenal's first nine successes in the FA Cup saw the side score at least once in the final, albeit in extra-time in 1971 against Liverpool, but the sequence came to an end in 2005 when they faced Manchester United.

The two sides failed to muster a goal in open play but it was the Gunners who held their nerve in the penalty shootout as Lauren, Freddie Ljungberg, Robin van Persie, Ashley Cole and Patrick Vieira were all on target from the spot to clinch a 10th win.

RIGHT: Steve Morrow scored the winner at Wembley in the 1993 League Cup final.

▼ ECSTASY IN EXTRA-TIME

A repeat of the 1950 final, the 1971 showdown between Arsenal and Liverpool at Wembley in May made history – both as the first final featuring the Gunners to go to extra-time and as the climax of the Club's first-ever league and cup double.

The match was goalless in the opening 90 minutes but the goals suddenly flowed in extra-time. Steve Heighway gave Liverpool the lead but substitute Eddie Kelly – the first replacement to feature in a final for the Gunners – equalized before Charlie George hit the winner in the 111th minute of the contest.

Arsenal had wrapped up the Division One title five days earlier courtesy of a 1–0 victory against Tottenham at White Hart Lane, making the success against Liverpool the Club's maiden double.

BELOW: The 1971 FA Cup final was the second leg of the Club's famous double.

ARSENAL'S FA CUP RECORD 1919–50

1919–20	Second Round (Lost 1–0, Bristol City)
1920–21	First Round (Lost 2–0, QPR)
1921–22	Quarter-Finals (Lost 2–1, Preston North End)
1922–23	First Round (Lost 4–1, Liverpool)
1923–24	Second Round (Lost 1–0, Cardiff City)
1924–25	First Round (Lost 1–0, West Ham United)
1925–26	Quarter-Finals (Lost 2–1, Swansea City)
1926–27	Runners-Up (Lost 1–0, Cardiff City)
1927–28	Semi-Finals (Lost 1–0, Blackburn Rovers)
1928–29	Quarter-Finals (Lost 1–0, Aston Villa)
1929–30	Winners (Won 2–0, Huddersfield Town)
1930–31	Fourth Round (Lost 2–1, Chelsea)
1931–32	Runners-Up (Lost 2–1, Newcastle United)
1932–33	Third Round (Lost 2–0, Walsall)
1933–34	Quarter-Finals (Lost 2–1, Aston Villa)
1934–35	Quarter-Finals (Lost 2–1, Sheffield Wednesday)
1935–36	Winners (Won 1–0, Sheffield United)
1936–37	Quarter-Finals (Lost 3–1, West Bromwich Albion)
1937–38	Fifth Round (Lost 1–0, Preston North End)
1938–39	Third Round (Lost 2–1, Chelsea)
1945–46	Third Round (Lost 6–1, West Ham)
1946–47	Third Round (Lost 2–0, Chelsea)
1947–48	Third Round (Lost 1–0, Bradford Park Avenue)
1948–49	Fourth Round (Lost 1–0, Derby County)
1949–50	Winners (Won 2–0, Liverpool)

FA Cup & League Cup Records – Sequences

▼ **RECORD UNBEATEN RUN**

Arsenal are one of the most successful sides in FA Cup history. Between January 1979 and May 1980, the Gunners set an incredible Club record of 21 consecutive games in the competition without suffering defeat.

The phenomenal run began when the team were drawn in the third round against Sheffield Wednesday. The initial clash at Hillsborough ended 1–1 but it was an era in which replays were unlimited and it would require a remarkable four more meetings between the two teams to pick a winner.

The first replay ended 1–1, the second 2–2 and the third 3–3, and it was only in the fourth rerun of the original tie that Arsenal finally emerged victorious courtesy of goals from Frank Stapleton and Steve Gatting.

BELOW: Terry Neill's side enjoyed huge success in the FA Cup

RIGHT: Liam Brady on the ball during the 1980 FA Cup semi-final against Liverpool.

Notts County and Nottingham Forest were both despatched without the need for a second match but the sixth-round clash with Southampton in March did go to a replay which the Gunners eventually won 2–0.

Arsenal saw off Wolves comfortably in the semi-final and their entertaining 3–2 victory over Manchester United in the final at Wembley took their unbeaten run in the FA Cup to 11 games.

Replays were the name of the game again the following season as the Gunners battled their way through to another final.

It took the side 180 minutes to overcome Cardiff in the third round in January and, although Brighton were beaten in the fourth round inside 90 minutes, it was a two-legged affair against Bolton in the next phase.

Watford fell 2–1 to Arsenal in the last eight but another epic, replay-laden contest awaited the team in the form of Liverpool in the semi-finals. The first clash was goalless while the

first and second replays finished 1–1 and it was only in the fourth game between the two that the Gunners did the business with a 1–0 win thanks to Brian Talbot's solitary goal.

Terry Neill's side were to lose the final to West Ham just nine days later, but their 21-match unbeaten sequence remains a record subsequent Arsenal teams have been unable to surpass or equal.

SEMI-FINAL SUCCESS

Between 2001 and 2005, the Gunners reached five successive FA Cup semi-finals, the most consistent run of reaching the last four in the Club's history.

Only their 2004 meeting with Manchester United at Villa Park, a narrow 1–0 defeat, failed to yield an appearance in the final itself.

Arsenal had previously battled through to the semis in three consecutive seasons twice, reaching the last four in 1971, 1972 and 1973 and again from 1978 to 1980.

▲ READING ROMP

Arsenal's phenomenal 7–5 victory over Reading in the fourth round of the League Cup in October 2012 set a new record for the highest aggregate score in the competition – but the match also saw the Gunners record another piece of football history.

The result booked them a place in the quarter-finals of the League Cup for a 10th consecutive season, a record that no other side can equal.

DAZZLING DOZEN

The Gunners' record-breaking triumph in the 2015 FA Cup final was the climax of two superb seasons of knockout football, as the team's victory over Aston Villa set a new club record of 12 successive victories in the competition.

The run began in the third round of the 2013–14 FA Cup when Arsenal beat old rivals Spurs at the Emirates in January, thanks to goals from Santi Cazorla and Tomas Rosicky, and continued with wins over Coventry, Liverpool and Everton.

It was nearly brought to an end in the semi-final against Wigan, but the Gunners emerged victorious 4–2 after a nerve-shredding penalty shootout, and made it six wins on the bounce after they beat Hull City 3–2 in the final.

Six more victories for Arsene Wenger's side en route to a successful defence of the trophy in 2015, including their quarter-final victory over Manchester United at Old Trafford, brought up the record-breaking dozen, which featured 31 goals for and just nine against.

The Gunners, of course, could also have recorded 12 consecutive wins when they won back-to-back FA Cups in 2002 and 2003, but they were held to 1–1 draw in the quarter-finals by Newcastle at St James' Park. The tie went to a replay and Arsenal's chance of establishing the record was gone.

ABOVE: Marouane Chamakh scored twice in extra-time in Arsenal's record 7–5 win over Reading in the League Cup in 2012.

ARSENAL'S FA CUP RECORD 1950–80

1950–51 – Fifth Round (Lost 1–0, Manchester United)
1951–52 – Runners-Up (Lost 1–0, Newcastle United)
1952–53 – Quarter-Finals (Lost 2–1, Blackpool)
1953–54 – Fourth Round (Lost 2–1, Norwich City)
1954–55 – Fourth Round (Lost 1–0, Wolverhampton Wanderers)
1955–56 – Quarter-Finals (Lost 3–1, Birmingham City)
1956–57 – Quarter-Finals (Lost 2–1, West Bromich Albion)
1957–58 – Third Round (Lost 3–1, Northampton Town)
1958–59 – Fifth Round (Lost 3–0, Sheffield United)
1959–60 – Third Round (Lost 2–0, Rotherham United)
1960–61 – Third Round (Lost 2–1, Sunderland)
1961–62 – Fourth Round (Lost 1–0, Manchester United)
1962–63 – Fifth Round (Lost 2–1, Liverpool)
1963–64 – Fifth Round (Lost 1–0, Liverpool)
1964–65 – Fourth Round (Lost 2–1, Peterborough United)
1965–66 – Third Round (Lost 3–0, Blackburn Rovers)
1966–67 – Fifth Round (Lost 1–0, Birmingham City)
1967–68 – Fifth Round (Lost 2–1, Birmingham City)
1968–69 – Fifth Round (Lost 1–0, West Bromwich Albion)
1969–70 – Third Round (Lost 3–2 Blackpool)
1970–71 – Winners (Won 2–1 aet, Liverpool)
1971–72 – Runners-Up (Lost 1–0, Leeds United)
1972–73 – Semi-Finals (Lost 2–1, Sunderland)
1973–74 – Fourth Round (Lost 2–0, Aston Villa)
1974–75 – Quarter-Finals (Lost 2–0, West Ham United)
1975–76 – Third Round (Lost 3–0, Wolverhampton Wanderers)
1976–77 – Fifth Round (Lost 4–1, Middlesbrough)
1977–78 – Runners-Up (Lost 1–0, Ipswich Town)
1978–79 – Winners (Won 3–2, Manchester United)
1979–80 – Runners-Up (Lost 1–0, West Ham United)

Other Domestic Cup Competitions

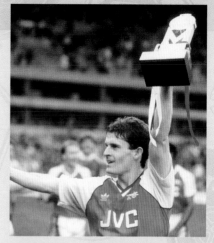

ABOVE: The Gunners were triumphant over Manchester United at Villa Park in 1988.

BARBOUR'S FINAL BRACE

Before turning professional in 1891, the amateurs of Arsenal used to compete in the Kent Senior Cup and won the inaugural competition in 1890. The Gunners faced Thanet Wanderers in March and claimed the trophy courtesy of goals from Humphrey Barbour (2) and Harry Offer.

Two weeks later Arsenal were celebrating more cup glory after beating Old Westminsters 3–1 in the final of the London Charity Cup, a competition that was finally disbanded in 1975, with the goals coming from Offer, W.E. Fry and Albert Christmas.

CAPITAL CUP

Although the Club no longer enters a side, Arsenal were crowned the London Senior Cup champions back in 1891 after beating a St Bartholomew's Hospital XI 6–0 in the final.

The Gunners had lost to Old Westminsters in the final 12 months earlier – their only other appearance in the showpiece – but made amends against Bartholomew's with the goals coming from David Gloak, Humphrey Barbour (2), Harry Offer, Peter Connolly and W.E. Fry.

EMIRATES EXCELLENCE

Since 2007 Arsenal have been fine-tuning their preparations for each new campaign at the two-day-long Emirates Cup and the Gunners have lifted the trophy three times in five attempts.

The side's first success was in 2007 when victories over Paris Saint-Germain and Inter Milan gave them the silverware and they were victorious once again in 2009 after beating Rangers and Atletico Madrid. Arsenal made it a hat-trick of wins 12 months later after drawing with AC Milan and overcoming Rangers.

The team's biggest victory since the start of the Emirates Cup came in 2009 when goals from Jack Wilshere (2) and Croatia striker Eduardo gave Arsene Wenger's side a 3–0 win. There was no Emirates Cup in 2012 as it clashed with the London Olympics.

CENTENARY CELEBRATIONS

The Mercantile Credit Centenary Trophy was a one-off tournament staged in 1988 to celebrate the centenary of the Football League. After battling through to the final, Arsenal became champions by beating Manchester United 2–1 in front of 22,182 supporters at Villa Park.

George Graham's side overcame Queens Park Rangers 2–0 in the quarter-finals before knocking out Liverpool 2–1 in the last four.

The final between two of the heavyweights of English football saw Paul Davis and Michael Thomas on target for the Gunners while Clayton Blackmore scored for United.

BELOW: Jack Wilshere in action against Rangers in Emirates Cup in 2009.

▶ THE NEXT GENERATION

Arsenal are the second most successful side in the history of the FA Youth Cup, lifting the trophy a total of seven times since its inception in 1953.

The Gunners' Under-18 side first won the competition in 1966 after beating Sunderland 5–2 on aggregate over two legs – with a team that featured future Arsenal legend Pat Rice.

Five years later the team were champions again after a 2–0 triumph against Norwich City and the trophy returned to Highbury in 1988, 1994, 2000 and 2001.

The Club's most recent success came in 2009 when a young Arsenal side demolished Liverpool 6–2 over two games.

The Gunners' most comprehensive aggregate success, however, was in 2001 when the team, including Jack Wilshere and Emmanuel Frimpong, overcame Blackburn Rovers 6–3 on aggregate, winning the first leg at home 5–0 before a 3–1 defeat in the return game.

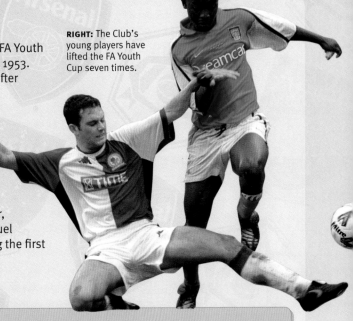

RIGHT: The Club's young players have lifted the FA Youth Cup seven times.

LUCKY THIRTEEN

In the Community Shield, the traditional season-opening game between the league and FA Cup winners, Arsenal faced Manchester City at Wembley in 2014 and the Club's resounding 3–0 victory saw the Gunners lift the trophy for a 13th time.

Twelve of those triumphs were outright victories – they shared the silverware with Tottenham after a goalless draw in 1991 – and the Club's haul of 13 puts the Gunners third on the all-time list of Community Shield winners.

The 2014 game was a repeat of the 1934 meeting between Arsenal and Manchester City, which finished 4–0 to the Gunners, giving the Club its record winning margin in the Community Shield.

BELOW: Santi Cazorla, Aaron Ramsey and Olivier Giroud pose with the Community Shield in the dressing room at Wembley after beating Manchester City 3–0.

ARSENAL'S FA CUP RECORD 1980–2014

1980–81 – Third Round (Lost 2–0, Everton)
1981–82 – Third Round (Lost 1–0, Tottenham Hotspur)
1982–83 – Semi-Finals (Lost 2–1, Manchester United)
1983–84 – Third Round (Lost 3–2, Middlesbrough)
1984–85 – Fourth Round (Lost 1–0, York City)
1985–86 – Fifth Round (Lost 3–0, Luton Town)
1986–87 – Quarter-Finals (Lost 3–1, Watford)
1987–88 – Quarter-Finals (Lost 2–1, Nottingham Forest)
1988–89 – Third Round (Lost 1–0, West Ham United)
1989–90 – Fourth Round (Lost 2–0, QPR)
1990–91 – Semi-Finals (Lost 3–1, Tottenham Hotspur)
1991–92 – Third Round (Lost 2–1, Wrexham)
1992–93 – Winners (Won 2–1 aet, Sheffield Wednesday)
1993–94 – Fourth Round (Lost 3–1 aet, Bolton Wanderers)
1994–95 – Third Round (Lost 2–0, Millwall)
1995–96 – Third Round (Lost 1–0, Sheffield United)
1996–97 – Fourth Round (Lost 1–0, Leeds United)
1997–98 – Winners (Won 2–0, Newcastle United)
1998–99 – Semi-Finals (Lost 2–1, Manchester United)
1999–2000 – Fourth Round (Lost 6–5 on penalties, Leicester City)
2000–01 – Runners-Up (Lost 2–1, Liverpool)
2001–02 – Winners (Won 2–0, Chelsea)
2002–03 – Winners (Won 1–0, Southampton)
2003–04 – Semi-Finals (Lost 1–0, Manchester United)
2004–05 – Winners (Won 5–4 on penalties, Manchester United)
2005–06 – Fourth Round (Lost 1–0, Bolton Wanderers)
2006–07 – Fifth Round (Lost 1–0, Blackburn Rovers)
2007–08 – Fifth Round (Lost 4–0, Manchester United)
2008–09 – Semi-Finals (Lost 2–1, Chelsea)
2009–10 – Fourth Round (Lost 3–1, Stoke City)
2010–11 – Quarter-Finals (Lost 2–0, Manchester United)
2011–12 – Fifth Round (Lost 2–0, Sunderland)
2012–13 – Fifth Round (Lost 1–0, Blackburn Rovers)
2013–14 – Winners (Won 3–2 aet, Hull City)
2014–15 – Winners (Won 4–0, Aston Villa)

FA Cup & League Cup Records – Miscellaneous

ABOVE: Robert Pires was a seven-time winner for Arsenal.

▲ SEVEN WINNER'S MEDALS

Arsenal legend Robert Pires won an amazing seven winners' medals during his stay with the Gunners. The France midfielder won three FA Cups (2002, 2003 and 2005) and two FA Community Shields (2002 and 2004) as well as his two Premier League winner's medals in 2001–02 and 2003–04.

MADJESKI MASSACRE

Arsenal's incredible 7–5 victory over Reading in the last 16 of the 2012–13 League Cup was the highest aggregate score in the history of the competition.

The record-breaking meeting in October saw the Gunners leak four unanswered goals in the first half before Theo Walcott scored to spark an unbelievable fightback just before the break.

Arsene Wenger's side emerged for the second half transformed and further strikes from Olivier Giroud, Laurent Koscielny and a last-minute second from Walcott levelled the scores at 4–4 and sent the match into extra-time.

Marouane Chamakh made it 5–4 before Reading rallied with a Pavel Pogrebnyak equalizer. But the drama was far from over, as Walcott and Chamakh both scored in the last minute to seal an improbable and record-breaking 7–5 triumph.

CUP DOUBLE

Arsenal made history in 1993 when they became the first Club ever to claim an FA Cup and League Cup double, beating Sheffield Wednesday in both finals.

The first instalment of the famous feat came in mid-April when the Gunners beat the Owls 2–1 at Wembley in the League Cup final courtesy of goals from Paul Merson and Steve Morrow. The two sides were back in north London a month later for the FA Cup final rematch.

The game went into extra-time after Ian Wright had opened the scoring only for David Hirst to equalize after the break and, with neither side able to make the breakthrough in the additional 30 minutes of play, a replay was required. Five days later they reconvened at Wembley.

Wright again opened the scoring, Wednesday again levelled in the second half (through Chris Waddle) and the game again headed into extra-time. But this time George Graham's side did score as Andy Linighan hit the winner in the penultimate minute and the Gunners had completed an unprecedented cup double.

RIGHT: Mexican striker Carlos Vela scored a hat-trick for the Gunners against Sheffield United in 2008.

CUP MARATHON

1979–80 saw Arsenal playing 18 times in the FA Cup and League Cup.

The Club played seven times to lose in the fifth round of the League Cup then added 11 fixtures in the FA Cup where they needed a replay to get past Cardiff City then two games to knock out Bolton. But it was the epic semi-final with Liverpool that really ratcheted up the number of games.

The first meeting finished goalless while the first and second replays ended 1–1 and it was only Brian Talbot's goal in the fourth meeting that could separate the two teams.

The Gunners lost the resulting final 1–0 to West Ham, the 18th domestic cup game in what was a record-breaking campaign.

▼ FORTRESS EMIRATES

Since the Club decamped to the Emirates in 2006, the new ground has witnessed some resounding victories in both domestic cup competitions.

The team's record winning margin in the FA Cup at the stadium is 4–0 and has been recorded twice.

The first time was in February 2009 against Cardiff City and the second occasion was against Coventry City a year later.

The Club's biggest League Cup win at the Emirates came in the Third Round of the competition in September 2008 when a young Gunners side despatched Sheffiled United 6–0 with a hat-trick from Carlos Vela, a brace from Nicklas Bendtner and a sixth from Jack Wilshere.

ARSENAL'S LEAGUE CUP RECORD 1966–2014

1966–67 – Third Round (Lost 3–1, West Ham United)
1967–68 – Runners-Up (Lost 1–0, Leeds United)
1968–69 – Runners-Up (Lost 3–1 aet, Swindon Town)
1969–70 – Third Round (Lost 1–0, Everton)
1970–71 – Fourth Round (Lost 2–0, Crystal Palace)
1971–72 – Fourth Round (Lost 2–0, Sheffield United)
1972–73 – Quarter-Finals (Lost 3–0, Norwich City)
1973–74 – Second Round (Lost 1–0, Tranmere Rovers)
1974–75 – Second Round (Lost 2–1 Leicester City)
1975–76 – Second Round (Lost 1–0, Everton)
1976–77 – Quarter-Finals (Lost 4–1, Middlesbrough)
1977–78 – Semi-Finals (Lost 2–1 on aggregate, Liverpool)
1978–79 – Second Round (Lost 3–1, Rotherham United)
1979–80 – Quarter-Finals (Lost 4–3, Swindon Town)
1980–81 – Fourth Round (Lost 1–0, Tottenham Hotspur)
1981–82 – Fourth Round (Lost 3–0, Liverpool)
1982–83 – Semi-Finals (Lost 6–3 on aggregate, Manchester United)
1983–84 – Fourth Round (Lost 2–1, Walsall)
1984–85 – Third Round (Lost 3–2, Oxford United)
1985–86 – Quarter-Finals (Lost 2–1, Aston Villa)
1986–87 – Winners (Won 2–1, Liverpool)
1987–88 – Runners-Up (Lost 3–2, Luton Town)
1988–89 – Third Round (Lost 3–1, Liverpool)
1989–90 – Fourth Round (Lost 3–1, Oldham Athletic)
1990–91 – Fourth Round (Lost 6–2, Manchester United)
1991–92 – Third Round (Lost 1–0, Coventry City)
1992–93 – Winners (Won 2–1, Sheffield Wednesday)

1993–94 – Fourth Round (Lost 1–0, Aston Villa)
1994–95 – Quarter-Finals (Lost 1–0, Liverpool)
1995–96 – Semi-Finals (Lost on away goals after 2–2 aggregate draw, Aston Villa)
1996–97 – Fourth Round (Lost 4–2, Liverpool)
1997–98 – Semi-Finals (Lost 4–3 on aggregate, Chelsea)
1998–99 – Fourth Round (Lost 5–0, Chelsea)
1999–2000 – Fourth Round (Lost 3–1 on penalties, Middlesbrough)
2000–01 – Third Round (Lost 2–1, Ipswich Town)
2001–02 – Quarter-Finals (Lost 4–0, Blackburn Rovers)
2002–03 – Third Round (Lost 3–2, Sunderland)
2003–04 – Semi-Finals (Lost 3–1 on aggregate, Middlesbrough)
2004–05 – Quarter-Finals (Lost 1–0, Manchester United)
2005–06 – Semi-Finals (Lost on away goals after 2–2 aggregate draw, Wigan Athletic)
2006–07 – Runners-Up (Lost 2–1 aet, Chelsea)
2007–08 – Semi-Finals (Lost 6–2 on aggregate, Tottenham Hotspur)
2008–09 – Quarter-Finals (Lost 2–0, Burnley)
2009–10 – Quarter-Finals (Lost 3–0, Manchester City)
2010–11 – Runners-Up (Lost 2–1, Birmingham City)
2011–12 – Fifth Round (Lost 1–0, Manchester City)
2012–13 – Quarter-Finals (Lost 3–2 on penalties, Bradford City)
2013–14 – Fourth Round (Lost 2–0, Chelsea)
2014–15 – Third Round (Lost 2–1, Southampton)

▼ FIVE-GOAL THRILLER

The League Cup abandoned its old two-legged format for the final in the 1966–67 season. Since the showpiece game became a one-off affair, Arsenal jointly hold the record for the highest aggregate scoreline.

They equalled the record in 1988 when they played Luton Town at Wembley. Brian Stein gave the Hatters a shock early lead but second-half goals from Martin Hayes and Alan Smith appeared to give the Gunners the upper hand – only for Danny Wilson and Stein again in the final minute to snatch a dramatic 3–2 victory.

The five-goal tally equalled the record set in the finals of 1967 and 1979, as well as the 1977 replay.

BELOW: Martin Hayes scores for the Gunners to draw level with Luton Town in the 1988 League Cup final. The game did not go the Gunners' way however, as Luton snatched a late winner.

RIGHT: Herbert Chapman, seen here in his playing days at Northampton Town, led Arsenal to their highest-ever winning scoreline in the FA Cup, 11–1 against Darwen in 1932.

▲ HAT-TRICK DOUBLE

The Gunners' biggest-ever win (12–0) in the FA Cup came against Ashford United in 1893 in the first qualifying round but the Club's heaviest victory in the competition proper came in January 1932 when they played Lancashire side Darwen.

The first-round clash at Highbury was nothing if not one-sided and, thanks to four goals from Cliff Bastin and a David Jack hat-trick, Herbert Chapman's side raced to a crushing 11–1 victory.

European Records

The Gunners first experienced European football during the 1963–64 season when they played in the Inter-Cities Fairs Cup and since that debut the Club has been a regular in Continental competition. This section is dedicated to all of Arsenal's greatest European achievements, as well as some of the team's inevitable disappointments.

BELOW: The Gunners famously lifted the UEFA Cup Winners' Cup in 1994.

RIGHT: Alan Smith celebrates after scoring the winner in the final against Parma in Copenhagen.

European Records – Biggest Wins

WRIGHT'S SEVEN-GOAL SALVO

Arsenal's first-ever competitive match in Europe was also one of the Club's biggest-ever wins.

The match came away from home against Danish side Stævnet in September 1963 in the first round of the Inter-Cities Fairs Cup, a forerunner of the UEFA Cup, and produced eight goals.

Billy Wright's side scored seven of them courtesy of hat-tricks from Geoff Strong and Joe Baker ... and the Gunners' European history had begun.

▼ PRAGUE'S EMIRATES EMBARRASSMENT

The Gunners have enjoyed some glorious European nights at Emirates but perhaps none more memorable than their clash with Slavia Prague in the group stages of the Champions League in October 2007. Arsenal were irresistible going forward, slicing through the Czech defence at will for a European Club-record 7–0 victory.

The writing was on the wall for the visitors after just five minutes when Cesc Fabregas hit a superb curling shot from the edge of the area and things went from bad to worse for Slavia midway through the first half when David Hubacek inadvertently poked the ball into his own net.

Theo Walcott made it 3–0 to Arsene Wenger's side before the break and the match was already over. The Gunners, however, were far from finished and the 60,000-strong crowd were treated to four more goals in the second half as Alexander Hleb, Walcott, Fabregas and Nicklas Bendtner piled on the misery.

▼ SUPERB IN THE SAN SIRO

Arsenal's biggest win away from home in the Champions League came in the group stages of the 2003–04 competition, a magnificent 5–1 triumph over Inter Milan at the San Siro on 25 November 2003.

The Italian giants had beaten the Gunners 3–0 at Highbury two months earlier and Arsene Wenger's team clearly had revenge on their minds.

Thierry Henry began the rout midway through the first half. Christian Vieri briefly equalized for the Italians before Freddie Ljungberg restored the advantage and Henry made it three with a stunning individual effort.

In the 86th minute, Edu grabbed the fourth and Robert Pires rubbed salt into the wound in injury-time with the fifth.

ABOVE RIGHT: Henry was twice on target as Inter Milan were humbled in the San Siro.

RIGHT: Walcott ripped the Slavia defence to shreds in the 2007–08 Champions League.

RIGHT: It was seventh heaven for Arsenal as they demolished Standard Liege in Belgium in 1993.

▶ SEVEN IN BELGIUM

The 7–0 annihilation of Slavia Prague is Arsenal's biggest Champions League win and equalled the Club's previous record European success, a 7–0 demolition of Standard Liege in the 1993–94 Cup Winners' Cup.

The Gunners qualified for the competition after their win over Sheffield Wednesday in the replay of the 1993 FA Cup final and lined up against the Belgians in the second leg of their second-round clash in the wake of a 3–0 victory in the first match.

Manager George Graham rested striker Ian Wright, one booking away from a suspension, but his side were no less potent in attack in the Stade Maurice Dufrasne, scoring seven unanswered goals on Belgian soil.

The 7–0 win was set up as early as the third minute when Alan Smith converted Paul Merson's inviting cross. Tony Adams, Ian Selley, Kevin Campbell (2), Merson and substitute Eddie McGoldrick all helped themselves and Arsenal went through to the third round with a 10–0 aggregate scoreline.

The victory clearly had a morale-boosting effect and the Gunners went on to win the Cup Winners' Cup after beating Parma in the final.

ARSENAL'S CHAMPIONS LEAGUE RECORD
1998–99 – Group Stage
1999–2000 – First Group Stage
2000–01 – Quarter-Finals (Lost on away goals after 2–2 aggregate draw, Valencia)
2001–02 – Second Group Stage
2002–03 – Second Group Stage
2003–04 – Quarter-Finals (Lost 3–2 on aggregate, Chelsea)
2004–05 – Last 16 (Lost 3–2 on aggregate, Bayern Munich)
2005–06 – Runners-Up (Lost 2–1, Barcelona)
2006–07 – Last 16 (Lost 2–1 on aggregate, PSV Eindhoven)
2007–08 – Quarter-Finals (Lost 4–3 on aggregate, Liverpool)
2008–09 – Semi-Finals (Lost 4–1 on aggregate, Manchester United)
2009–10 – Last 16 (Lost 6–3 on aggregate, Barcelona)
2010–11 – Last 16 (Lost 4–3 on aggregate, Barcelona)
2011–12 – Last 16 (Lost 4–3 on aggregate, AC Milan)
2012–13 – Last 16 (Lost on away goals after 3–3 aggregate draw, Bayern Munich)
2013–14 – Last 16 (Lost 3–1 on aggregate, Bayern Munich)
2014–15 – Last 16 (Lost 3–3 on away goals, Monaco)

◀ DEPORTIVO CRUSHED

Spain is the most successful European country in terms of trophies won, but the Gunners have claimed a Spanish scalp 10 times in the Club's history.

The team's most emphatic victory over La Liga opposition was in March 2000 when Deportivo La Coruna came to Highbury for the first leg of a UEFA Cup fourth-round clash.

Arsene Wenger gambled by leaving Tony Adams, Ray Parlour and Kanu on the bench. But his side still proved too powerful for the Spanish visitors as Lee Dixon, Thierry Henry (2), Kanu from the bench and Dennis Bergkamp all scored in a 5–1 romp.

WEMBLEY ADVENTURE

Between 1998 and 2000 Arsenal relocated to Wembley for their Champions League fixtures. When they qualified for the competition for the first time, during their temporary residency at the home of English football, their biggest win came against Swedish side AIK.

The two teams met in the group stages in September 1999 and Freddie Ljungberg opened the scoring after 28 minutes. The visitors equalized but the Gunners registered a record 3–1 Wembley win courtesy of injury-time goals from Thierry Henry and Davor Suker.

LEFT: Lee Dixon was on the score sheet as Spanish side Deportivo La Coruna were thumped 5–1 at Highbury in 2000.

European Records – Biggest Defeats

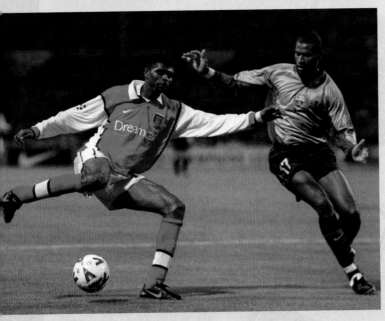

ABOVE: The Gunners were far from their best against Barcelona at Wembley in October 1999.

◀ FOUR UP FOR BARCELONA

Arsenal relocated to Wembley for European nights during the 1989–99 and 1999–2000 seasons and in the six games they played at the home of the England team, the Gunners were beaten three times. The worst defeat was a 4–2 loss to Barcelona in the group phases in October 1999.

Rivaldo and Luis Enrique put the Spanish ahead and although Dennis Bergkamp pulled one back before half-time, Barcelona stretched their lead through Luis Figo and Phillip Cocu after the break and Marc Overmars' 84th-minute strike was no more than a consolation.

ITALIAN WOE

Arsenal played three seasons in the old Cup Winners' Cup, lifting the trophy in 1994 and finishing as runners-up in 1980 and 1995. In total the side lost just twice in the now defunct tournament, suffering their biggest defeat – a 3–2 reverse – against Sampdoria in Italy at the semi-final stage in April 1995.

▶ MILAN HIT FOUR

Arsenal were beaten just twice in the Champions League during the 2011–12 campaign and the second of those defeats proved to be the Gunners' heaviest loss in the revamped competition.

The opposition were Italian giants AC Milan at the San Siro in February in the last 16 of the tournament. Arsene Wenger's side found themselves trailing after just 15 minutes when Kevin-Prince Boateng struck a superb long-range effort. A brace from Brazilian Robinho either side of half-time did further damage while a late penalty from Swedish striker Zlatan Ibrahimovic condemned Arsenal to a 4–0 defeat and their biggest-ever Champions League failure.

The Gunners took revenge three weeks later in the second leg at Highbury with a 3–0 triumph – but it was not enough to earn the side a quarter-final place.

LEFT: AC Milan were too strong for Arsene Wenger's side in Italy in February 2012.

PORTUGUESE PITFALL

Before the introduction of the Champions League in 1992–93, Arsenal enjoyed two seasons of European Cup football, in 1971–72 and then again in 1991–92. In 10 fixtures, the team was beaten four times and the heaviest of those was a 3–1 extra time loss to Portuguese side Benfica at Highbury in November 1991.

INTER-CITIES DISAPPOINTMENT

Arsenal's first three seasons of European football came in the Inter-Cities Fairs Cup and in 24 outings in the competition, they suffered defeat just six times.

The team's debut campaign in 1963–64 saw Billy Wright's team beaten 3–1 by Standard Liege seven days before Christmas and the Gunners equalled that record Inter-Cities reverse during their 1969–70 campaign, losing 3–1 to Anderlecht in April.

SPARTAK SMASH GUNNERS

The Club's largest loss in any competitive European match came in the UEFA Cup in 1982–83. Arsenal faced Spartak Moscow at Highbury in September and, having lost the first leg in Russia a fortnight earlier, Terry Neill's team desperately needed to win the rematch.

Unfortunately things didn't go according to plan as the visitors smashed five goals past goalkeeper George Wood. Lee Chapman and a Spartak own-goal briefly gave the Highbury faithful something to cheer, but at full-time the Gunners had been beaten 5–2.

► IRRESISTIBLE INTER

The Gunners' biggest reverse at home in the Champions League also came against a team from Milan but this time it was Inter who inflicted it.

The game at Emirates came in September 2003 in the opening fixture of the group stages and the home side found themselves on the back foot on 22 minutes when Julio Ricardo Cruz opened the scoring.

Three minutes later Andy van der Meyde doubled the advantage and when Thierry Henry had a penalty superbly saved by Francesco Toldo, the writing was on the wall. Obafemi Martins added Inter Milan's third before the break and, although there were no further goals in the second half, the Gunners crashed to their biggest home defeat in the competition.

RIGHT: Messi singlehandedly knocked Arsenal out of the 2009–10 Champions League.

► MESSI MAULS ARSENAL

The Gunners reached the knockout stages of the Champions League for a fourth successive season in 2009–10 but their involvement in the tournament came to an unceremonious end after they were beaten 4–1 by Barcelona in the Nou Camp.

The two teams locked horns in Spain just six days after a 2–2 draw at Emirates in the first leg of their quarter-final encounter and when Nicklas Bendtner scored, after just 18 minutes, Arsenal were dreaming of a place in the last four.

They hadn't, however, reckoned with the genius of Lionel Messi who transformed the tie with a first-half hat-trick and a fourth after the break to seal a 4–1 triumph and condemn the Gunners to their worst loss in the knockout stages of the Champions League.

BELOW: Freddie Ljungberg was unable to stop the Gunners losing 3–0 to Inter at Highbury in 2003.

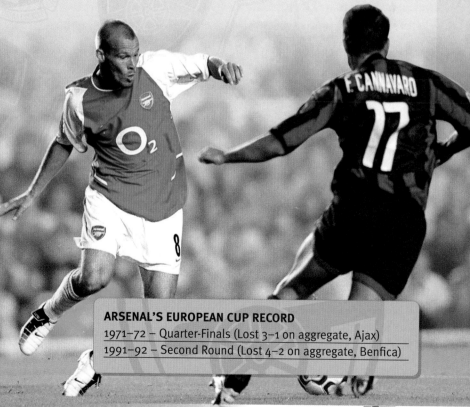

ARSENAL'S EUROPEAN CUP RECORD

1971–72 – Quarter-Finals (Lost 3–1 on aggregate, Ajax)

1991–92 – Second Round (Lost 4–2 on aggregate, Benfica)

European Records – Champions

▶▶ MEE MAKES HISTORY

Arsenal's first taste of European glory came in the 1969–70 season when Bertie Mee's side entered the Inter-Cities Fairs Cup and, despite their inexperience of Continental football and a side exclusively featuring English and Scottish players, battled through all the way to the final.

The Gunners had little problem despatching Irish opponents Glentoran 3–1 on aggregate in the first round and a 3–0 victory over two games against Portuguese side Sporting Lisbon, next up, eased the team into round three.

French club Rouen stood in the way of a place in the quarter-finals and, after a goalless draw in the first leg at Highbury, Arsenal were heavily indebted to a goal from Jon Sammels at the Stade Robert Diochon in January to ease the team into the last eight.

Romanian side FCM Bacau proved no match for the Gunners in the quarter-finals, losing 9–2 on aggregate, and in their debut campaign Mee's team found themselves in the semi-finals.

Ajax, who were to lift the European Cup just 12 months later, lined up against Arsenal in the last four but were swept aside in the first leg at Highbury as goals from Sammels and Charlie George (2) secured a priceless 3–0 win. The Dutch side exacted a degree of revenge in Amsterdam in the second leg with a 1–0 success seven days later but it was not enough to prevent the Gunners reaching the final.

Belgian club Anderlecht, 2–1 aggregate winners over Inter Milan in the semis, were the only remaining hurdle but Arsenal's prospects of silverware looked bleak after the first leg in the Constant Vanden Stock Stadium as the home side recorded a 3–1 victory. Ray Kennedy grabbed a late 82nd-minute consolation but the Gunners knew they still needed a vastly improved performance in the return match at Highbury.

An early goal to settle the nerves was top of the agenda in north London in late April and Eddie Kelly provided it after 25 minutes. John Radford levelled the tie on aggregate midway through the second half and just a minute later Sammels settled the issue with his sixth goal of the campaign.

Ajax had no reply and, 84 years after the Club was founded, Arsenal were lifting a European trophy.

RIGHT: Manager Bertie Mee secured Arsenal's first ever European trophy in 1970.

BELOW: George Armstrong celebrates Jon Sammels' winning goal against Anderlecht in the 1970 Inter Cities Fairs Cup final.

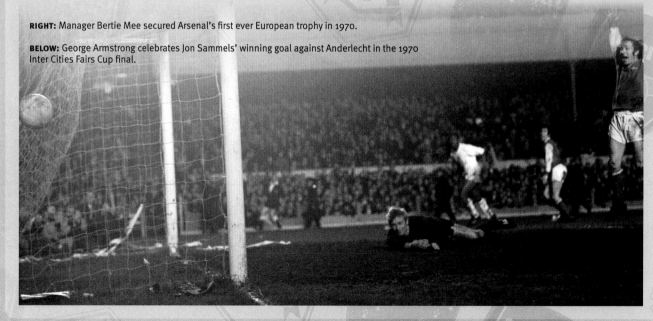

SMITH STRIKE SEALS SILVERWARE

The Gunners' triumph over Sheffield Wednesday in the 1993 FA Cup final at Wembley earned the Club a place in the Cup Winners' Cup the following season, the second time the Gunners had entered the competition.

The team were drawn against Danish side Odense in the first round. After a 2–1 victory in the first leg away from home courtesy of goals from Ian Wright and Paul Merson, George Graham's team ground out a 1–1 draw at Highbury to progress.

The second round saw the Gunners face Standard Liege but the Belgians were simply outclassed in both legs, losing 3–0 at Highbury before slumping to a one-sided 7–0 defeat at their Stade Maurice Dufrasne in early November as six different players got on the score sheet.

Italy's Torino were the quarter-final opponents and the Serie A outfit provided a far sterner test of Arsenal's credentials. The first leg in Turin finished goalless and the tie was only finally settled at Highbury when captain Tony Adams became an unlikely hero with the only goal of the match on 66 minutes.

The semi-final against Paris Saint-Germain was equally tense. A Wright goal earned the Gunners a 1–1 draw in Paris and, although Kevin Campbell was on target after just seven minutes at Highbury, Arsenal could not break down the PSG defence again and

had to endure a nervous 83 minutes before the final whistle confirmed they were through to the final.

It was Italian opposition once again for Graham and his team in the shape of Parma, the defending champions. Joint top-scorer Wright was suspended for the match in the Parken Stadium in Copenhagen but the back four which had conceded just three times in the earlier rounds remained *in situ* for the Anglo-Italian clash.

There was to be just one goal in the game and it came after 22 minutes. Parma captain Lorenzo Minotti mis-hit a clearance which fell to Alan Smith, who unleashed an instinctive, deadly left-foot volley that beat Luca Bucci in goal. The Gunners' back four shackled the threat of Gianfranco Zola and Faustino Asprilla for the rest of the match, and after 90 minutes Adams was preparing to lift the Cup Winners' Cup for the first time in the Club's history.

ABOVE: Arsenal beat Parma to win the Cup Winners' Cup in 1994 and made their mark on European football.

LEFT: Alan Smith proudly lifts the Cup Winners' Cup after an historic night in Denmark.

ARSENAL'S UEFA CUP RECORD
1978–79 – Third Round (Lost 2–1 on aggregate, Red Star Belgrade)	
1981–82 – Second Round (Lost on away goals after 2–2 aggregate draw, Genk)	
1982–83 – First Round (Lost 8–4 on aggregate, Spartak Moscow)	
1996–97 – First Round (Lost 6–4 on aggregate, Borussia Monchengladbach)	
1997–98 – First Round (Lost 2–1 on aggregate, PAOK)	
1999–00 – Runners-Up (Lost 4–1 on penalties, Galatasaray)	

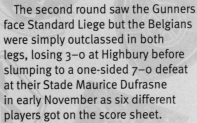

European Records – Sequences

▶ LEHMANN'S LONG RUN

Jens Lehmann is the proud holder of the Champions League record for the longest time a goalkeeper has gone without conceding a goal, going a unprecedented 853 minutes without picking the ball out of the back of the net between February 2005 and September 2006.

The German keeper's unbelievable streak began in the last 16 of the 2004–05 campaign. Arsenal were defeated 3–1 by Bayern Munich away from home, with Lehmann beaten by Hasan Silihamidzic for the third goal in the 65th minute in the Olympiastadion but it was to be 20 months before another player scored against him.

Lehmann kept a clean sheet in the second leg against the Germans and, after missing the opening two group phase games in 2005–06, he returned to the side and successfully kept Sparta Prague, Real Madrid, Juventus and Villarreal at bay as Arsenal reached the final.

Arsene Wenger's side conceded two in the final against Barcelona but both goals came after the German had been sent off in the 18th minute for bringing down Samuel Eto'o – and so, albeit in bizarre circumstances, his unbeaten sequence continued.

He was finally beaten in the opening game of 2006–07 when Boubacar Sanogo scored a 90th minute consolation goal for Hamburg at the Imtech Arena, ending 853 minutes of glorious goalkeeping.

Lehmann's achievement eclipsed the previous record of 658 minutes set by Edwin van der Sar when he was an Ajax player in the 1990s.

▶ EUROPEAN EXILE

Following the Club's first foray into European football during the 1963–64 season in the Inter-Cities Fairs Cup, Arsenal's longest absence from European competition came in the 1970s when the Gunners spent six seasons reluctantly concentrating solely on domestic matters.

The side was eliminated from the European Cup at the quarter-final stage by Ajax on 22 March 1972 and did not feature in a UEFA tournament again until they lined up against Lokomotive Leipzig on 13 September 1978 in the first round of the UEFA Cup.

There was a nine-year exile from European action between 1982 and 1991 but six years of that absence were due to the ban on English clubs following the Heysel Stadium disaster.

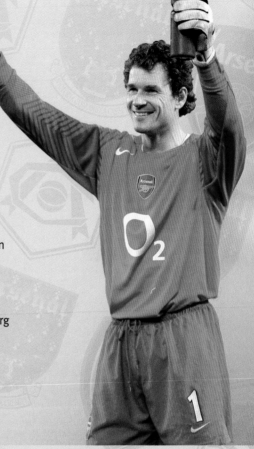

ABOVE: Jens Lehmann went more than 14 hours without conceding a Champions League goal.

BELOW: Alan Sunderland in action against Lokomotive Leipzig in the 1978–79 UEFA Cup campaign.

ABOVE: Liam Brady surges forward in the European Cup Winners' Cup against Valencia in 1980. On this occasion, the Gunners succumbed to a penalty shootout.

CLEAN SHEET RECORD

The Gunners hold the Champions League record for the most consecutive clean sheets in the competition, going an amazing 10 matches during the 2005–06 campaign without allowing the opposition to score.

The miserly defensive streak started on 18 October 2005 in the third game of the group phase when Arsenal travelled to the Czech Republic to face Sparta Prague and returned to London with a 2–0 triumph.

The remaining three group games saw Sparta beaten 3–0 at Highbury, Swiss side FC Thun 1–0 away from home and Ajax held goalless in north London.

Real Madrid failed to breach the Gunners' defence in either leg of their last-16 meeting, as did Juventus in two quarter-finals clashes. Villarreal also fired blanks home and away in the semi-finals and it was not until the 76th minute of the final against Barcelona, when Samuel Eto'o scored, that Arsene Wenger's side finally conceded.

Before Eto'o, the last player to score against the team in the Champions League was Ajax's Markus Rosenberg in the 71st minute of the group game in September, meaning Arsenal had gone 995 minutes without conceding.

AC Milan had held the previous record, registering seven consecutive clean sheets in the 2004–05 season.

▶ UEFA CUP MILESTONE

Arsenal finished UEFA Cup runners-up in 2000 and it is no surprise that the team's longest unbeaten run in open play in the competition came en route to the final.

The sequence began with a 2–0 quarter-final, first-leg defeat of Werder Bremen at Highbury. The Germans were despatched 4–2 in the return match while Lens were beaten home and away in the semi-final.

The final in Copenhagen saw the Gunners face Galatasaray and, although it was the Turkish team who lifted the trophy, they only did so after beating Arsene Wenger's side in a penalty shootout, meaning Arsenal had still set a Club record of five UEFA Cup fixtures without defeat in open play.

▲ UNBOWED IN EUROPE

Arsenal had a real affinity with the UEFA Cup Winners' Cup – winning the competition once and twice finishing as runners-up – and between September 1979 and April 1995 the Club went an incredible 25 games in the tournament without suffering defeat in open play.

The remarkable streak began in September in the 1979–80 season with a 2–0 first-round, first-leg victory against Turkish side Fenerbahce at Highbury, and the side marched all the way to the final without loss. They were eventually beaten in a dreaded penalty shootout by Valencia but their unbeaten record inside 120 minutes remained intact.

The Gunners were back in Cup Winners' Cup action in 1993–94 and lifted the trophy without being beaten, extending the sequence to 18 games.

The 1994–95 campaign saw Arsenal reach the semi-finals with four wins and two draws and the run reached a phenomenal 25 matches when they overcame Sampdoria 3–2 in the first leg of their last-four encounter at Highbury.

It was finally ended in the second leg a fortnight later when the Italians emerged 3–2 winners in the Stadio Luigi Ferraris in Genoa, although Arsenal still reached the final after overcoming the home side in a penalty shootout.

BELOW: Thierry Henry and the Gunners were in impressive form during their 1999–2000 UEFA Cup campaign.

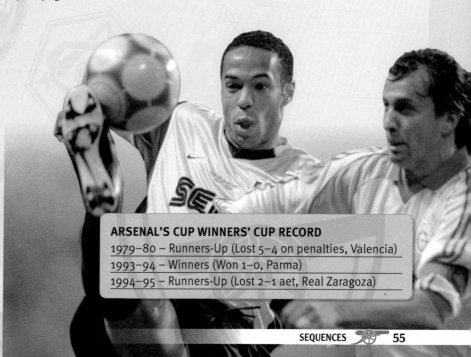

ARSENAL'S CUP WINNERS' CUP RECORD

1979–80 – Runners-Up (Lost 5–4 on penalties, Valencia)

1993–94 – Winners (Won 1–0, Parma)

1994–95 – Runners-Up (Lost 2–1 aet, Real Zaragoza)

European Records – Miscellaneous

RECORD EIGHT VICTORIES

The Gunners won eight matches en route to the 2006 Champions League final, equalling the previous Club record of eight victories in a European campaign, set in 1969–70 when they won the Inter-Cities Fairs Cup.

In terms of a winning percentage, their feat of 1969–70 was the more impressive, with eight wins in 12 games compared to eight in 13 fixtures in 2005–06.

DEADLY CHAMAKH

Only three players have scored in six consecutive Champions League fixtures and the distinction of being the first man to achieve the feat belongs to former Gunners striker Marouane Chamakh.

The Moroccan forward began his prolific sequence as a Bordeaux player in the knockout stages of the 2009–10 competition, finding the back of the net against Olympiacos and Lyon twice.

He signed for Arsenal on a free transfer in the summer of 2010 and continued his deadly form in front of goal with strikes in successive appearances for the Club in the group phase against Braga, Partizan Belgrade and Shakhtar Donetsk.

Since Chamakh's record-breaking achievement, Galatasary's Burak Yilmaz (2012–13) and Real Madrid's Cristiano Ronaldo (2012–13) have also hit the net in six successive Champions League appearances.

ABOVE: John Lukic rolled back the years in Arsenal's 1–1 draw with Lazio at the Stadio Olimpico.

LUKIC AGAINST LAZIO

The oldest player to represent the Club in a competitive European fixture is goalkeeper John Lukic, who was 39 years and 311 days old when he was named in the starting XI for Arsenal's Champions League clash with Lazio in October 2000.

BELOW: Marouane Chamakh enjoyed a fine run in front of goal in 2010.

NATIONAL PRIDE

Since making their European debut, Arsenal have faced opposition from 24 different countries and are yet to suffer a defeat against clubs from 10 of those nations.

Teams from Croatia, Cyprus, the Czech Republic, Norway, Romania, Scotland, Serbia, Sweden, Switzerland and Turkey have all unsuccessfully tried to beat the Gunners over the years in a total of 39 games.

In terms of overall victories against sides from one country, Italian teams are Arsenal's favourite opposition. The Club have faced Italian teams 33 times in European competition and recorded 16 wins, nine draws and just eight defeats.

FANTASTIC BACK FOUR

The Gunners' progress to the final of the 2006 Champions League was built on a superb defensive effort and the four goals Arsene Wenger's side conceded that season represent the Club's lowest tally ever in the competition. Arsenal played 13 Champions League games in 2005–06 but only FC Thun and Ajax and Barcelona were able to find a way through the Gunners' back four.

▶ BENDTNER ON TARGET

Although they were eliminated by Barcelona at the quarter-final stage, the 2009–10 season was Arsenal's most prolific ever, with the side scoring 26 goals in 12 matches.

The Gunners racked up five in their aggregate victory over Celtic in the third qualifying round, and scored 12 more in finishing top of Group H. Their 6–2 demolition of Porto in the last 16 added to the tally and, although they were knocked out by Barcelona in the last eight, they still managed three over two legs against the reigning Spanish champions.

The goals were evenly shared among the squad. Nicklas Bendtner top-scored with five, Cesc Fabregas weighed in with four while Samir Nasri registered a treble. In total, 13 different Arsenal players found the back of the net during the campaign.

▶ MARVELLOUS MACLEOD

The 1963–64 season saw Arsenal venture into Europe for the first time and their first match was against Danish side Stævnet in Copenhagen in the first round of the Inter-Cities Fairs Cup.

The Gunners triumphed 7–1 and, while Geoff Strong and Joe Baker made the headlines with a hat-trick apiece, it was Johnny MacLeod, a £400,000 signing from Hibernian, who made history with the Club's first-ever goal in a competitive European fixture.

Almost a month later winger Alan Skirton joined MacLeod in the record books when he became the first Gunner to score a European goal at Highbury as the side despatched Stævnet in the return leg.

ABOVE: Johnny MacLeod scored the Club's first ever goal in Europe in the 1963–64 season.

TEENAGER WILSHERE SETS NEW MARK

The youngest-ever player to feature for Arsenal in a European match was Jack Wilshere when he was named in the squad for the Champions League group stage clash with Dynamo Kiev at Emirates in November 2008.

The England midfielder started on the bench but was introduced to the action after 77 minutes in place of Carlos Vela, becoming the youngest European Gunner at the age of 16 years and 329 days.

It was only Wilshere's fourth appearance for the first team and broke the previous record set by Cesc Fabregas.

LEFT: Nicklas Bendtner was the Gunners' top scorer in the 2009–10 Champions League with five goals.

ARSENAL'S INTER-CITIES FAIRS CUP RECORD
1963–64 – Second Round (Lost 4–2 on aggregate, RFC de Liege)
1969–70 – Winners (Won 4–3 on aggregate, Anderlecht)
1970–71 – Quarter-Finals ((Lost on away goals after 2–2 aggregate draw, Cologne)

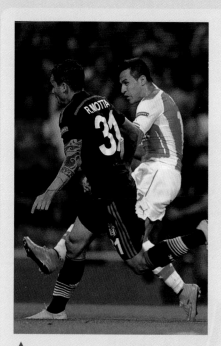

CONTINENTAL CONSISTENCY

The Gunners are yet to lift the Champions League trophy, but they remain one of the most consistent sides in the competition.

Arsenal's 1–0 aggregate victory over Turkish side Besiktas in the play-offs in August 2014 saw the Club qualify for the group stages of the tournament for the 17th season in succession, a record only Real Madrid and Manchester United have surpassed with 18 consecutive campaigns.

Arsene Wenger's side then finished second in Group D behind Borussia Dortmund to reach the last 16 for the 15th successive season. Only 10-time European champions Real Madrid

LONDON LANDMARK

When the Gunners beat Villarreal 1–0 on aggregate in the last four of the Champions League in 2006, they became the first Club from the capital to reach the final of European football's leading competition.

Tottenham had made the last four of the old European Cup in 1962 only to lose to Benfica 4–2 on aggregate, while Chelsea reached the semi-finals of the Champions League in 2004 and 2005, but it was Arsenal who set the record as the first London team to progress all the way to the final.

LEFT: Alexis Sanchez scored the only goal of the tie against Besitkas to take Arsenal into the Champions League group stages in 2014–15.

EMIRATES OPENER

Arsenal played their first competitive European match at Emirates in August 2007 when they faced Croatian side Dinamo Zagreb in the third qualifying round of the Champions League.

The Gunners were already 3–0 up following the first leg two weeks earlier, and they ran out 2–1 winners in north London to book their place in the group stages.

Freddie Ljungberg on 79 minutes and Mathieu Flamini in the final minute of the game were on target for Arsene Wenger's side, making Ljungberg the Gunners' first player to score a European goal at Emirates.

boast a better record in reaching the latter stages of the competition.

The team's subsequent third-place finish in the 2014–15 Premier League ensured they will play in the Champions League for an 18th consecutive season in 2015–16 and leaves them sixth on the competition's all-time appearance list.

OVERMARS' EUROPEAN OPENER

Netherlands winger Marc Overmars holds the distinction as the first Arsenal player to score a Champions League goal for the Club, netting in the side's 1–1 draw with Lens in September 1998.

Arsenal qualified for the competition for the first time in 1998–99 after winning the Premier League the previous season and Overmars was on target in the Stade Felix Bollaert in the opening game of the group phase to earn his place in the record books. The Dutchman stroked home Emmanuel Petit's slide-rule pass in the 51st minute in France, but it was not quite enough to earn Arsene Wenger's side all three points, with Lens equalizing in the final minute.

RIGHT: Marc Overmars opened the Club's Champions League account against Lens, in 1998.

RED CARD FIRST

Jens Lehmann made 200 appearances for the Club between 2003 and 2011 but the German international will probably want to forget his performance in the Champions League final against Barcelona in 2006.

The Gunners' goalkeeper was sent off in the 18th minute of the game in the Stade de France in Paris for a foul on striker Samuel Eto'o, becoming the first player to see red in a Champions League final.

BENDTNER'S BARRAGE

A Champions League hat-trick is a rare commodity and the first player to hit the fabled treble for the Gunners was Nicklas Bendtner, in March 2010.

The opposition was Porto at Emirates, in the last 16, and the Danish striker opened his account in the 10th minute when he pounced on a loose ball following a fine run from Andrey Arshavin. He doubled his tally 15 minutes later after more good work from Arshavin and completed his hat-trick in the final minute of the match from the penalty spot.

HENRY HITS FIRST

Arsenal's first two appearances in the Champions League resulted in elimination at the first group phase but Arsene Wenger's side did make it through to the quarter-finals in 2000–01, facing Spanish side Valencia.

The first leg at Highbury saw the Gunners emerge 2–1 winners, with Thierry Henry's 58th-minute opener the first-ever goal for the Club in the knockout stages of the competition.

RIGHT: Nicklas Bendtner hit a Champions League treble against Porto in 2010.

PART 2
Player Records

Football may be a game of 11 versus 11 but it's inevitable that individuals will make their mark and this chapter looks at the players who have rewritten the record books while wearing the red and white shirt.

The first six pages focus on the Club's most prolific and predatory marksmen over the years – from Thierry Henry's record haul of Arsenal goals, to Ted Drake's amazing exploits during the 1934–35 season, the Gunners' leading hat-trick heroes and Alan Smith's four-goal salvo in the European Cup.

The middle section is devoted to the likes of David O'Leary, Tom Parker and Ray Parlour who made Arsenal history with their number of appearances for the Club – the loyal servants who just kept on playing.

The Gunners' biggest transfers

– from David Jack's British-record £10,890 move from Bolton in 1928 up to the recent past and Nicolas Anelka's massive £22.5 million switch to Real Madrid in 1999 – chart the Club's transfer dealings.

The final pages focus on the players from Great Britain and Ireland, and more recently those from beyond these shores, to have earned international recognition during their Arsenal careers, while the chapter also includes details of Alan Skirton's milestone appearance for the Club during the 1965–66 season.

ABOVE: Ted Drake (right) shoots during a match against Brentford in 1938.

RIGHT: David O'Leary (left) and Tony Adams celebrate Arsenal's 1990–91 League title success.

Player Records – Goalscoring

Goals win matches and over the years Arsenal have been blessed with some of the game's most prolific strikers – players who just couldn't stop scoring. From Cliff Bastin to Thierry Henry and Doug Lishman to Ian Wright, this section celebrates the Gunners whose eye for goal was without equal.

ABOVE: Bobby Gould made history in 1968 when he scored against Leicester after coming off the bench.

GOULD STANDARD

Substitutions were first allowed in English football in the 1965–66 season but it was not until August 1968 that an Arsenal replacement came off the bench to score. The player who made history was striker Bobby Gould, who came on for George Graham in the Gunners' Division One clash with Leicester City and found the back of the net twice in a 3–0 victory.

RECORD-BREAKING HENRY

The most prolific striker ever to pull on the famous red and white shirt of Arsenal, Thierry Henry scored 228 times in 377 appearances for the Gunners, to become the only player to surpass the 200-goal landmark in the Club's history. Surprisingly, it took the legendary Frenchman 10 games to open his Arsenal account following his £9 million move from Juventus in the summer of 1999, but once the legendary Frenchman had hit the winner against Southampton in September, coming off the bench at The Dell on 71 minutes and scoring just eight minutes later, the goals continued to flow with breathtaking regularity and style.

Henry reached a century of goals for the Club in his fourth season in England with a brace in a 4–0 demolition of Birmingham City at St Andrews in January 2003, and he reached the 150 milestone with a four-goal salvo against Leeds United at Highbury in April 2004.

On 18 October 2005, he became Arsenal's greatest-ever goalscorer. The game was a Champions League clash with Sparta Prague and, with his first of the evening, Henry equalled Ian Wright's previous record haul of 185. His second in a 3–0 victory saw him surpass the record Wright had set eight years and 35 days earlier, earning the Frenchman a unique place in the Club's illustrious history.

He hit the 200 mark in February 2006 with another goal at Birmingham while his 228th and final strike came exactly six years later while he was on loan back to the Gunners from the New York Red Bulls, hammering home an injury-time winner for Arsène Wenger's side at Sunderland in the Premier League.

The Frenchman still holds many other scoring records for the Club but his record-breaking career tally of 228 is undoubtedly his greatest.

LEFT: Thierry Henry registered the 100th goal of his Arsenal career in 2003 against Birmingham.

SEVENTH HEAVEN

Ted Drake's achievements in the 1934–35 campaign were phenomenal but his feat in December 1935 was almost unbelievable, scoring a Club-record seven goals in a single match. The unfortunate opponents were Aston Villa in a Division One clash at Villa Park and the final scoreline was 7–1 to the Gunners, with Drake netting all the goals for George Allison's team. According to contemporary reports, however, the striker could have actually had eight goals, had one of his efforts not struck the crossbar and the referee ruled the deflected ball did not cross the line.

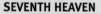

▶ SENSATIONAL SEASON FOR DRAKE

The great Ted Drake spent 11 superb seasons with the Gunners in the 1930s and 1940s and the Southampton-born centre-forward still holds the Club record for both the most goals and the most league goals scored in a single season. Unsurprisingly, he achieved his historic double in the same campaign, Arsenal's 1934–35 Division One title-winning season. In just 41 appearances, Drake contributed 42 of the 115 league goals the Gunners scored that year, and he took his overall tally to a record-breaking 44 with an FA Cup goal against Brighton & Hove Albion and another strike in the Charity Shield against Manchester City.

TWELVE-MATCH STREAK

The most consistent Gunner in terms of scoring in consecutive appearances for the Club is Ian Wright, who was on target in 12 matches on the bounce during the 1994–95 campaign. His amazing sequence began in mid-September, when he scored in Arsenal's 3–1 win in Cyprus against Omonia in the first round of the European Cup Winners' Cup and he subsequently scored against Newcastle in the league and twice against Hartlepool United in the League Cup.

West Ham, Omonia in the second leg and Crystal Palace all failed to stop the striker scoring and, although he missed the second leg against Hartlepool, Wright was back in business away to Wimbledon in the league before helping himself to a brace in a 3–1 league victory over Chelsea at Highbury. Goals against Danish club Brondby home and away in the European Cup Winners' Cup and Coventry in the league followed, and the prolific forward made it 12 matches in a row with a goal when he found the back of the net from the penalty spot in Arsenal's 2–1 win against Leicester at Filbert Street. Manchester United finally managed to shackle Wright in a goalless draw at Highbury at the end of November but his return of 16 goals in 12 successive games remains a Club record.

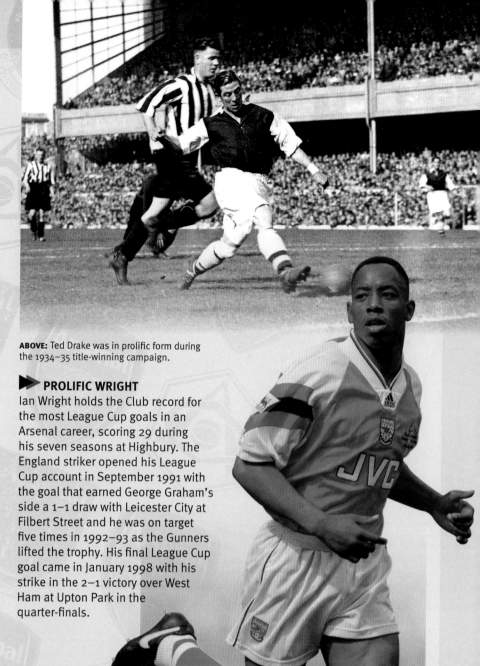

ABOVE: Ted Drake was in prolific form during the 1934–35 title-winning campaign.

▶ PROLIFIC WRIGHT

Ian Wright holds the Club record for the most League Cup goals in an Arsenal career, scoring 29 during his seven seasons at Highbury. The England striker opened his League Cup account in September 1991 with the goal that earned George Graham's side a 1–1 draw with Leicester City at Filbert Street and he was on target five times in 1992–93 as the Gunners lifted the trophy. His final League Cup goal came in January 1998 with his strike in the 2–1 victory over West Ham at Upton Park in the quarter-finals.

RIGHT: The League Cup proved a happy hunting ground for Ian Wright.

TOP 10 GOALSCORERS

	App	Goals
Thierry Henry (1999–2007, 2012)	377	228
Ian Wright (1991–98)	288	185
Cliff Bastin (1929–46)	396	178
John Radford (1962–76)	481	149
Ted Drake (1934–45)	184	139
Jimmy Brain (1923–31)	232	139
Doug Lishman (1948–56)	244	137
Robin van Persie (2004–12)	278	132
Joe Hulme (1926–38)	374	125
David Jack (1928–34)	208	124

HAT-TRICK HEROES

Twenty-five different players have scored three or more hat-tricks in competitive games for Arsenal since the Club was formed in 1886. Although Joseph Heath isn't on that list, he does hold the distinction as the player to score the first-ever league treble for the Gunners.

His brilliant triple came in a 4–0 victory over Walsall Town Swifts in a Second Division clash at Plumstead in September 1893 and he went on to register three more hat-tricks that season in friendlies against Chatham, London Caledonians and Crusaders.

The first-ever treble at Highbury was scored by Harry King in a 6–0 demolition of Grimsby Town in November 1914, one of the four hat-tricks of his Gunners career.

Dutch striker Dennis Bergkamp recorded the first hat-trick of Arsene Wenger's managerial reign at the Club in a 3–3 draw with Leicester City in August 1997, while the first treble of the Emirates era went to Emmanuel Adebayor in the 5–0 mauling of Derby County a decade later.

The youngest Arsenal player to hit the target three times in a single match was John Radford, who was just 17 years and 315 days old when the Gunners beat Wolves 5–0 at Highbury in January 1965.

Overall, Jack Lambert and Jimmy Brain head the career list with 12 Arsenal hat-tricks apiece. Ted Drake and Ian Wright both recorded 11 while Thierry Henry scored eight.

ABOVE: Joe Baker was on target 36 times for the Gunners in 1963.

DEADLY DRAKE

Three players currently hold the record for the most goals for the Gunners in a calendar year. Yorkshireman Jack Lambert set the original mark back in 1930 when he was on target 36 times, but just five years later Ted Drake equalled his 12-month tally, while Liverpudlian Joe Baker joined the list in 1963.

HENRY IN EUROPE

Thierry Henry was the spearhead for some of Arsenal's greatest nights in Europe during his eight-year stay in north London and his 42 glorious goals remains a record return for the Club.

His first-ever European goal for the Gunners came on 22 September 1999 when he came off the bench for Marc Overmars at Highbury to score in a 3–1 victory against Swedish side AIK Solna. He was on target seven more times during the campaign to register his most prolific season for the Club.

The French striker was also to the fore during 2005–06 as Arsenal reached the Champions League final, with five goals in 11 appearances, and it was his famous strike against Real Madrid at the Bernabeu that saw the Gunners knock out the Spanish giants in the last 16 of the competition. He was also on target in the quarter-final triumph against Juventus.

In total, 35 of Henry's record-breaking 42 European goals came in the Champions League, while his last strike for the Club was in September 2006 in a 2–0 victory over Porto at Emirates.

LEFT: John Radford was still a teenager when he hit his first hat-trick for the Club.

FABULOUS FABREGAS

The youngest goalscorer in the Club's history is Cesc Fabregas, who was just 16 years and 212 days old when he was on target for Arsenal in their 5–0 win over Wolverhampton Wanderers at Highbury in a fifth-round League Cup clash.

The Spanish midfielder also holds the record as the Gunners' most youthful scorer in both league and European football.

He hit his first Premier League goal for the Club aged 17 years and 113 days against Blackburn Rovers in August 2004 while his maiden European strike came in the Champions League clash with Rosenborg at Highbury in December the same year – aged 17 years and 303 days.

▶ FOUR FOR SMITH

Henry holds the record for the most career European goals but Alan Smith holds the distinction as the player to have scored the most goals in a single European game for the Gunners. The England striker scored four in a 6–1 thrashing of FK Austria Wien at Highbury in the European Cup in September 1991.

RIGHT: Alan Smith was in deadly form in the 1991–92 European Cup campaign.

BELOW: The 2011–12 Premier League season was Robin van Persie's most prolific.

OLD-TIMER

The oldest player to find the back of the net for Arsenal is English winger Jock Rutherford, scoring in a 2–0 win over Sheffield United in Division One in September 1924. Rutherford was just 13 days short of celebrating his 40th birthday.

FASTEST TO 100 ARSENAL GOALS

Ted Drake (1934–45) – 108 appearances
Ian Wright (1991–98) – 143 appearances
Jimmy Brain (1923–31) – 144 appearances
Jack Lambert (1926–33) – 149 appearances
Joe Baker (1962–66) – 152 appearances
Reg Lewis (1935–53) – 152 appearances
David Jack (1928–34) – 156 appearances
Doug Lishman (1948–56) – 163 appearances
David Herd (1954–61) – 165 appearances
Cliff Bastin (1929–46) – 174 appearances

◀ PREMIER LEAGUE RECORD

Thierry Henry and Robin van Persie jointly hold the Club record for the most goals in a Premier League season. Henry scored 30 league goals in the 2003–04 campaign as Arsene Wenger's side were crowned champions while van Persie emulated the Frenchman's achievement in 2011–12 to finish as the division's leading marksman.

BASTIN'S CUP EXPLOITS

Arsenal's third-highest scorer of all time, Cliff Bastin is also the Club's leading marksman in the FA Cup – with 26 goals in 42 appearances between 1929 and 1947.

The Gunners won the FA Cup twice during the outside-left's Highbury career and, although Bastin didn't score in either final, his four goals in eight appearances in 1929–30 and six in seven in 1935–36 were pivotal in the team's progress to Wembley.

He also holds the record as Arsenal's youngest scorer in an FA Cup tie, hitting the net in a 2–0 win against Chelsea in the third round at the age of 17 years and 303 days.

GOALS GALORE

Dutch striker Robin van Persie and England star Ian Wright jointly hold the Premier League record for scoring against the highest number of different sides in a single season, with the two former players both hitting the target against 17 of the 19 other top-flight clubs.

Wright first set the record during the Gunners' 1996–97 campaign when only Manchester United and Sunderland succeeded in stopping him in front of goal, and van Persie emulated his feat in 2011–12 when he hit the net against every Premier League team except Manchester City and Fulham.

EXTRA-TIME EDDIE

The 1971 FA Cup final was a magical moment in Arsenal's history, with victory in extra-time against Liverpool at Wembley completing the fabled league and cup double for the first time.

The match, however, was also noteworthy for Eddie Kelly's strike in the 101st minute, the first time a substitute had scored in an FA Cup final. The Scottish midfielder came on for Peter Storey after 64 minutes at Wembley and his goal levelled the match after Steve Heighway had put Liverpool in front, paving the way for Charlie George's late winner.

ABOVE: Victory over Liverpool saw Arsenal lift the FA Cup for a fourth time in 1971.

BELOW: Van Persie found the back of the net 132 times in 278 games during his eight-year Arsenal career.

LEFT: Olivier Giroud netted his 50th goal for the Gunners in February 2015.

ANFIELD ANNIHILATION

Brazilian Julio Baptista spent a season on loan at Arsenal in 2006–07 and, although the midfielder's spell in English football was brief, he still found time to set a Club record for the most goals in a League Cup match.

He set the record in January 2007 when Arsene Wenger's side travelled to Anfield to face Liverpool in the fifth round, scoring twice either side of half-time for a personal haul of four goals in the side's remarkable 6–3 victory. Amazingly, Baptista also had a penalty saved by Jerzy Dudek as Liverpool crashed to their worst home defeat in 76 years.

▲ HALF-CENTURY MILESTONE

Olivier Giroud became the latest Arsenal player to score 50 goals for the Club when he was on target against Crystal Palace in February 2015. The Frenchman's first goal for the Gunners came in September 2012 in the League Cup against Coventry, while his 50th saw the striker join 47 other players to have registered the half-century for the Gunners.

SILVA LINING

Brazilian midfielder Gilberto Silva registered a modest 24 goals in 244 appearances over six years for the Gunners, but he still holds the record as the scorer of the fastest-ever goal in the Club's history.

His amazingly rapid effort came in the group stages of the 2002–03 Champions League against PSV Eindhoven and when Silva converted Thierry Henry's cross for the opening goal of what proved to be a 4–0 victory, there had been a mere 20.07 seconds of play.

ABOVE: Danny Welbeck scores one of his three goals against Galatasaray in October 2014. His was the first hat-trick by an Arsenal player for 21 months.

▲ DANNY ENDS THE DROUGHT

The 2013–14 campaign was the first since Arsene Wenger's debut season at the Arsenal helm in 1996–97 in which no Gunner registered a hat-trick. The drought, which had lasted 21 months, was finally brought to an end in October 2014 when Danny Welbeck netted three times in the 4–1 defeat of Galatasaray in the group stages of the Champions League at the Emirates.

In the process the England star became the 20th player to record a hat-trick under Wenger, following in the footsteps of Dennis Bergkamp, Ian Wright, Nicolas Anelka, Nwankwo Kanu, Marc Overmars, Ray Parlour, Thierry Henry, Sylvain Wiltord, Jermaine Pennant, Robert Pires, Freddy Ljungberg, Julio Baptista, Emmanuel Adebayor, Carlos Vela, Andrey Arshavin, Nicklas Bendtner, Theo Walcott, Robin van Persie and Santi Cazorla.

MOST ARSENAL HAT-TRICKS

Jack Lambert (1926–33)	12
Jimmy Brain (1923–31)	12
Ted Drake (1934–45)	11
Ian Wright (1991–98)	11
Thierry Henry (1999–2007, 2012)	8
David Herd (1954–61)	7
David Jack (1928–34)	7
Doug Lishman (1948–56)	7
John Radford (1962–76)	6
Ronnie Rooke (1946–49)	5
Joe Baker (1962–66)	5

Player Records – Appearances

Injury, age and loss of form can all curtail a professional career but some Arsenal players have defied all these obstacles to clock up a breathtaking number of games for the Club. This section looks at the players who refused to quit.

ABOVE: David O'Leary spent almost two decades in the Arsenal ranks, making him a legend at the Club.

▶▶ EIGHTEEN YEARS FOR O'LEARY

Republic of Ireland defender David O'Leary holds the record for the most appearances for Arsenal, playing 722 times for the Club between 1975 and 1993 in a glittering career which saw him claim two Division One winner's medals, as well as two FA Cups and two League Cups.

Signed as an apprentice in 1973, the centre-half graduated through the Club's reserve team ranks, and just three months after his 17th birthday he was handed his first team debut by manager Bertie Mee – in the opening fixture of the 1975–76 season against Burnley at Turf Moor. He made an instant impression on the side and went on to play 26 more times in the league for the Gunners in his first season.

The youngest player ever to reach both the 100 and 200-match milestones, O'Leary made his 400th appearance for the Club at the age of 26 and surpassed George Armstrong's previous record of 621 senior games in November 1989 when he played in the dramatic 4–3 victory over Norwich City at Highbury.

His last game for the Club was the 1993 FA Cup final replay against Sheffield Wednesday at Wembley, when he came off the bench after 81 minutes to replace Ian Wright in the Gunners' 2–1 extra-time victory. He signed for Leeds United on a free transfer in July 1993 after 18 years at Arsenal, bringing to an end a superb career in which he also set a Club milestone of 558 league appearances.

RIGHT: Tom Parker was an incredibly consistent performer for the Club during the 1920s.

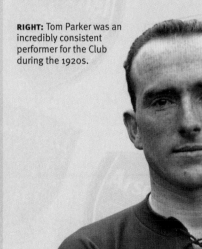

◀◀ RELIABLE PARKER

Signed from Southampton for £3,250 in March 1926, right-back Tom Parker captained Arsenal to their first major trophy – the 1930 FA Cup – and also holds the record for the most consecutive appearances in Gunners history.

His unbroken sequence of games began against Blackburn Rovers in April 1926, a game Arsenal won 4–2 at Highbury, and continued until Boxing Day 1929 when he was in the side that lost 2–1 to Portsmouth in north London.

In total Parker played in 172 consecutive matches for the Gunners. In his seven seasons with the Club, he missed just six games.

TEENAGE STAR

The youngest player to appear for the Gunners in an FA Cup match is Stewart Robson. The young midfielder registered the milestone in the Gunners' 1–0 loss against Tottenham at White Hart Lane in the third round of the 1981–82 competition, only 57 days after he had turned 17.

EXPERIENCED GUNNER

The oldest player to wear the Arsenal shirt in a competitive match is Jock Rutherford, who was 41 years and 159 days old when he featured against Manchester City at Highbury in March 1926.

The outside-right signed for the Club from Newcastle in 1913 and a decade later left to become the manager of Stoke City. He resigned from his new role after just two months and returned to Highbury as a player. He hung up his boots in 1925 but was tempted out of retirement for a third stint as an Arsenal player later the same year, paving the way for his record-setting appearance against Manchester City.

▼ PARLOUR'S PREMIER LEAGUE MILESTONE

A product of the Arsenal junior ranks, Ray Parlour joined the Club as a trainee in 1989 and, with 333 games on his impressive CV, the midfielder is the most-experienced-ever Gunner in terms of Premier League appearances.

Parlour made his first team debut in the old First Division in January 1992 but the first of his 333 Premier League matches came the following season when he was selected for the clash with Liverpool at Anfield in August.

The midfielder went on to feature heavily in all three of the Club's Premier League title triumphs, playing 34 times in 1997–98, 27 in 2001–02 and a further 25 in 2003–04.

His final Premier League appearance for the Gunners came in the penultimate game of the 2003–04 season, a 1–0 victory over Fulham at Craven Cottage.

ABOVE: Jock Rutherford (front row, first player on the left), continued to play into his forties.

LEFT: Ray Parlour set a Club record for Premier League appearances.

CHAMPIONS LEAGUE RECORD

Thierry Henry has played more Champions League games for the Club than any other player, appearing 78 times in European football's marquee competition.

The Frenchman made his Gunners debut in the tournament as an 81st-minute substitute for Dennis Bergkamp in a goalless draw against Fiorentina in the group stages in 1999, while his first start for the Club came 12 months later in a 1–0 victory over Sparta Prague.

His last Champions League game was during his loan spell at Emirates during the 2011–12 season, replacing Theo Walcott at half-time in the Gunners' 4–0 loss in Italy to AC Milan in February.

TOP 10 APPEARANCES

	App	Goals
David O'Leary (1973–93)	722	14
Tony Adams (1983–2002)	669	48
George Armstrong (1961–77)	621	68
Lee Dixon (1988–2002)	619	25
Nigel Winterburn (1987–2000)	584	12
David Seaman (1990–2003)	564	0
Pat Rice (1966–80)	528	22
Peter Storey (1965–77)	501	17
John Radford (1964–76)	481	149
Peter Simpson (1960–78)	477	15

ABLE SEAMAN

Only five goalkeepers have made over 300 appearances for the Club in Arsenal's history and David Seaman stands head and shoulders above his rivals in terms of total number of games played.

The England custodian was signed from Queens Park Rangers for a British record fee of £1.3 million in 1990 and made his first team debut on the opening day of the 1990–91 campaign against Wimbledon at Plough Lane. Seaman was ever-present in the league for the Gunners throughout the season, conceding just 18 goals in 38 matches as George Graham's side claimed the title.

He spent 13 years as an Arsenal player and his final appearance was a fittingly triumphant send-off, keeping a clean sheet as the Gunners beat Southampton 1–0 in the 2003 FA Cup final at Wembley.

In total, Seaman played a Club-record 564 times for Arsenal. Welsh keeper Jack Kelsey is second on the all-time list with 352 appearances in the 1950s and 1960s, while Irish legend Pat Jennings is third with 327. Bob Wilson played 308 times for the Gunners while James Ashcroft featured in 303 games for the Gunners at the start of the 20th century.

John Lukic and George Swindin both narrowly missed out on the 300-match career milestone, playing 298 and 297 times respectively.

▼ SWEET SIXTEEN

The youngest player to feature in the Arsenal first team is Cesc Fabregas after Arsene Wenger selected the Spanish playmaker for the Club's League Cup clash with Rotherham United at Emirates in October 2003 at the age of 16 years and 177 days. Fabregas played 85 minutes of the 1–1 draw before being substituted.

RIGHT: David Seaman joined Arsenal from Queens Park Rangers in the summer of 1990.

BELOW: Cesc Febregas broke into the Gunners' first team as a 16-year-old.

AMAZING ARMSTRONG

George Armstrong is third on the all-time list of appearances for the Gunners, with a magnificent career tally of 621 matches, and also holds the unique distinction of having played exactly 500 league games.

The winger made his debut as a teenager in a First Division clash with Blackpool at Bloomfield Road in February 1962 and, although it was his only appearance for George Swindin's team that season, he was in the starting XI for new manager Billy Wright for the opening game of the 1962–63 campaign against Leyton Orient.

Over the next 15 years, Armstrong was a fixture in the Gunners' team and made his 500th and final league appearance for the Club in a 3–2 win over Manchester United at Old Trafford in the final game of the 1976–77 season.

He signed for Leicester City in the summer of 1977 but returned to Highbury in 1990 as part of the reserve team coaching staff.

THE 300 CLUB

When Theo Walcott came off the Emirates bench in the second half of Arsenal's Premier League clash with Sunderland in May 2015, replacing Jack Wilshere in the 67th minute, he joined an exclusive group of players who have made 300 appearances for the Gunners.

Walcott had joined Arsenal from Southampton in January 2006 for an initial fee of £5 million (eventually rising to £12 million). By the start of the 2014–15 season, he had become the longest-serving member of the squad. He became the 49th player in the Club's history to reach the 300-game milestone – and the eighth to do so during Arsene Wenger's reign as manager. A total of 190 of his 300 games came in the starting XI.

Walcott made two more appearances in 2014–15, including a place in the starting XI for the FA Cup victory over Aston Villa (in which he scored Arsenal's opening goal in a 4–0 victory), to take his tally to 302, just one behind Cesc Fabregas on the Gunners' all-time list.

ABOVE: George Armstrong is third on Arsenal's all-time appearance list.

DUTCH DELIGHT

The first 17 players on the all-time Arsenal appearance list all hail from Britain or Ireland, making Dutchman Dennis Bergkamp in 18th the foreign player with the most career games for the Club.

Signed from Inter Milan for £7.5 million in June 1995, the striker made his league debut in August in a 2–0 victory against Everton at Goodison, and for his 11 seasons in north London he was a key figure in one of the most successful eras of the Club's history.

He retired at the end of the 2005–06 campaign, bidding farewell to the Gunners in May with an 11-minute cameo appearance from the bench in a 4–2 win against Wigan at Highbury.

It was his 423rd and final appearance for Arsenal, eclipsing the 406 games Frenchman Patrick Vieira played for the Club.

RIGHT: Dennis Bergkamp scored 120 goals in his 423 games for the Club.

ARSENAL APPEARANCE RECORDS

Most League Games: 558, David O'Leary

Most Premier League Games: 333, Ray Parlour

Most Champions League Games: 79, Thierry Henry

Most League Cup Games: 70, David O'Leary

Most Consecutive Games: 172, Tom Parker (3 April 1926–26 December 1929)

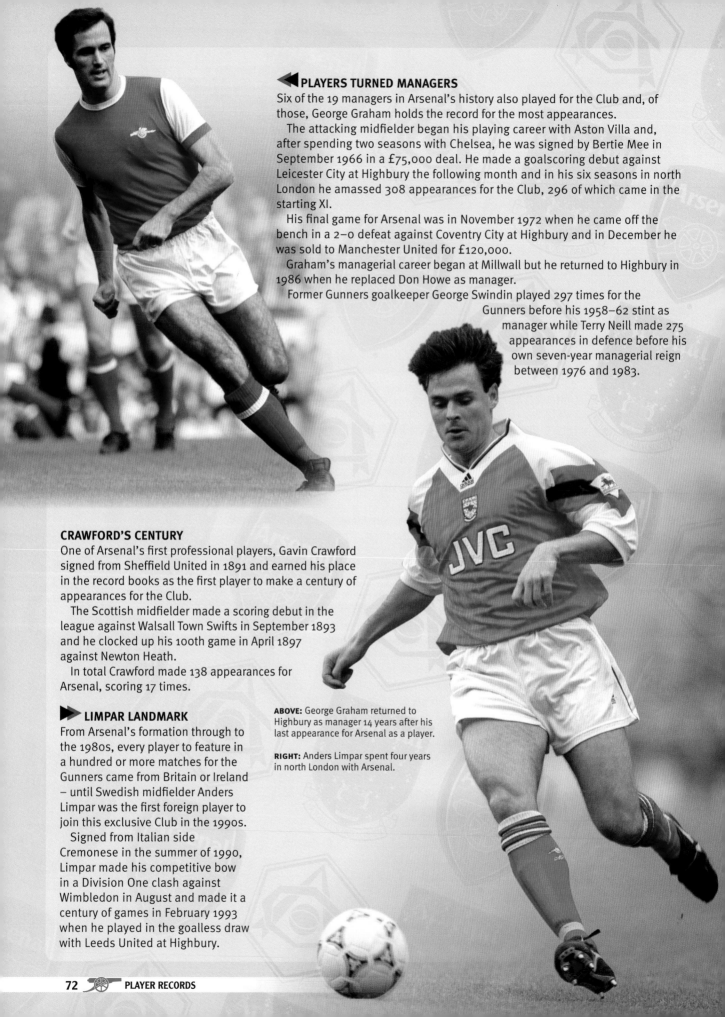

◀◀ PLAYERS TURNED MANAGERS

Six of the 19 managers in Arsenal's history also played for the Club and, of those, George Graham holds the record for the most appearances.

The attacking midfielder began his playing career with Aston Villa and, after spending two seasons with Chelsea, he was signed by Bertie Mee in September 1966 in a £75,000 deal. He made a goalscoring debut against Leicester City at Highbury the following month and in his six seasons in north London he amassed 308 appearances for the Club, 296 of which came in the starting XI.

His final game for Arsenal was in November 1972 when he came off the bench in a 2–0 defeat against Coventry City at Highbury and in December he was sold to Manchester United for £120,000.

Graham's managerial career began at Millwall but he returned to Highbury in 1986 when he replaced Don Howe as manager.

Former Gunners goalkeeper George Swindin played 297 times for the Gunners before his 1958–62 stint as manager while Terry Neill made 275 appearances in defence before his own seven-year managerial reign between 1976 and 1983.

CRAWFORD'S CENTURY

One of Arsenal's first professional players, Gavin Crawford signed from Sheffield United in 1891 and earned his place in the record books as the first player to make a century of appearances for the Club.

The Scottish midfielder made a scoring debut in the league against Walsall Town Swifts in September 1893 and he clocked up his 100th game in April 1897 against Newton Heath.

In total Crawford made 138 appearances for Arsenal, scoring 17 times.

▶ LIMPAR LANDMARK

From Arsenal's formation through to the 1980s, every player to feature in a hundred or more matches for the Gunners came from Britain or Ireland – until Swedish midfielder Anders Limpar was the first foreign player to join this exclusive Club in the 1990s.

Signed from Italian side Cremonese in the summer of 1990, Limpar made his competitive bow in a Division One clash against Wimbledon in August and made it a century of games in February 1993 when he played in the goalless draw with Leeds United at Highbury.

ABOVE: George Graham returned to Highbury as manager 14 years after his last appearance for Arsenal as a player.

RIGHT: Anders Limpar spent four years in north London with Arsenal.

TOURE THE TRAILBLAZER

Arsenal have become a genuinely global side in recent years and this was reflected in the seven-year Highbury career of Kolo Toure, whose 326 appearances for the Gunners is a record for a non-European player. The Ivory Coast centre-half joined Arsenal from African side ASEC Mimosas in 2002 and made 26 Premier League appearances in his debut season. He remained a first choice for Arsene Wenger for the following six years in north London and before leaving for Manchester City, in 2009, he won the Premier League and two FA Cups.

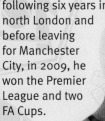

HOMEGROWN HERO

Cesc Fabregas joined the Arsenal Academy as a 16-year-old in September 2003 and less than three years later made his 100th appearance for the Club, making him the most recent homegrown player in Arsenal history to reach a century of games for the Gunners.

The Spaniard reached the milestone when he featured in the Champions League clash with Dynamo Zagreb in early August 2006, joining an illustrious list of young players to graduate through the Club's junior ranks to first-team football and 100 or more senior appearances.

The midfielder clocked up 300 matches under Arsene Wenger against Blackpool at Bloomfield Road in April 2011, but little more than two months later he returned to his native Spain when he signed for Barcelona.

JOHN FIRST TO 400

Just 20 players have reached the 400-game milestone for the Club and the first to do so was Welsh midfielder Bob John. A member of the Gunners side that won the title in 1931, 1933 and 1934 and the FA Cup in 1930, John signed from Caerphilly in January 1922 and spent 15 years in London before retiring.

He reached the 400-match mark in the 1932–33 season and made 470 appearances in total for the Club, placing him 11th on the all-time list.

RIGHT: Bob John's Arsenal career lasted 15 years.

ABOVE: Kolo Toure arrived at Highbury in 2002, making his debut against Liverpool in the Community Shield.

ARSENAL APPEARANCE RECORDS
YOUNGEST PLAYERS
Overall: Cesc Fabregas
(16 years 177 days v Rotherham Utd, League Cup, Oct 2003)
League: Jack Wilshere
(16 years 256 days v Blackburn, Sept 2008)
Premier League: Jack Wilshere
(16 years 256 days v Blackburn, Sept 2008)
Europe: Jack Wilshere
(16 years 329 days v Dynamo Kiev, Champions League, Nov 2008)
FA Cup: Jack Wilshere
(17 years 2 days v Plymouth, Jan 2009)
OLDEST PLAYERS
Overall: Jock Rutherford
(41 years 159 days, v Man City, League, March 1926)
League: Jock Rutherford
(41 years 159 days, v Man City, March 1926)
Premier League: Jens Lehmann
(41 years 151 days v Blackpool, April 2011)
Europe: John Lukic
(39 years 311 days v Lazio, Champions League, Oct 2000)

Player Records – Transfers

Arsenal have always attracted marquee players but quality invariably comes at a price and this section focuses on the milestone transfer fees the Club has paid to sign some of the game's biggest names.

▼ JACK'S FIVE-FIGURE DEAL

Arsenal have been involved in a British-record transfer deal five times in the Club's history and hit the headlines for the first time in October 1928 when manager Herbert Chapman secured the services of Bolton Wanderers inside-forward David Jack.

The previous record was the £5,500 fee paid by Sunderland to South Shields for England full-back Warney Cresswell six years earlier but Chapman had to dig deep to persuade Bolton to sell Jack and after prolonged negotiations the two clubs agreed on a figure of £10,890, the first time any player in the world had moved clubs for a five-figure sum.

Jack's reputation preceded him – he had become the first player ever to score at Wembley in the 1923 FA Cup final, and had a tally of 144 goals in 295 league appearances for Wanderers – but he arrived at Highbury aged 29 and the sceptics questioned whether Chapman had got value for money in the deal.

In his six seasons with the Gunners, Jack proved he was worth every penny. He finished his first season in the capital as the side's top scorer, with 25 goals in 31 games and he was an integral part of the team that beat Huddersfield 2–0 in the 1930 FA Cup final, the Club's first major trophy.

His most prolific campaign came in 1930–31 when he netted 34 times as Arsenal were crowned First Division champions. He would go on to add two further championship medals to his collection after the title triumphs of 1932–33 and 1933–34.

Jack finally hung up his boots in 1934 at the age of 35, having scored a remarkable 124 times in 208 games in all competitions – costing the Club roughly £88 for each goal during his Highbury career.

▼ HUGE PROFIT ON ANELKA

No club likes to see its best players leave, but there was no arguing with the financial logic behind Arsene Wenger's decision to sell Nicolas Anelka to Real Madrid in 1999 for £22.5 million, then a record fee involving a British side.

The young French striker had cost the Gunners a modest £500,000 when Wenger had signed him from Paris Saint-Germain two years earlier. After helping Arsenal clinch the 1997–98 Premier League title with six goals in 26 appearances, he left Highbury for Spain for 45 times what they paid for him.

LEFT: Nicolas Anelka was sold to Real Madrid in the summer of 1999 after two seasons at Highbury.

LEFT: David Jack became the first player ever to command a five-figure transfer fee.

BERGKAMP JOINS GUNNERS

The fourth time Arsenal were involved in a British-record deal was in 1995 – and it was arguably the Club's greatest piece of business, as it saw Dennis Bergkamp join the Gunners.

The Dutchman arrived at Highbury in a £7.5 million move from Italian giants Inter Milan, smashing the previous mark of £2.5 million paid for Ian Wright in 1991 and John Hartson four years later. In his 11 seasons with the Club Bergkamp certainly did not disappoint.

His debut season saw the striker on target 11 times in 33 league appearances and he was the Club's top scorer with 16 in 1997–98 as Arsenal claimed the Premier League title for the first time. Bergkamp won three league titles and four FA Cups with the Gunners and in total the sublimely-talented forward made 423 appearances, scoring 120 goals.

The love affair finally came to an end in 2006 when he called time on his playing career – and on more than a decade of Arsenal service.

BELOW: Alan Ball became Club captain following his £220,000 transfer from Everton.

ABOVE: Dennis Bergkamp's performances for the Club justified his record price tag.

BONUS BALL

Arsenal famously won the league and FA Cup double in 1970–71 but manager Bertie Mee was not one to rest on his laurels – and in December 1971 he persuaded the Highbury board to spend £220,000 on signing Alan Ball from Everton.

The deal eclipsed the previous British transfer record – the £200,000 Tottenham paid West Ham for Martin Peters almost two years earlier – and although Ball did not win a trophy with the Club, he was a hugely influential player who made 217 starts in five seasons in north London.

Ball was named captain for the 1973–74 season, and in a period of transition for the Club he was a key figure as the team preserved their top-flight status.

BRITISH TRANSFER RECORD

A decade after the Gunners made history by signing David Jack, they again set a new British transfer record when they paid Wolverhampton Wanderers £14,500 for the privilege of signing Welshman Bryn Jones in March 1938.

The inside-forward scored on his Division One debut for the Club, in a 2–0 win over Portsmouth at Highbury in August, but the outbreak of the Second World War the following year and the suspension of league football interrupted his Gunners career.

Jones served in the Royal Artillery during the conflict but, when competitive football resumed in 1946, he was 34 years old and past the peak of his powers.

He did play seven times during the1947–48 season as Arsenal were crowned champions but it was not enough to earn him a winner's medal and in 1949 he was sold to Norwich City.

ARSENAL'S FIVE BRITISH RECORD TRANSFERS

Player	From	To	Date	Fee
David Jack	Bolton	Arsenal	Oct 1928	£10,890
Bryn Jones	Wolves	Arsenal	Mar 1938	£14,500
Alan Ball	Everton	Arsenal	Dec 1971	£220,000
Dennis Bergkamp	Inter Milan	Arsenal	Jun 1995	£7.5m
Nicolas Anelka	Arsenal	Real Madrid	Jul 1999	£22.5m

RECORD-BREAKING OZIL

Success in the modern game comes at a price and the Gunners proved they were as hungry as ever for silverware in September 2013 when they smashed the Club's transfer record to bring German playmaker Mesut Ozil from Real Madrid to the Emirates on a five-year contract.

The deal to prise the midfielder away from the Spanish giants cost Arsenal £42.5 million, and in the process almost trebled the Club's previous highest transfer, the £15 million upfront fee that they paid Russian side Zenit St Petersburg to sign midfielder Andrey Arshavin in the January window in 2009.

At the time, Ozil's move to Arsenal made him the second most expensive recruit ever to an English club behind Fernando Torres, who cost Chelsea £50 million when he joined from Liverpool in 2011. Ozil has since slipped to third on the all-time list following Angel di Maria's £59.7 million move from Real Madrid to Manchester United in August 2014.

SIX-FIGURE MARINELLO

When the Gunners signed David Jack back in 1928, they became the first Club ever to pay five figures for a player. Forty-two years later Arsenal invested their first-ever six figure fee when Scottish striker Peter Marinello arrived at Highbury.

The then 19-year-old forward signed from Hibernian in January 1970 for £100,000 and made an instant impression on English football with a goal on his debut against Manchester United at Old Trafford.

Sadly, that was to be the highlight of a disappointing career in north London as Marinello struggled to break into the first team on a regular basis, and in July 1973 he left for Portsmouth – having made just 51 appearances and scoring five times in three seasons with the Gunners.

LEFT: Peter Marinello struggled to find form at Highbury after his switch from Hibs.

BELOW: Mesut Ozil signed for Arsenal from Real Madrid ahead of the 2013–14 campaign in a record-breaking £42.5 million deal.

COSTLY CUSTODIAN

Goalkeepers don't tend to command the same high transfer fees as their outfield counterparts but David Seaman was an exception to the rule when he signed from Queens Park Rangers in 1990, a deal which cost Arsenal £1.3 million.

The transfer set two new records at the same time, making Seaman both the Gunners' first seven-figure player and the world's most expensive goalkeeper at the time.

The England star settled quickly into his new surroundings, and in his first season at Highbury he conceded a miserly 18 goals in 38 Division One games as Arsenal were crowned champions. Seaman went on to add two more Championship winner's medals, four FA Cups, a League Cup and the Cup Winners' Cup to his collection.

In total, the keeper spent 13 years at Arsenal and made 564 appearances for the Club before a swan-song season with Manchester City and his retirement in 2004.

▶ TEENAGE TALENT

Young talent comes at a premium and Arsenal certainly had to dig deep to sign Alex Oxlade-Chamberlain in the summer of 2011, agreeing a £12 million deal with Southampton to make the winger the most expensive teenager in the Club's history.

The youngster signed a three-year deal with the Gunners in August, five days after celebrating his 18th birthday and in the process broke the record set by Theo Walcott five years earlier as the most costly teenage recruit.

The deal agreed to bring Oxlade-Chamberlain to Emirates from St Mary's saw Arsenal pay £7 million up front with another £5 million due depending on performance-related targets. The Walcott transfer was initially also reported as a £12 million deal but was subsequently revised down to £9.1 million when Southampton agreed to an early but lower settlement.

▶ FAREWELL FABREGAS

The sale of Cesc Fabregas to Barcelona in the summer of 2011 brought to an end one of the most protracted transfer sagas in the Club's history – and earned Arsenal the biggest transfer fee it has ever received for a player.

The reported headline fee for the Spanish midfielder was £35 million but in reality Barcelona paid £25.4 million in advance to sign Fabregas, with the balance of the deal dependent on appearances and his new side's success in La Liga and the Champions League over the course of his contract.

But even allowing for the reduced down payment, the deal still eclipsed the £24 million the Gunners received when Robin van Persie joined Manchester United in August 2012.

ABOVE: Cesc Fabregas returned to Spain in 2011 but cost Barcelona a record fee.

LEFT: The Club were looking to the future when they signed Alex Oxlade-Chamberlain in 2011.

MILLIONAIRE FRENCHMAN

The advent of the Premier League sparked a sharp rise in transfer fees in English football and Arsenal followed the trend when they bought Thierry Henry to the Premier League from Juventus for £11 million, the first instance of the Club paying an eight-figure fee for a new player.

The prolific Frenchman swapped Turin for London in 1999 and proceeded to rewrite the record books in eight glorious years with the Gunners, eventually finishing as the Club's all-time top goalscorer with 228 in 337 appearances.

Two league titles and three FA Cup triumphs were no more than his scintillating performances deserved, and many still regard Henry as the Premier League's finest-ever foreign recruit.

Player Records – Miscellaneous

From the first Gunner to see red in a competitive game at Emirates, to Alan Skirton's unprecedented substitute appearance against Northampton and Alex Manninger's Premier League clean sheet record, this section looks at the players who made their own little bit of Arsenal history.

▶ RED CARD RECORD

Patrick Vieira was a famously combative presence in the Gunners' midfield between 1996 and 2005 and it's perhaps no surprise that the Frenchman holds the dubious distinction of being the Arsenal player to receive the most Premier League red cards.

In total, Vieira was sent off eight times in his 279 league appearances for the Club. His first dismissal came in January 1998 in a 2–2 draw with Coventry City at Highfield Road – for dissent after conceding a penalty for handball.

He began the 2000–01 season with successive sending-offs in the two opening fixtures, against Sunderland and Liverpool, while his eighth and final red card was in September 2003 in the goalless draw with Manchester United at Old Trafford – for fouling Ruud van Nistelrooy.

The Frenchman also set a Club record for the most yellow cards in the Premier League, with 72 – which means he was cautioned on average every 3.88 games. His first yellow came in only his second appearance for the Club, in September 1996.

RIGHT: Patrick Vieira was no stranger to the wrath of referees during his Highbury career.

BELOW: Olivier Giroud scored twice for Arsenal as they eased past Middlesbrough 2–0 in the 2014–15 FA Cup fifth round.

▼ AT THE DOUBLE

When French striker Olivier Giroud scored both goals in Arsenal's 2–0 victory over Middlesbrough in the fifth round of the FA Cup in February 2015, it was the 200th time in the Arsene Wenger era in which a Gunner had recorded a brace in a competitive match.

The first incident of a Wenger player scoring two goals in a match came in October 1996 when Ian Wright beat Tim Flowers twice at Ewood Park in a 2–0 victory over Blackburn Rovers, while Thierry Henry holds the record for most braces under Wenger, bagging 42 of them during his eight-year association with the Club.

FANTASTIC FABREGAS

Cesc Fabregas was a talisman for Arsenal during his eight years with the Club and his impact on the side is borne out by the team's phenomenal record in matches in which he scored.

The Spanish midfielder scored 57 goals for the Gunners in all competitions and on only one occasion did Arsenal suffer defeat when he found the back of the net.

That match was the 2005 Community Shield clash with Chelsea at the Millennium Stadium, a game the Blues won 2–1 thanks to two Didier Drogba goals.

In total Arsenal were unbeaten in the 49 league, European and cup games in which Fabregas was on target, winning 41 of them.

McDONALD'S TREBLE

Goalkeeper Hugh McDonald holds the distinction of being the first player to enjoy three different spells with the Club, amassing a total of 103 games for the Gunners between 1906 and 1913.

The Scottish custodian first signed for Arsenal in January 1906 as an understudy for England keeper Jimmy Ashcroft but, after making just two league appearances, he joined Brighton & Hove Albion at the end of the year.

McDonald spent two years on the south coast but returned to London in 1908 when Ashcroft was sold to Blackburn Rovers. He would be the Club's first-choice goalkeeper for two seasons, making 74 appearances in the league.

He was on the move again in 1910 when he was transferred to Oldham Athletic but, after a brief spell with Bradford Park Avenue, he was back at Arsenal in 1912 for a third time. It was to prove only a season-long reunion, however, and after 18 more league games for the Club he left to play for Fulham.

LEFT: Alan Skirton's substitute appearance was a watershed in the tactics of the game.

STRIKERS STEP UP

The 2014–15 season was a good one for both Olivier Giroud and Alexis Sanchez in front of goal as both Arsenal forwards registered significant scoring achievements.

Giroud was in superb form in the Premier League in February and April, and his goals in consecutive games against Crystal Palace, Everton, QPR, West Ham, Newcastle and Liverpool made him the first player to score in six successive league matches for the Club since Emmanuel Adebayor in 2008.

Sanchez was top scorer for the Club in all competitions in 2014–15 with 25 after his £31.7 million transfer from Barcelona, making him the first Arsenal player since Thierry Henry in 1999–2000 to break the 20-goal barrier in his first season.

ABOVE: Alexis Sanchez scored 25 goals in his debut season for Arsenal in 2014–15.

SKIRTON'S BENCHMARK

The 1965–66 season was the first in English football in which managers could make substitutions. Winger Alan Skirton became the first player in Arsenal's history to come off the bench in a competitive match when they played Northampton Town in September 1965.

The Gunners had already played nine Division One games without manager Billy Wright having to turn to the bench, but that all changed at Highbury against the Cobblers when Skirton was introduced to the action. Wright made six more substitutions over the course of the season, centre-half Peter Simpson leading the way with three appearances as a replacement.

CESC FABREGAS SEASON-BY-SEASON

	League	Cup	Europe	Goals
2003–04	0	3	0	1
2004–05	33	8	5	3
2005–06	35	2	13	5
2006–07	38	6	10	4
2007–08	32	3	10	13
2008–09	22	1	10	3
2009–10	27	1	8	19
2010–11	25	6	5	9
Total:	212	30	61	57

◤ MARVELLOUS MANNINGER

Austrian goalkeeper Alex Manninger made a modest 63 starts during his five-year stint in north London but he still holds the record for most consecutive clean sheets in the Premier League after debut.

His first Premier League appearance came in January 1998 when Arsenal beat Southampton 3–0 at Highbury. Eight days later the Austrian shut Chelsea out and kept a third consecutive clean sheet against Crystal Palace. A goalless draw with West Ham at Upton Park in March and a 1–0 victory away at Wimbledon extended the sequence and he made it six Premier League clean sheets in his first six games when a series of superb saves helped earn Arsene Wenger's side a 1–0 win over Manchester United at Old Trafford.

His feat remains a record – although his seventh league game for the Gunners did end in a thumping 4–0 defeat against Liverpool at Anfield.

DREADFUL DEBUT

Jason Crowe made just three appearances for the Club before he was transferred to Portsmouth in 1999 – and the full-back's debut was definitely one to forget.

His first team bow came as a substitute in extra-time during Arsenal's League Cup clash with Birmingham City at Highbury in October 1997. The 21-year-old had been on the pitch for just 33 seconds when referee Uriah Rennie showed him a red card for a high tackle on a Blues player. It remains the fastest dismissal on debut in the Club's history.

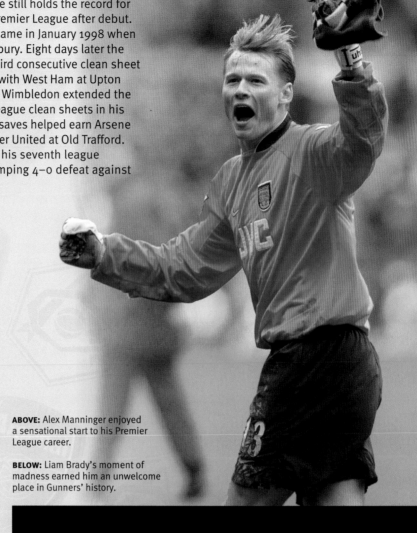

ABOVE: Alex Manninger enjoyed a sensational start to his Premier League career.

BELOW: Liam Brady's moment of madness earned him an unwelcome place in Gunners' history.

◤ BAD BOY BRADY

Republic of Ireland international Liam Brady was a cultured presence in the Gunners' midfield for seven years during the 1970s – but there was nothing stylish about his behaviour in Arsenal's Division One clash with Stoke City at the Victoria Ground in March 1977.

Midway through the first half, Brady was brought down by Stoke's Steve Waddington. Rather than allow the referee to punish the Potters player, the Irishman got up and struck him in the face with his forearm. The official was far from impressed and showed Brady a straight red card, making him the first Arsenal player ever to be sent off in a competitive match.

The Gunners were on a seven-match losing streak, but much to Brady's relief his team-mates held on for a 1–1 draw despite their numerical disadvantage.

BOULD NEW ERA

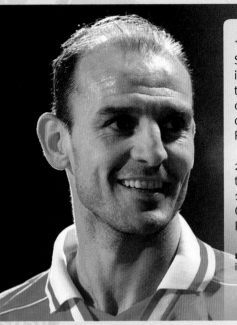

Steve Bould scored just eight times in his 372 career appearances for the Gunners but the long-serving centre-half does hold the distinction of having scored Arsenal's first-ever Premier League goal.

The defender was on target in the 28th minute of his side's 4–2 defeat to Norwich City at Highbury in August 1992, with the first of 40 goals the Gunners scored in their inaugural Premier League campaign.

LEFT: Steve Bould was the first on target in the inaugural Premier League season.

YELLOW PERIL

The 1976–77 season in English football saw the introduction of yellow and red cards – and George Armstrong became the first Arsenal player to be booked, on 25 August 1976.

The Gunners winger was cautioned during a 3–1 victory over Norwich City at Carrow Road but was quickly followed into the referee's book by team-mates Pat Rice, Liam Brady and David O'Leary.

LEFT: Rarely in trouble with referees, George Armstrong's yellow card against the Canaries in 1976 was history-making.

MAGNIFICENT MESUT

Mesut Ozil became the Gunners' record signing when he joined Arsenal from Real Madrid for £42.5 million in September 2013 and his first goal for Arsenal the following month also made Club history.

The German was on target for Arsene Wenger's side in a 2–0 home victory over Napoli in the Champions League and in the process Ozil became the 50th Arsenal player to score at the Emirates.

SENDEROS SENDING-OFF

The Club's debut 2006–07 season at Emirates failed to produce a single red card for an Arsenal player, making Philippe Senderos the first Gunner to get sent off at Ashburton Grove.

The Swiss defender made history in September 2007 against Portsmouth in the Premier League, getting his matching orders in the 50th minute for a professional foul on Pompey striker (and former Gunner) Kanu.

Fortunately for Senderos, Arsene Wenger's side were still too strong for the visitors, running out 3–1 winners.

FIRST PREMIER LEAGUE GOALSCORER

1992–93 – Steve Bould (2–4 v Norwich City, 15 August)
1993–94 – Ian Wright (1–0 v Tottenham, 16 August)
1994–95 – Kevin Campbell (3–0 v Manchester City, 20 August)
1995–96 – Ian Wright (1–1 v Middlesbrough, 20 August)
1996–97 – John Hartson (2–0 v West Ham, 17 August)
1997–98 – Ian Wright (1–1 v Leeds United, 9 August)
1998–99 – Emmanuel Petit (2–1 v Nottingham Forest, 17 August)
1999–2000 – Dennis Bergkamp (2–1 v Leicester, 7 August)
2000–01 – Lauren (2–0 v Liverpool, 21 August)
2001–02 – Thierry Henry (4–0 v Middlesbrough, 18 August)
2002–03 – Thierry Henry (2–0 v Birmingham, 18 August)
2003–04 – Thierry Henry (2–1 v Everton, 16 August)
2004–05 – Dennis Bergkamp (4–1 v Everton, 15 August)
2005–06 – Thierry Henry (2–0 v Newcastle, 14 August)
2006–07 – Gilberto Silva (1–1 v Aston Villa, 19 August)
2007–08 – Robin van Persie (2–1 v Fulham, 12 August)
2008–09 – Samir Nasri (1–0 v West Bromwich, 16 August)
2009–10 – Denilson (6–1 v Everton, 15 August)
2010–11 – Pepe Reina OG (1–1 v Liverpool, 15 August)
2011–12 – Theo Walcott (2–8 v Manchester United, 28 August)
2012–13 – Lukas Podolski (2–0 v Liverpool, 2 September)
2013–14 – Olivier Giroud (1–3 v Aston Villa, 17 August)
2014–15 – Laurent Koscielny (2–1 v Crystal Palace, 16 August)

Player Records – International

Welshman Caesar Jenkyns became Arsenal's first ever international in 1896 and this section celebrates the records and feats of the Club's players who have followed in his footsteps and represented their countries.

The Gunners have boasted hundreds of internationals and their unprecedented tally of 15 players at the 2006 World Cup finals in Germany was more than any other Club in the world.

From goalkeeper Jimmy Ashcroft, the Club's first England cap in 1906, to the magnificent midfield duo of Emmanuel Petit and Patrick Vieira, the first Gunners to play in a World Cup final in 1998, and German centurion Lukas Podolski, Arsenal players have consistently been at the forefront of the international game.

These pages also commemorate some of the Gunners' more unusual achievements, including Paddy Sloan's unique career as a dual international in the 1940s, Gerry Keyser's game for the Netherlands in the 1930s which began a new chapter in Arsenal history and the infamous 'Battle Of Highbury' against Italy.

The section concludes with a nod to the increasingly global nature of the Gunners' squad and the trailblazing players such as Christopher Wreh, Junichi Inamoto and Frank Simek who have come to north London from far and wide to play for the Club.

BELOW RIGHT: Adams leads England out in September 2000 for the final international played at the old Wembley Stadium.

BELOW LEFT: Tony Adams was a stalwart for England for more than a decade, making 66 appearances between 1987 and 2000.

RIGHT: Adams and Dennis Bergkamp briefly put club allegiances aside when England faced the Netherlands at Euro 96.

▶ KEEPING IT IN THE FAMILY

The first father and son to play for England were George Eastham Senior and George Eastham, the latter winning his 19 caps for his country in the 1960s while he was an Arsenal player.

Eastham Senior played just once for the Three Lions when he was a Bolton player, featuring in a 1–0 victory over Holland in May 1935. His son made his Three Lions debut 28 years later in the 1–1 draw with Brazil at Wembley, making the Easthams the first family to supply England with two generations of players.

▶ SANSOM'S RECORD

Arsenal signed Kenny Sansom from Crystal Palace in the summer of 1980 and the full-back still holds the Club record for the number of England caps amassed while a Gunner.

The defender made his international debut against Wales in May 1979 while he was still a Palace player but 12 months later, and after eight more appearances for his country, he made the switch from Selhurst Park to Highbury.

In total, Sansom won 77 of his 86 England caps while he was with Arsenal, featuring in the 1982 and 1986 World Cup finals and the 1988 European Championship campaign in West Germany.

The first and only goal of his Three Lions career came in a 5–0 win over Finland in a World Cup qualifier in October 1984 at Wembley while his final appearance was against the USSR in June 1988 in Frankfurt.

Eastham Junior was part of Sir Alf Ramsey's squad for the 1966 World Cup campaign and, although he did not play in the tournament in which England were crowned world champions, he was retrospectively awarded a winners' medal by FIFA in 2009.

He scored twice for the Three Lions in his 19 appearances. His second international goal came in his final game, a 2–0 friendly victory over Denmark in Copenhagen in July 1966 – just eight days before England's opening game of the World Cup finals.

RIGHT: George Eastham proudly followed in his father's footsteps when he played for England in the 1960s.

BELOW: With 77 appearances while with Arsenal, Kenny Sansom is still the Gunners' most capped English player.

ENGLAND FIRST

Signed by Harry Bradshaw from Gravesend United in the summer of 1900, goalkeeper Jimmy Ashcroft spent eight years with Arsenal and in his sixth season at the Club he became the first-ever Gunner to represent England.

His Three Lions debut came in the opening fixture of the British Home Championship in February 1906 against Ireland in Belfast. A brace from Dicky Bond and further strikes from Arthur Brown, Stanley Harris and Samuel Day earned England a 5–0 victory.

Ashcroft kept his place in the side and another clean sheet in a 1–0 win over Wales at the Arms Park in Cardiff a month later and he won his third and final cap in April 1906 against Scotland at Hampden Park in Glasgow. This time, however, the Liverpool-born keeper was unable to shut out the opposition as Scotland won 2–1.

WORLD CUP BREAKTHROUGH

England first sent a team to the World Cup in 1950 but it was not until 1982 that English players from Arsenal represented the Three Lions in the finals.

The Gunners who led the way were Graham Rix and Kenny Sansom, who both played in the Ron Greenwood starting XI that beat France 3–1 at the Estadio San Mames in Bilbao in June 1982.

CAPTAIN JACK

A key figure in Arsenal's emergence as a major force in English football in the 1930s, David Jack also holds the distinction of being the first Gunners player to captain England.

The famous inside-right won his first four caps as a Bolton Wanderers player but he made a record-breaking £10,890 transfer to Highbury in October 1928, and in April 1930 he led England out for the first time in the Home Championship clash with Scotland at Wembley.

England won the game 5–2 and Jack wore the captain's armband for the Three Lions in three more matches: a 3–3 draw with Germany in Berlin and goalless draws with Austria and Wales.

BELOW: David Jack (front row, second left) was the first Arsenal player to captain England.

ABOVE: Goalkeeper Jimmy Ashcroft blazed the trail for Arsenal players with the Three Lions, making his debut against Ireland in 1906

BATTLE OF HIGHBURY

Arsenal hold the record for the most players from a single club to represent England in an international, supplying seven of the Three Lions XI that faced Italy at Highbury in November 1934.

The seven Gunners were Frank Moss, George Male, Eddie Hapgood, Wilf Copping, Ray Bowden, Ted Drake and Cliff Bastin and – in an ill-tempered and violent game that became known as the "Battle of Highbury" – England beat the World Cup holders 3–2.

Manchester City's Eric Brook scored the first two goals while Drake added the third as early as the 12th minute.

TOP 10 MOST CAPPED ENGLAND PLAYERS

Ashley Cole	107 caps
Kenny Sansom	86
David Seaman	75
Sol Campbell	73
Alan Ball	72
Tony Adams	66
David Platt	62
Martin Keown	43
Tony Woodcock	42
Theo Walcott	40
Note: not all caps were won while playing at Arsenal	

DELAYED DEBUT

Leslie Compton won just two caps for England but his first international appearance set a Three Lions record for the oldest outfield debutant ever.

The Gunners centre-half was 38 years and 64 days old when he played for England in the team's 4–2 victory against Wales at Roker Park in November 1950, eclipsing Newcastle United's 35-year-old Frank Hudspeth as the Three Lions' oldest first-timer.

Wanderers goalkeeper Alex Morten is the oldest-ever England debutant at 41 years and 113 days (set in 1873) but Compton remains the most senior outfield player in the history of the national side.

CAMPBELL ON TARGET

Only one Arsenal player has ever scored for England in a World Cup finals game – and the honour is held by Sol Campbell after his effort for the Three Lions against Sweden in 2002.

The central defender scored with a 24th-minute header against the Swedes in the Saitama Stadium in Japan in the group stages to earn Sven-Goran Eriksson's side a 1–1 draw.

Former Gunners Paul Mariner and Matthew Upson have also scored for England in the finals but neither were with Arsenal at the time they found the net.

Mariner scored in a 3–1 defeat of France in Bilbao at the 1982 World Cup in Spain, two years before he signed for the Gunners from Ipswich Town, while Upson's effort against Germany at the 2010 finals in South Africa came seven years after he'd left Highbury for Birmingham City.

ABOVE: Leslie Compton left it late to play for his country in a full international, making his debut two months into his 39th year.

CAPTAIN FANTASTIC

Tony Adams won 66 caps for England in an international career that spanned 13 years and the legendary Gunner holds the record for captaining the Three Lions at the most matches in European Championship finals.

The centre-half was named skipper by manager Terry Venables for the Euro 96 tournament and he led the side against Switzerland, Scotland and the Netherlands in the group stages.

He also wore the captain's armband for the quarter-final victory over Spain in a penalty shootout, and in the agonizing defeat to Germany in another shootout at Wembley. His five Championship appearances as skipper remains a Three Lions record.

Adams was also the first Arsenal player to captain England in the finals.

EUROPEAN BOW

Adams was the first Gunner to lead England at the European Championships. He and Highbury team-mate Kenny Sansom were the first Arsenal players to play for the Three Lions at the finals.

The duo made their Championship debut at the 1988 tournament in West Germany, playing in the Three Lions' 1–0 defeat against the Republic of Ireland in Stuttgart.

RIGHT: Tony Adams was an inspirational leader for both club and country.

BASTIN'S DOZEN

Cliff Bastin scored 178 times in 396 appearances for the Gunners while his 12 goals for England in 21 games is still a record for an Arsenal player.

The iconic outside-left was first capped by the Three Lions against Wales in November 1931 and in May 1933 he opened his England account in a 1–1 draw with Italy in Rome. He scored two braces for his country, the first coming just seven days after the Italy game when he was on target twice in a 4–0 demolition of Switzerland in Berne. His second double was in February 1935 in the 2–1 defeat of Ireland at Goodison Park.

LEFT: Cliff Bastin's 12-goal haul for England remains a Club record.

England lost only twice when Bastin scored, a 2–1 reverse against Wales at Ninian Park in October 1936 and a 2–1 defeat to Switzerland in May 1938. His final goal for the Three Lions came later that month, in a 4–2 rout of France in Paris.

Former Gunners David Platt and Tony Woodcock both scored more goals for England but they were not Arsenal players for the whole of their international careers.

Midfielder Platt scored 27 international goals but only one – his strike in the 3–0 defeat of Hungary at Wembley in May 1996 – came while he was at Highbury.

Woodcock found the back of the net 16 times in England colours but the first seven of his goals came while he was playing in Germany for Cologne. He signed for Arsenal in the summer of 1982 and hit nine England goals as a Gunner before returning to Cologne in 1986.

TEENAGE KICKS

Theo Walcott made history in May 2006 when he became the youngest player ever to represent the senior England side. Signed to Arsenal from Southampton in January 2006, the winger was just 17 years and 75 days old when he came off the bench in the Three Lions' clash with Hungary at Old Trafford, replacing Michael Owen after 65 minutes.

Walcott's appearance eclipsed the previous record of 17 years and 111 days set by Wayne Rooney against Australia in February 2003.

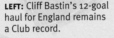

LEFT: Theo Walcott beat Wayne Rooney's record as England's youngest debutant.

CLIFF BASTIN'S ENGLAND GOALS

England 1 Italy (3 May 1933)

England 4 (2 goals) Switzerland 0 (20 May 1933)

England 3 Scotland 0 (14 April 1934)

England 2 (2 goals) Northern Ireland 1 (6 February 1935)

England 3 Germany 0 (4 December 1935)

England 1 Wales 2 (17 October 1936)

England 3 Northern Ireland 1 (18 November 1936)

England 6 Germany 3 (14 May 1938)

England 1 Switzerland 2 (21 May 1938)

England 4 France 2 (26 May 1938)

DUAL INTERNATIONAL

Inside-forward Paddy Sloan signed for Arsenal from Tranmere Rovers in 1947 and has the unusual claim to fame of having represented both the Republic of Ireland and Northern Ireland at full international level.

Sloan's curious international career began in 1945, while he was still a Tranmere player when he was selected by the Irish Football Association, the governing body of the game in Northern Ireland, to play against England at Windsor Park. He won his second cap against Wales at Ninian Park in May the following year.

Following his move to Highbury, however, he was called up by the Football Association of Ireland to tour with the Republic of Ireland side in the summer of 1946, playing in a 3–1 defeat to Portugal in Lisbon and a shock 1–0 victory over Spain in Madrid.

In April 1947 he made a third and final appearance for Northern Ireland against Wales in Belfast.

IRISH LEGENDS

Niall Quinn (92), Liam Brady (72) and Frank Stapleton (71) all won more caps for the Republic of Ireland than David O'Leary – but the centre-half appeared in more games than any of them for the Republic while he was an Arsenal player.

All 68 of O'Leary's caps came while he was at Highbury. The highlight of his international career was at the 1990 World Cup in Italy when he scored the winning penalty in the shootout against Romania, in the last 16 of the tournament.

WORLD CUP MILESTONE

The inaugural World Cup was staged in Uruguay in 1930, but it was not until the 1958 instalment of the competition in Sweden that Arsenal players were involved.

The two trailblazers were inside-half Dave Bowen and goalkeeper Jack Kelsey, who were both named in the Wales XI to face Hungary in the tournament opener at the Jernvallen Stadium in June. Wales drew the match 1–1 and eventually qualified for the quarter-finals.

Both Bowen and Kelsey were subsequently in the side that lost 1–0 in the last eight to Brazil in Gothenburg – to a Pele goal.

ABOVE: Paddy Sloan played for both the Republic of Ireland and Northern Ireland in a five-match international career.

BELOW: Jack Kelsey was the first goalkeeper to concede a World Cup goal scored by Brazil's legendary Pele.

HAIL CAESAR

Jimmy Ashcroft was the first Arsenal player to be capped by England, in 1906, but a full decade before his appointment with the Three Lions it was Welshman Caesar Jenkyns who earned the distinction of being the Club's first-ever full international.

The centre-half from Powys joined the Club from Small Heath in April 1895, three years after making his Wales debut, and in March 1896 he became the Gunners' first international when he was selected to play against Scotland in Dundee.

He won eight caps for his country but spent just one season with Arsenal, ending his association with the Club in May 1896 when he signed for Newton Heath.

BELOW: Chesterfield-born Bob Wilson headed north of the border to kickstart his international career.

ABOVE: Caesar Jenkyns (back row, fourth left) was Woolwich Arsenal's first international, playing for Wales, during his one season with the Club.

SCOTTISH SWITCH

A veteran of 308 games for Arsenal, goalkeeper Bob Wilson was born in Chesterfield but played twice for Scotland, becoming the first Englishman in almost a century to be selected by the SFA.

Wilson's parents both hailed from north of the border and a change in the rules on eligibility in 1970 paved the way for his Scotland debut against Portugal in a European Championship qualifier in Glasgow in October 1971. His second cap came against the Netherlands in Rotterdam two months later.

In total, 18 players have represented Scotland while on the books at Arsenal.

RICE'S RECORD

Belfast-born Pat Rice holds the Club record for the most caps for Northern Ireland, playing 49 internationals for his country between 1968 and 1979.

The full-back won his first cap against Israel in September 1968 while his final appearance for Northern Ireland was against England in a European Championship qualifier in October 1979.

Just behind Rice are former Gunner Sammy Nelson, who played 47 times for Northern Ireland, and Terry Neill, who won 44 caps.

A CENTURY OF CAPS

The likes of Thierry Henry, Patrick Vieira and Ashley Cole have gone on to reach the 100 international appearances milestone after leaving the Club – but Lukas Podolski is the only man with a century of caps to play for Arsenal.

The midfielder played his 100th game for Germany in a 2–1 victory over Denmark in the group stages of Euro 2012 and officially became a Gunners player on 1 July.

He won his 102nd cap in a World Cup qualifier against the Faroe Islands in September 2012 to become the first Arsenal international centurion.

▶▶ THE FRENCH CONNECTION

Thierry Henry graced Highbury and subsequently Emirates for eight glorious seasons – and during his record-breaking spell in north London he also set the Club record for the most caps accumulated by an Arsenal player.

The striker played for France 123 times between 1997 and 2010, and 81 of his caps were earned while he was a Gunner. His international debut came as a 20-year-old against South Africa in October 1997, while his first game for *Les Bleus* after signing for Arsenal was against Scotland at Hampden Park in March 2000, where he scored in a 2–0 victory.

Henry continued to represent his country after joining Barcelona in 2007 but his 81 appearances while with Arsenal remains a record. He scored 38 goals in those 81 matches, which is also an Arsenal milestone.

Compatriot Patrick Vieira is second on the all-time list with 79 games for France during his nine-year association with the Club.

WORLDWIDE GUNNERS

Up to October 2012, Gunners players past, future and present had represented 43 different countries beyond Britain and Ireland at international level.

France led the way with 18 capped players who had also represented Arsenal in their career while the Netherlands were second on the list with six. Brazil and Sweden were joint third with five international Gunners.

BELOW: Thierry Henry became a *Les Bleus* legend while he was at Highbury.

◀ VICTORIOUS VIEIRA

Legendary midfielder Patrick Vieira is the most successful international player in terms of silverware in Arsenal's history. The Frenchman lifted the 1998 World Cup and 2000 European Championship with *Les Bleus* and made it an unprecedented hat-trick of trophies in 2001 when France beat Japan in the final of the 2001 Confederations Cup.

Vieira scored the only goal of the match in the 30th minute of the match against the hosts in the Yokohama International Stadium to seal his trophy treble.

LEFT: Patrick Vieira won three major international trophies during his Arsenal career, including helping France to claim the FIFA Confederations Cup against Japan in 2001.

ABOVE: The Gunners' Mesut Ozil, Lukas Podolski and Per Mertesacker celebrate after Germany's triumph in the 2014 World Cup Final.

LEFT: John Kosmina signed for Arsenal from his hometown club Adelaide City.

◄ FINAL FIRST

The first Arsenal players to play in a World Cup final were Emmanuel Petit and Patrick Vieira, who both featured in France's 3–0 victory over Brazil in Paris in July 1998.

Petit was named in Aime Jacquet's starting XI for the clash with the South Americans in the Stade de France and scored the third goal in injury-time in a famous 3–0 triumph. Vieira started the match on the bench but entered the fray after 74 minutes when he replaced Youri Djorkaeff.

Midfielder Cesc Fabregas emulated the achievement 12 years later when he was part of the Spanish squad that won the 2010 World Cup in South Africa. Named on the bench for the final against the Netherlands in Johannesburg, Fabregas came on for Xabi Alonso in the 87th minute as the game headed towards extra-time.

In 2014, Mesut Ozil, Lukas Podolski and Per Mertesacker joined the Club's growing list of world champions as Germany defeated Argentina 1–0 in extra-time of the World Cup final in the Maracana Stadium in Brazil.

Ozil started the match in Rio de Janeiro and was replaced in the 120th minute by Mertesacker, while Podolski was an unused substitute as Germany were crowned champions for a fourth time. Alan Ball, Thierry Henry, Robert Pires and Gilberto Silva have all won World Cup winner's medals – but not while they were with the Gunners.

◄ AUSTRALIAN ARRIVAL

The only Australian international to play for the Gunners is John Kosmina, a £20,000 buy from Adelaide City in March 1978. Capped 60 times by the Socceroos, the striker made just one league appearance for the Club, as a substitute in a 2–2 draw with Leeds United at Highbury in August 1978, and headed back to Australia the following year when he signed for the West Adelaide Hellas club.

MOST CAPS AS AN ARSENAL PLAYER	
Thierry Henry (France)	81 caps
Patrick Vieira (France)	79
Kenny Sansom (England)	77
David Seaman (England)	72
David O'Leary (Republic of Ireland)	68
Robin van Persie (Netherlands)	68
Tony Adams (England)	66
Freddie Ljungberg (Sweden)	60
Nicklas Bendtner (Denmark)	60
Cesc Fabregas (Spain)	58

EUROPEAN CHAMPIONS

France's 2–1 victory over Italy in the final of Euro 2000 saw Patrick Vieira and Thierry Henry become the first Arsenal players to claim the European Championship crown.

The midfielder and the striker were both in the starting XI for the clash in Rotterdam, a game the French won 2–1 in extra-time courtesy of David Trezeguet's golden goal.

Future Gunners Robert Pires and Sylvain Wiltord also featured in the final, signing for the Club after France's triumph.

Midfielder Cesc Fabregas is Arsenal's only other European Championship winner, claiming the title with Spain in 2008 after a 1–0 victory against Germany in Vienna. Santi Cazorla also played in the match in the Ernst-Happel-Stadion, four years before signing for Arsenal from Malaga.

John Jensen was in the Danish side that beat Germany 2–0 in the final of the 1992 European Championship and became an Arsenal player two months later when George Graham signed him from Brondby.

 ## EASTERN PROMISE

Three international players from Asia have represented the Gunners. Japanese midfielder Junichi Inamoto led the way when he signed for Arsenal from Gamba Osaka in the summer of 2001, and a decade later compatriot Ryo Miyaichi signed his first professional contract with the Club.

South Korea winger Park Chu-Young became Arsenal's third Asian signing in August 2011 when he signed from Monaco, making his debut in a 3–1 League Cup victory over Shrewsbury at Emirates in September.

 ## THE HALF-CENTURY

A total of 12 players have won 50 or more caps for their respective countries while they were on Arsenal's books. The first player to reach the milestone was England full-back Kenny Sansom, while the most recent was Danish striker Nicklas Bendtner.

The other players on the elite list are Thierry Henry, Patrick Vieira, David Seaman, David O'Leary, Robin van Persie, Tony Adams, Freddie Ljungberg, Cesc Fabregas, Gilberto Silva and Ashley Cole.

ABOVE: Junichi Inamoto had already been capped by Japan when he arrived at Highbury.

LEFT: Nicklas Bendtner of Denmark is one of a dozen Gunners to play 50 international matches.

ABOVE: Christopher Wreh swapped Liberia for London when he signed for the Gunners.

CONTINENTAL CUSTODIAN

Dutch goalkeeper Gerry Keyser was the first non-British or Irish player to represent Arsenal in competitive action and made 12 league appearances for Herbert Chapman's side in the 1930–31 season as the Gunners were crowned Division One champions for the first time.

Keyser spent just one season at the Club, and after brief spells with Charlton and QPR he returned to the Netherlands to play for Ajax. It was during his time in Amsterdam that he won two caps for Holland in 1934, making him the first (albeit former) Gunner to play international football for a non-Home Nations team.

AMERICAN CONTINGENT

Six full South American internationals have played for the Gunners, with Brazilians Silvinho, Edu, Gilberto Silva, Julio Baptista and Andre Santos and Argentina's Nelson Vivas all pulling on the famous red and white shirt.

Central America is represented by Mexico's Carlos Vela, who made 62 appearances for the Club between 2008 and 2012, while the only international player from North America is USA defender Frank Simek whose one game for Arsenal came in a League Cup clash against Wolves in December 2003.

AFRICAN PIONEER

South African winger Daniel Le Roux was the first player from Africa to play for Arsenal, in the 1950s, but it was not until 1997 that the Gunners had a full African international in their ranks. Signed by Arsene Wenger from Monaco in a £300,000 deal, the player was Liberian striker Christopher Wreh.

The West African spent three seasons at Highbury, winning the 1997–98 Premier League and starting in the 1998 FA Cup final victory over Newcastle. His international career spanned seven years, winning 36 caps for the Lone Stars.

Le Roux did represent South Africa in his career but his appearances came during the side's amateur era.

In addition to Liberia, nine further African nations have supplied the Gunners with current or future international players. The countries are Togo, Senegal, Ivory Coast, Libya, Guinea, Ghana, Cameroon, Morocco and Nigeria.

GLOBAL INFLUENCE

The 2006 World Cup in Germany saw Arsenal supply 15 players to their respective countries, more than any other club.

Three Gunners represented England – Ashley Cole, Sol Campbell and Theo Walcott – while Kolo Toure and Emmanuel Eboue were on duty for the Ivory Coast. Johan Djourou and Philippe Senderos were selected by Switzerland while Cesc Fabregas and Jose Antonio Reyes were part of the Spain squad.

The other Arsenal players at the tournament were Jens Lehmann (Germany), Freddie Ljungberg (Sweden), Robin van Persie (Holland), Gilberto Silva (Brazil), Thierry Henry (France) and Emmanuel Adebayor (Togo).

RIGHT: Dutch goalkeeper Gerry Keyser broke the mould when he joined Arsenal ahead the 1930–31 season.

MOST INTERNATIONAL HONOURS AS AN ARSENAL PLAYER

Patrick Vieira – 3 (1998 World Cup, Euro 2000, 2001 Confederations Cup)

Thierry Henry – 2 (Euro 2000, 2003 Confederations Cup)

Sylvain Wiltord – 2 (2001, 2003 Confederations Cup)

Cesc Fabregas – 2 (Euro 2008, 2010 World Cup)

Robert Pires – 2 (2001, 2003 Confederations Cup)

Gilberto Silva – 2 (2005 Confederations, 2007 Copa America)

Lauren – 2 (2000 Olympics, 2002 Africa Cup of Nations)

PART 3
Other Records

Arsenal are one of the best-supported teams in the world and over the years hundreds of thousands of fans have streamed through the turnstiles to watch the Gunners in action.

The first pages of this chapter detail all the Club's record attendances – from the modest days of matches on Plumstead Common in the 1880s to the crowds seen at Emirates since Arsenal moved into their state-of-the-art new home in the summer of 2006.

Next up is a review of the achievements of the Club's managers with a special focus on George Graham and Arsene Wenger, the two most successful coaches in Arsenal's history and the winners of 13 major trophies between them.

The Gunners' stadiums from the old Invicta Ground, the team's 93-year love affair with Highbury and the recent relocation to Ashburton Grove are detailed in the middle section before four pages devoted to the north London derby and Arsenal's enduring and passionate rivalry with neighbours Tottenham.

The chapter ends with miscellaneous Club records, including the side's landmark European firsts, its unique role in the development of televised football, Australian John Kosmina's bizarre claim to Gunners fame and details of the last time the Club started a game with 11 Englishmen in the starting line-up.

ABOVE: Highbury's fabled marble hall, with its bust of legendary manager Herbert Chapman.

RIGHT: The Gunners faithful show their true colours as Arsenal begin a new era at Emirates.

Other Records – Attendances

From the record 73,295 fans who were at Highbury in 1935 for the visit of Sunderland to the 60,023 supporters in attendance for the first-ever competitive match at Emirates, this section focuses on the biggest crowds in Arsenal's history.

▶ **WEMBLEY WOE**

The Gunners' first two seasons of Champions League football saw the Club hierarchy take the decision to play "home" games at Wembley rather than Highbury. The team's supporters flocked in their thousands to watch.

The record attendance for a Wembley game was the 73,707 who watched Arsene Wenger's side tackle Lens in the group stages of the competition in November 1998.

Unfortunately Arsenal were unable to deliver the win the crowd craved and slipped to a 1–0 defeat after a Mickael Debeve goal – a result which saw them eliminated from that season's tournament.

The Gunners played six Champions League group phase games at Wembley between September 1998 and October 1999 with an aggregate total of 438,072 supporters attending the matches.

ABOVE: Wembley was packed when French side Lens were the opponents in 1998.

BELOW: The League Cup visit of Shrewsbury Town failed to capture the imagination of the Gunners faithful.

▼ **LEAGUE CUP LOW**

The early rounds of the League Cup do not always produce the most glamorous of matches and Arsenal's third-round clash with Shrewsbury Town certainly failed to capture the imagination as a record-low crowd of 46,539 turned up at Emirates for the game in September 2011.

Arsene Wenger selected an experimental side but, despite the empty seats at Emirates, his unfamiliar team still ran out 3–1 winners against their League Two opponents with the goals coming from Kieran Gibbs, Yossi Benayoun and Alex Oxlade-Chamberlain.

EMIRATES ERA

The first-ever competitive match staged at Emirates saw Aston Villa travel to north London for the opening game of the 2006–07 Premier League campaign. But the christening of the new stadium in August didn't go exactly according to plan.

A crowd of 60,023 swelled the Club's new home, but an Olof Mellberg goal for Villa threatened to spoil the party, and the Gunners faithful were grateful when Gilberto Silva's 84th-minute equalizer saved the day.

HIGHBURY HIGH

Arsenal spent 93 years at Highbury before relocating from London N5 to Emirates in the summer of 2006. The biggest crowd ever to cram into the famous old stadium was the 73,295 who watched the Gunners play Sunderland in a First Division clash in March 1935.

The Wearsiders had beaten George Allison's side 2–1 at Roker Park earlier in the season, but hopes of exacting revenge at Highbury fell flat as Arsenal were held to a goalless draw by the visitors.

FEWEST FANS

The 1960s was a relatively lean period for Arsenal and the lack of success on the pitch was reflected by the meagre crowd of just 4,554 who were at Highbury to watch the side play Leeds United in the First Division in May 1966.

It was a record low attendance and the lack of support didn't do Billy Wright's side any favours as the Gunners crashed to a 3–0 defeat, with two goals from Jim Storrie and one from Jimmy Greenhoff.

ABOVE: Sunderland goalkeeper Jimmy Thorpe kept a clean sheet when he played in front of Highbury's record crowd, 73,295, in 1935.

ABOVE: The move to Emirates Stadium in 2006 has seen Arsenal's attendances soar.

TICKET BONANZA

The 1934–35 season was undoubtedly a good one for Arsenal on the pitch as George Allison's side claimed the Division One title for a fourth time in the Club's history.

The Gunners' accountants were also extremely happy, with the Club generating an estimated £100,000 in gate receipts over the course of the season, the first time an English side had reached six figures for ticket sales.

One of the biggest crowds of the campaign was the 70,544 at Highbury who paid to watch the north London derby against Spurs in October. Their loyalty was rewarded as the Gunners crushed the old rivals 5–1 courtesy of a Ted Drake hat-trick.

The record attendance of the season, however, came for the Sunderland match in March. The Wearsiders were Arsenal's main title rivals and the importance of the game was reflected by the 73,295 who packed Highbury to watch what turned out to be a goalless draw.

HOME ATTENDANCES – HIGHEST
Highbury
73,295 v Sunderland, 9 March 1935 (League)
Emirates Stadium
60,161 v Manchester United, 3 November 2007 (Premier League)
Wembley Stadium
73,707 v RC Lens, 25 November 1998 (Champions League)

ABOVE: The Invincibles celebrate their record-breaking achievement before collecting the Premiership trophy at Highbury in May 2004.

► LEAGUE DEBUT

The Manor Ground in Plumstead was Arsenal's home for 20 years from 1893 and the stadium was the venue for the Gunners' first-ever Football League fixture.

The Division Two match in September 1893 saw Newcastle United in town and goals from Walter Shaw and Arthur Elliott were enough to earn Arsenal a 2–2 draw in front of a 10,000-strong crowd.

Attendances fluctuated over the rest of the Second Division campaign with a modest 2,000 turning up to watch the 3–1 victory over Grimsby Town in September, while a season-best 13,000 were in the stands for the 2–1 defeat against Notts County in March.

The biggest crowd of the year, however, was in November for the FA Cup third qualifying-round encounter with Millwall, a game which attracted an impressive gathering of 20,000 fans to the Manor Ground.

The Gunners players responded admirably to the support, winning the tie 2–0 courtesy of goals from wing-half Fred Davis and outside-left Charles Booth.

▲ PREMIER LEAGUE HIGH

Arsenal's phenomenal, all-conquering 2003–04 season saw Arsene Wenger's Invincibles wrap up the Premier League title by the end of April with a 2–2 draw with Tottenham at White Hart Lane. But it was not until the final day of the season that the side were officially presented with the trophy.

The presentation was scheduled after the Gunners' clash with Leicester City at Highbury in May. After goals from Thierry Henry and Patrick Vieira sealed a 2–1 victory and preserved the side's incredible unbeaten record, the silverware was handed over.

Captain Vieira was the first to hold the trophy in front of a crowd of 38,419, the highest attendance at Highbury in Premier League history.

BELOW: The Manor Ground in Plumstead witnessed the start of Arsenal's Football League adventure in 1893, but this match against Liverpool was in 1906.

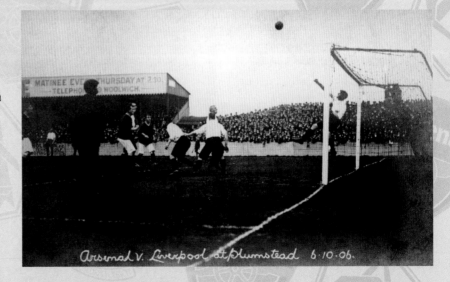

Arsenal v. Liverpool at Plumstead 6·10·06.

SECOND-TIER FAREWELL

Arsenal's long and proud record as a top-flight club began in 1919 after the end of the Second World War, making their Division Two clash with Nottingham Forest in April 1915 the Gunners' last lower-league game.

The match at Highbury saw George Morrell's team thrash the visitors 7–0, with Harry King scoring four. A crowd of 10,000 were on hand to witness the Club's farewell to the Second Division.

HIGHBURY DEBUT

The Gunners bid farewell to the Manor Ground in Plumstead in the summer of 1913 and headed north of the river, relocating to Highbury and signalling a new era for the Club.

The first-ever competitive match at the stadium saw George Morrell's team play Leicester Fosse in a Division Two clash in early September 1913, and a 20,000-strong crowd flocked to the new ground to see the action.

The visitors threatened to spoil the party with a first-half goal but a George Jobey strike and an Archie Devine penalty, awarded for handball, ensured Arsenal christened their new home in appropriate winning style.

ABOVE: Arsenal goalkeeper George Swindin prepares to block a header from Manchester United's Jimmy Delaney, watched by a League-record crowd of 83,260 at United's temporary Maine Road home

HIGHBURY SWANSONG

The last-ever competitive match to be staged at Highbury was Arsenal's Premier League clash with Wigan in May 2006, a game that drew a crowd of 38,359 for an emotional afternoon in the Club's history.

A Thierry Henry hat-trick and a Robert Pires goal sealed a 4–2 victory for the Gunners.

The attendance for the Wigan match was 219 bigger than the crowd of 38,140 who poured through the turnstiles for Arsene Wenger's first match in charge at Highbury, a goalless draw with Coventry in October 1996.

▲ GUNNERS TREBLE

The three highest attendances in the history of the old Division One were all for matches featuring Arsenal, underlining the enduring popularity of the Club.

The First Division's crowd record was set in January 1948 when Tom Whittaker's side headed north to face Manchester United, a game witnessed by 83,260 supporters and one which the Gunners drew 1–1 courtesy of a goal from striker Reg Lewis.

Arsenal's visit to Stamford Bridge to play Chelsea in October 1935 attracted the division's second-highest-ever attendance with 82,905 fans, and it was another 1–1 stalemate thanks to a Jack Crayston strike.

Another trip to Manchester in February 1935 – this time to face City at Maine Road – drew Division One's third-biggest crowd with 79,491 spectators – and yet again the points were shared as Ray Bowden scored in the 1–1 draw.

◄ DERBY RECORD

Tickets for the north London derby are invariably snapped up within minutes of going on sale but the 1991 FA Cup semi-final between Arsenal and Tottenham presented a record number of fans with the opportunity to watch the two old rivals do battle.

Wembley was chosen as the neutral venue for the last-four showdown, meaning 77,893 supporters were able to watch the game.

Unfortunately for the Gunners contingent in the record crowd, it was Spurs who emerged 3–1 winners and were back at Wembley for the final a month later.

LEFT: The 1991 north London derby at Wembley was watched by a record crowd

HOME ATTENDANCES – LOWEST
Highbury
4,554 v Leeds United, 5 May 1966 (League)
Emirates Stadium
46,539 v Shrewsbury Town, 20 September 2011 (League Cup)
Wembley Stadium
71,227 v AIK Solna, 22 September 1999 (Champions League)

OLYMPIC VENUE

As well as playing host to England, Highbury was also used as a venue for the 1948 Olympics and hosted two matches during the course of the Games.

The first, at the end of July, saw the Great Britain side dramatically beat the Netherlands 4–3 after extra-time in the first round in front of a 21,000-strong crowd.

The quarter-final showdown between Denmark and Italy six days later, however, proved even more popular – with 25,000 fans in attendance as the Danes beat the Azzurri 5–3 to book their place in the last four at Wembley.

CHARITY BEGINS AT HOME

The Charity Shield became English football's traditional season opener at Wembley in 1974, but before the game was switched to the home of the England team Arsenal contested the fixture at Highbury five times.

The first time saw George Allison's team demolish Manchester City 4–0 in November 1934 in front of a crowd of 10,888, while the final Highbury instalment of the Charity Shield – a 3–1 victory over Blackpool in October 1953 – was watched by 39,853 fans.

The record crowd for the fixture, however, was in attendance for the game against Preston North End in September 1938 when 40,296 supporters packed Highbury to witness Ted Drake score twice in a 2–1 triumph.

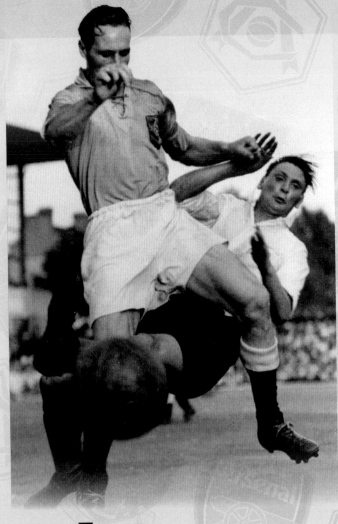

RIGHT: Highbury staged two matches at the 1948 Olympic Games: this first-round match between Great Britain and the Netherlands and a quarter-final tie.

CUP CONNECTION

During its 93-year-long life, Highbury was chosen as the neutral venue for a total of 12 FA Cup semi-finals.

The opening last-four clash at the ground saw Portsmouth beat Aston Villa in March 1929 while the last semi-final was between Chelsea and Wimbledon in April 1997, a game the Blues won 3–0 in front of 32,674 spectators.

BELOW: FA Cup semi-finals were held at Highbury for 58 years, but with all semi-finals now at Wembley, Emirates (top) isn't needed.

FIGHT NIGHT

In the football fraternity, 1966 is famed for England's pulsating extra-time victory over West Germany at Wembley in the World Cup – but in the same year Highbury played host to another famous sporting occasion, the second fight between Henry Cooper and Muhammad Ali.

The ring was built in the middle of the pitch at Highbury and 45,973 tickets were sold for the world heavyweight championship bout. Sadly for the Cooper fans, the fight was stopped by the referee in the sixth round due to a cut over the English champion's left eye. Ali retained his title.

INTERNATIONAL DUTY

England played matches at Highbury 12 times during the ground's lifetime and five times the games attracted 50,000-plus crowds to roar on the Three Lions.

The first time was in December 1931 when 55,000 thronged the Gunners' home to watch England demolish Spain 7–1 in a friendly. Three years later there were 56,044 supporters at the ground to witness a 3–2 win against the Italians courtesy of goals from Eric Brook (2) and Arsenal striker Ted Drake, a game which became known as the "Battle of Highbury".

The record attendance for an England game at Highbury, however, was in November 1950 when Yugoslavia were the visitors to north London. The game was watched by 61,000 people and ended in a 2–2 draw thanks to a brace from legendary Bolton Wanderers centre-forward Nat Lofthouse.

ABOVE: Henry Cooper and Muhammad Ali did battle at Highbury back in 1966.

RARE RUGBY VISIT

The Australian rugby league side embarked on its third tour of Britain in 1921 and in October the Kangaroos made an unlikely appearance at Highbury against England.

The rest of the matches were staged in the north of the country or Wales, but the tourists headed south for the eighth game of their trip, attracting 12,000 spectators to witness a rare game of rugby league in the capital – and a 6–5 victory for England.

BELGIAN MATCH

The second of England's visits to Highbury to play Belgium in March 1923 was also their first full home match against a side outside Great Britain and Ireland.

The Three Lions were far more accustomed to playing Wales, Scotland and Ireland, but found the new opposition to their liking, despatching the Belgians 6–1 in front of 25,000 delirious England supporters.

BELOW: A dozen internationals were played at Highbury, N5, starting with the 1931 clash between England and Spain.

ARSENAL'S TOP FIVE ATTENDANCES

83,260	Manchester United v Arsenal	17/01/1948	(Division 1)
82,905	Chelsea v Arsenal	12/10/1935	(Division 1)
79,491	Manchester City v Arsenal	23/02/1935	(Division 1)
75,952	Chelsea v Arsenal	09/10/1937	(Division 1)
74,918	Manchester City v Arsenal	10/04/1937	(Division 1)

Other Records – Managers

This section is devoted to the records, milestones and trophies of the Club's managers from Scotsman Thomas Mitchell in the late 1880s, the Gunners' first professional coach, to the arrival of Arsene Wenger in 1996.

ABOVE: George Morrell's seven-year reign as manager was not a successful one.

ABOVE: Harry Bradshaw took the Gunners into the First Division for the first time.

▲ MORRELL'S MISERY

Famously Arsenal have been relegated just once in the Club's illustrious history – and George Morrell holds the unfortunate distinction of being the manager who oversaw the season in which they went down.

Appointed manager in February 1908, the Scot was forced to sanction the sale of some of the Club's leading players to balance the books, and eventually the exodus of talent caught up with Arsenal.

Morrell's team flirted with relegation during the 1909–10 campaign, only to escape the drop with an 18th-place finish. But there was no hiding place in 1912–13 when the side finished rock-bottom with just three victories in 38 league games.

The manager stayed with the Gunners despite the disappointment.

The Club relocated to Highbury and, although the side failed to secure an automatic return to the top-flight in 1913–14, the team's fifth-place finish the following season proved enough to earn an unusual return to Division One and a degree of redemption for Morrell.

Fifth place, of course, would not have won automatic promotion, but league football was suspended in 1915 due to the First World War. When competitive football returned in 1919, Arsenal were included in a new First Division that been expanded from 20 to 22 teams.

The decision to elevate the Gunners was partly based on the strength of Morrell's fifth place and, although he had resigned at the end of the 1914–15 campaign, it provided a happy footnote to what otherwise might have been a wholly miserable managerial career.

▲ BRADSHAW'S TRIUMPH

The Gunners' third professional manager, Harry Bradshaw, arrived in north London in August 1899 from his home-town club of Burnley and earned his place in the Arsenal record books as the first man to mastermind a successful promotion campaign.

His groundbreaking achievement came in the 1903–04 season when he steered the Gunners into second place in the final Division Two table, finishing a single point behind champions Preston North End and earning the Club a place in the top tier of English football for the first time.

His team won 21 of their 34 league fixtures during the campaign and were beaten just six times. Bradshaw's side were the division's most prolific scorers with 91 goals, Irish forward Tommy Shanks top-scoring in the league with 24.

Bradshaw also holds the distinction of being the first Arsenal manager to take charge of the team for 100 games, but left the Club at the end of the 1903–04 campaign when he accepted a lucrative offer to join Fulham.

PLAYER TURNED BOSS

The first man to play for Arsenal and then go on to manage the Club was Tom Whittaker, a wing-half for the Gunners for six years after the end of the First World War and subsequently the team's manager in the wake of the Second World War.

Born in Aldershot, Whittaker signed for the Gunners in 1919 and made his debut in a 1–0 defeat to West Bromwich Albion at the Hawthorns in April 1920. In total he clocked up 70 games for the Club, but his playing career was prematurely cut short by a persistent knee injury and his appearance against West Ham at Highbury in March 1925 was to be his last.

After his enforced retirement, Whittaker studied physiotherapy before legendary boss Hebert Chapman appointed him Arsenal's first team trainer in 1927. Twenty years later he was given the job of manager, succeeding George Allison.

His nine-year Highbury reign was certainly a highly successful one, with the Gunners winning the 1947–48 Division One title in his first season at the helm. He claimed a second title for the Club in 1952–53 while his team were also triumphant in the 1950 FA Cup final, beating Liverpool 2–0 at Wembley courtesy of a brace of goals from Reg Lewis.

Whittaker died of a heart attack in October 1956, at the age of 58, but his successful transition from player to manager remains a milestone in the Gunners' history.

MITCHELL'S BRIEF REIGN

Arsenal's first-ever full-time manager, Scotsman Thomas Mitchell, joined the Club in August 1897, replacing "secretary-manager" Sam Hollis and ushering in a new professional coaching era for the Club.

Hailing from Dumfries, Mitchell was secretary at Blackburn Rovers for 12 years before accepting his new position with the Gunners and, although his short tenure was to end in March 1898 when he resigned, the team rose from 10th to fifth in Division Two under his guidance.

Arsenal played 26 times in total under Mitchell in all competitions, winning 14 games and drawing four. His reign remains the shortest of all of the Club's permanent rather than interim or caretaker bosses.

BELOW: Tom Whittaker made a successful transition from Gunners player to Arsenal manager.

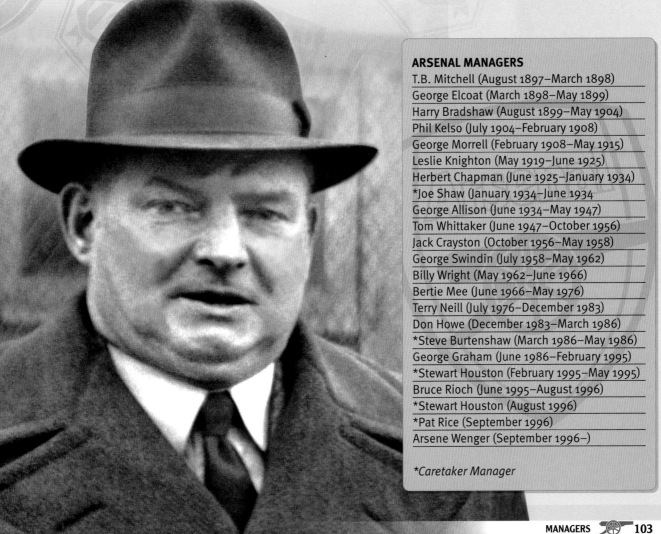

ARSENAL MANAGERS

T.B. Mitchell (August 1897–March 1898)

George Elcoat (March 1898–May 1899)

Harry Bradshaw (August 1899–May 1904)

Phil Kelso (July 1904–February 1908)

George Morrell (February 1908–May 1915)

Leslie Knighton (May 1919–June 1925)

Herbert Chapman (June 1925–January 1934)

*Joe Shaw (January 1934–June 1934

George Allison (June 1934–May 1947)

Tom Whittaker (June 1947–October 1956)

Jack Crayston (October 1956–May 1958)

George Swindin (July 1958–May 1962)

Billy Wright (May 1962–June 1966)

Bertie Mee (June 1966–May 1976)

Terry Neill (July 1976–December 1983)

Don Howe (December 1983–March 1986)

*Steve Burtenshaw (March 1986–May 1986)

George Graham (June 1986–February 1995)

*Stewart Houston (February 1995–May 1995)

Bruce Rioch (June 1995–August 1996)

*Stewart Houston (August 1996)

*Pat Rice (September 1996)

Arsene Wenger (September 1996–)

*Caretaker Manager

◤ HERBERT'S CUP HEROICS

Herbert Chapman is remembered and revered in Arsenal folklore for many reasons, but perhaps his greatest achievement was his pivotal role in securing the first major trophy in Gunners history.

A journeyman inside-forward, the Yorkshireman joined the Club in the summer of 1925 after managerial spells with Northampton Town, Leeds City and Huddersfield Town (where he won four Division One titles and the FA Cup). Almost as soon as he arrived at Highbury, Arsenal's fortunes began to turn.

In his first season in north London, the Gunners narrowly missed out on a first league title when they finished as runners-up behind Chapman's old side the Terriers. The Club's wait for silverware would not continue for much longer.

Chapman's moment of truth came in the 1930 FA Cup final against Huddersfield. Arsenal had already despatched Chelsea, Birmingham, Middlesbrough, West Ham and Hull en route to Wembley and goals from Alex James and Jack Lambert – both Chapman signings – ensured the journey was not wasted as they ran out 2–0 winners.

Under his astute and tactically innovative leadership, the Gunners famously went on to claim the First Division title for the first time in 1930–31 and again in 1932–33. But the FA Cup triumph was the major breakthrough the Club had been waiting for since it had turned professional in 1891.

Chapman died suddenly in early 1934 after a brief illness, but his part in Arsenal's emergence as a heavyweight of English football is commemorated forever in the shape of a bronze statue of the ground-breaking Yorkshireman outside Emirates Stadium.

RIGHT: Herbert Chapman was the mastermind behind Arsenal's first major trophy triumph.

RIGHT: Bertie Mee made history in 1970–71 when his side completed the coveted Double for the first time.

◀ END OF THE DROUGHT

Bertie Mee was Arsenal manager for a decade between 1966 and 1976 and his Highbury reign made history when the Gunners claimed the fabled League and FA Cup double for the first time.

Two successive but losing League Cup final appearances in 1968 and 1969 hinted at bigger and brighter things to come and when Mee's side won the 1970 Inter-Cities Fairs Cup, the Club's first piece of European silverware, to end a 17-year trophy drought, his team was almost at the peak of its powers.

The best, however, was yet to come and in 1970–71 Arsenal dominated. The league was a tightly-contested affair with Leeds United, but a Gunners surge towards the end of the campaign, in which they won eight of their closing 10 fixtures, was enough to secure the title – a point ahead of their Yorkshire rivals.

The climax of the season found Mee's team facing Liverpool at Wembley in the FA Cup final and, although the match went into extra-time, Charlie George's 112th-minute goal saw Arsenal complete the first double of the 20th century.

Mee remained at Highbury for five more years, in the process becoming the first man to manage the Club in 500 games.

ABOVE: Stewart Houston twice took charge of Arsenal as caretaker manager.

LOYAL SERVANT

The only man to manage Arsenal twice, albeit briefly, is Stewart Houston who took charge at Highbury in 1995 in a caretaker capacity and again in 1996 on an interim basis.

The Scotsman joined the Club in 1990 as George Graham's assistant manager, but when his compatriot was sacked in February 1995 Houston stepped into the breach for the remainder of the 1994–95 season.

He stood aside that summer to make way for Bruce Rioch, but was elevated once again to caretaker manager when Rioch was dismissed in August 1996. The plan was for Houston to take charge of first team affairs until the arrival of Arsene Wenger from Grampus Eight in Japan. But the offer of the manager's job at QPR proved too tempting and he moved to Loftus Road in September, three weeks before the Frenchman's accession.

In total, Houston took charge of the side in 25 games during his two caretaker stints, winning nine matches and drawing five.

▶ YOUNG GUN

Terry Neill's seven-year stint as Arsenal manager saw the Club lift the 1979 FA Cup, but his reign is also notable for two other landmark achievements – he remains the youngest-ever man to coach the Gunners and he was also the first non-English or Scottish manager in the Club's history.

The Belfast-born centre-back spent 11 years at Highbury as a player, and three years after hanging up his boots he returned to the Club as manager at the age of 34.

Overall the Northern Irishman was in charge at Arsenal for 416 games, and as well as the FA Cup triumph he steered the team to the final of the 1979–80 Cup Winners' Cup against Valencia.

BELOW: Terry Neill was just 34 when he succeeded Bertie Mee in the Highbury hot seat.

GLORIOUS GRAHAM

The most successful manager in Arsenal's history prior to the Arsene Wenger era, George Graham claimed six major trophies during nine celebrated and hugely successful years in the Highbury dugout, eclipsing even the great Herbert Chapman, George Allison, Tom Whittaker and Bertie Mee in terms of silverware.

The Scot spent 15 years at Highbury in total and, although his stint in the Gunners midfield yielded three trophies in the early 1970s, it was his reunion with the Club as manager between 1986 and 1995 that confirmed his legendary status.

Graham cut his managerial teeth at Millwall before his return to Arsenal and in his first season at the helm he ended the Club's eight-year wait for a trophy when he led his new side to victory in the final of the League Cup, beating Liverpool 2–1 at Wembley.

His coaching philosophy was to build from the back, and it reaped dividends with a second League Cup success in 1993 and the First Division title in 1988–89 and 1990–91.

Those triumphs put Graham ahead of his predecessors, but the final major act of his association with Arsenal was arguably his most significant as the Gunners won the 1994 Cup Winners' Cup. The Club had won the Inter-Cities Fairs Cup in 1970 under Bertie Mee, but it was not a UEFA-sanctioned competition, making Graham's 1994 success the first time Arsenal had lifted an official UEFA trophy.

The team despatched Danish side Odense and Belgians Standard Liege in the early rounds before edging past Torino 1–0 on aggregate in the quarter-finals courtesy of a Tony Adams strike in the second leg at Highbury. Paris Saint-Germain were beaten in the last four and defending champions Parma were the opponents in the final, staged at the Parken Stadium in Copenhagen in front of a 34,000 strong crowd.

Striker Alan Smith made the breakthrough in the first half with a superb volley after a mistake by the Italian defence, and for the rest of the match Graham's famed back four held firm as Parma pressed and Arsenal were champions.

The Gunners reached the final again 12 months later only to lose to Real Zaragoza in extra-time, but Graham had been sacked three months earlier, bringing down the curtain on an era in which the Scot had re-established the Club among the elite of English football.

BELOW: George Graham (with David O'Leary, left) made the Gunners a force to be reckoned with in English football.

OPPOSITE: Arsene Wenger with the FA Cup after his side's 4–0 victory over Aston Villa in the 2015 FA Cup final.

THE WONDER OF WENGER

The arrival of Arsene Wenger in north London in October 1996 from Japan was greeted with a mixture of anticipation and apathy. The new manager may have won the French League Championship and French Cup with Monaco but, following Bruce Rioch's ill-fated season-long reign at Highbury, he was not the household name many of the Arsenal faithful yearned for.

"The Professor", however, was unperturbed and the revolution he instigated at the Club was to see the Gunners enjoy the most prolific period in their history. Now, by any measure, Wenger is Arsenal's most successful and significant manager.

His first game in charge was away to Blackburn Rovers at Ewood Park on 12 October 1996 in the Premier League. Ian Wright scored both goals in a 2–0 win, but the 1997–98 campaign was Wenger's first full season and

saw his increasingly cosmopolitan side dethrone Manchester United as champions. The icing on the cake was the subsequent 2–0 win over Newcastle in the FA Cup final and, less than two years after his appointment, Wenger had already emulated Bertie Mee's legendary 1971 double feat.

It was, of course, merely the beginning of a tide of silverware. Three more FA Cups and two further Premier League titles would follow, while the second double in 2001–02 and the staggering Invincibles season of 2003–04 cemented the Frenchman's place at the very top of the pantheon of the Club's great managers.

In October 2009, he surpassed George Allison's record of 4,748 days as the Gunners' manager. The team's stunning 5–3 win at Stamford Bridge against Chelsea in October 2011 was his 500th victory in all competitions

at the helm, while the Premier League clash with Chelsea in March 2014 saw him take charge of the side for the 1000th time in his illustrious career.

In reaching the 1000-game milestone, the Frenchman had presided over 572 victories and just 193 defeats.

His long list of individual awards includes Premier League Manager of the Season in 1998, 2002 and 2004, his 2006 induction into the English Football Hall of Fame, an honorary OBE and the accolade of World Coach of the Decade, awarded by the International Federation of Football History & Statistics. His success on the pitch and his astute dealings in the transfer market are also credited with helping to fund the Club's 2006 move from Highbury to Emirates.

Wenger's reign has comprehensively rewritten the record books since he moved to north London.

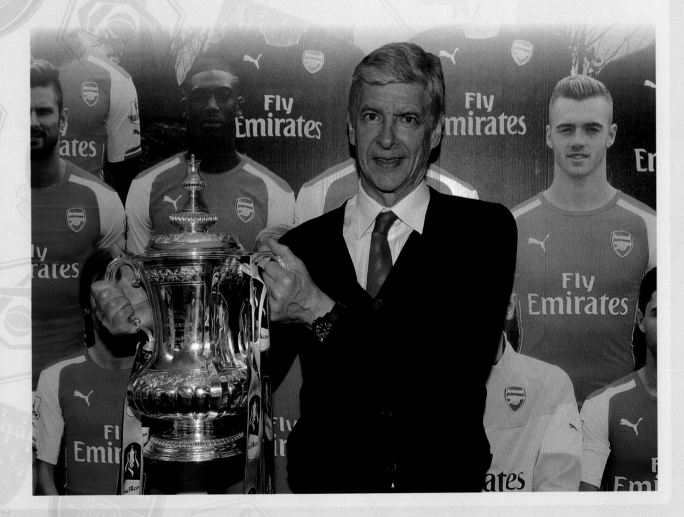

Other Records – Stadiums

Arsenal have played at six different grounds since the Club was founded in the 19th century and this section details all of the Gunners' homes from their early days on Plumstead Common to the £390 million Emirates Stadium.

COMMON PEOPLE

Arsenal's first "home" in the late nineteenth century was the open expanse of Plumstead Common in south-east London. But it was far from the height of luxury and, less than 12 months after the Club was founded, they were quickly on the move ahead of the 1887–88 season.

The Gunners won their first recorded match 6–1 against Erith in January 1887 and, although they were to play only a handful of games on the Common before relocating, it was to prove a happy albeit brief hunting ground – seven days later Arsenal demolished Alexandra United 11–0 in a friendly.

GROUND SWITCH

The Gunners' second home – the aptly named Sportsman Ground – was hardly more developed than their first and they spent just six months on the edge of Plumstead Marshes before they were on the move again.

The Club rented the Sportsman Ground from a local pig breeder and they played their first game there – a 5–1 victory over Alexandra United – in October 1887. But the pitch had a tendency to flood and the side's 5–0 win over Ascham in March 1888 was the Club's last fixture at the ground before the pigs reclaimed their old stamping ground.

▼ MANOR MOVE

Arsenal's itinerant existence continued in 1888 when they rented the Manor Ground in Plumstead, ignoring the inconvenient fact that a large open sewer ran along the southern side of the pitch.

By the Club's early standards, their two-year stay at the Manor Ground was relatively long. But with the players forced to change in the nearby Railway Tavern, the ambitious Gunners realized they needed a more modern facility and in 1890 they packed their bags once again.

BELOW: In 1893 Arsenal raised £4,000 to buy and redevelop the Manor Ground and the stadium regularly attracted 10,000 fans.

▲ TO THE MANOR REBORN

It was a case of déjà vu in 1893 when Arsenal returned to the Manor Ground. This time, though, after raising £4,000 through a share issue to buy 13-and-a-half acres of land for development, the Club was the owner rather than a temporary tenant.

Work quickly began on a large iron stand to house 2,000 fans and, with the terraces and military wagons that were wheeled in as viewing platforms for the big matches, the new-look Manor Ground was now capable of accommodating up to 20,000 supporters.

Thanks to scores of volunteers who worked tirelessly over the summer, the redevelopment was finished in time for the Club's debut in the 1893–94 Second Division. In the space of six years, Arsenal had grown from an amateur side into a fully fledged Football League team.

Around 10,000 descended on the new ground for the league

opener against Newcastle United in September 1893 and the team christened the stadium with a 2–2 draw, courtesy of goals from inside-left Arthur Elliott and striker Walter Shaw.

The average gate during the Club's historic 1893–94 campaign was 6,000, while the highest attendance for a league match was the 13,000 who turned out to watch the visit of Notts County in March.

The Gunners spent 20 years at the Manor Ground, but crowds dwindled towards the end of their stay and just 3,000 were there to witness the final game, a 1–1 stalemate with Middlesbrough, in April 1913.

Arsenal were in financial trouble and new owner Sir Henry Norris decided the Club needed a new, more lucrative home. The Gunners were set to head north of the river and the Manor Ground quickly fell derelict. The old stand was demolished and the land redeveloped.

ABOVE: A packed Manor Ground watches Arsenal take on Liverpool during the 1905–06 season.

TRADING UP

The Invicta Ground in Plumstead was the Club's home between 1890 and 1893. With a stand that could house 1,500 spectators and terraces that were big enough for 3,000 more supporters, it signalled a new era for Arsenal.

Initially the average crowd was a modest 1,000, but a friendly game against Scottish Cup holders Hearts in March 1891 saw a record 12,000 fans in attendance.

The ground's owner first charged the Gunners an annual rent of £200. But after the Club turned professional in 1891 and were elected to the Football League two years later, the charges suddenly went up to £350 plus tax per year and the Arsenal accountants decided it was high time to seek alternative accommodation.

ARCHITECTURAL RIVALRY

Arsenal's move to Highbury would ignite a long-standing rivalry with neighbours Tottenham. But in 1913 the Gunners were more than happy to turn to renowned architect Archibald Leith, the man who had designed White Hart Lane, to draw up the first plans for the Club's new home.

The stadium was hurriedly built over the summer of 1913. It featured a stand on the east side of the pitch and banked terracing on the other three sides.

The total cost was £125,000 and although it was not completely finished in time for the opening game of the 1913–14 season – the team's 2–1 win over Leicester Fosse in September in the old Second Division – Highbury was open for business.

BUMS ON SEATS

The late 1980s and 1990s saw the last major improvements to Highbury, with the remodelling of the Clock End during the 1988–89 season which saw the addition of a roof and executive boxes, while the North Bank was demolished at the end of the 1991–92 campaign to make way for a new all-seater stand.

THE FINAL COUNT

The last-ever fixture at Highbury saw Arsene Wenger's side defeat Wigan Athletic 4–2 in May 2006, the 2,010th and final competitive match at the stadium that was the Club's home for more than nine decades.

Over those 93 years, the Gunners scored a grand total of 4,038 goals and won 1,196 games. They lost just 339 matches and conceded a miserly 1,955 goals.

The club's overall league record reads: played 1,689, won 981, drawn 412 and lost 296, while the team won 92 of the 142 FA Cup ties held in N5.

Only nine teams came to the stadium and went away victorious in 76 European fixtures, while Arsenal triumphed in four of the five Charity Shield games held at Highbury before the annual game was moved to Wembley.

HANDS OF TIME

The construction of a roof over the North Stand presented Arsenal with the dilemma of what to do with the famous Highbury Clock that could no longer be accommodated at that end of the ground. In 1935 it was agreed to relocate the huge timepiece to the College End, the southern side of the stadium.

The clock had been the idea of manager Herbert Chapman and initially it provided supporters with a 45-minute countdown during games – until the Football Association deemed that it undermined their referees and the Club were forced to change it to a conventional design.

The "striking" feature, however, proved so popular among the fans that College End was informally renamed the Clock End, and when the Club reluctantly moved to Emirates in 2006, they took the iconic clock with them.

Until the 1950s, the Gunners were at the mercy of the sun when it came to staging matches, but in 1951 that all changed when the Club installed the first floodlights at Highbury.

Arsenal were the second English club (after Southampton) to experiment with artificial illumination and the lights were first put to the test in September in a friendly against Israeli side Hapoel Tel Aviv.

A healthy crowd of 44,385 turned out to watch the match – and a Cliff Holton hat-trick which secured a 6–1 victory for Tom Whittaker's side.

ABOVE: The introduction of floodlights in the 1950s added a new dimension to Highbury.

HOLY ORDERS

Arsenal owner Sir Henry Norris was desperate to increase the Club's potential supporter base. After considering relocating to Battersea and Harringay, he took the brave decision to invest in a plot of land in Highbury and the Gunners left south London for the north of the capital.

Norris negotiated a 21-year lease at a price of £20,000 and, despite initial opposition from local residents and other football clubs in the area,

BELOW: In April 2007 a building site was all that remained of Arsenal Stadium, Highbury to generations of Gunners.

the builders were commissioned and work began on the new stadium.

There were, however, restrictions. Norris leased the land from St John's College of Divinity and an initial condition of the deal was that Arsenal would not schedule matches for either Christmas Day or Good Friday. It was also agreed that no alcoholic drinks would be sold at the ground. The Club eventually bought the site outright in 1925 for £64,000 and the restrictions were lifted.

▼ HOME IMPROVEMENT

The 1930s saw the first significant addition to Leith's original design and in 1932 a West Stand, designed by Claude Waterlow Ferrier and William Binnie, was opened by the Prince of Wales (later King Edward VIII) after a £45,000 investment by the Club.

Four years later Arsenal decided to demolish Leith's old East Stand and replace it with a state-of-the-art edifice that could seat 4,000 spectators and boasted terracing for 17,000 more at a cost of £130,000. At the same time the North Bank terrace was given a roof and Highbury began to resemble a thoroughly modern stadium.

ARSENAL'S RECORD AT HIGHBURY

	P	W	D	L	F	A
League	1,689	981	412	296	3,372	1,692
FA Cup	142	92	32	18	305	123
League Cup	98	69	14	15	195	74
Europe	76	50	17	9	153	60
Charity Shield	5	4	0	1	13	6
TOTAL	2,010	1,196	475	339	4,038	1,955

▶ RECORD ATTENDANCES

Arsenal said goodbye to Highbury to increase match day capacity and the supporters have responded in their millions since the move across north London.

In the Club's first Premier League season at the ground, a grand total of 1,140,863 fans came through the turnstiles – an average of a 60,045-strong crowd for each of the Gunners' 19 league fixtures.

The biggest gate of the season came in March for the visit of Reading when 60,132 supporters filled the stadium to watch their side win 2–1, courtesy of a Gilberto Silva penalty and a Julio Baptista goal.

The second-highest attendance was the 60,128 spectators who witnessed Arsenal beat Manchester United 2–1 in January, while 60,115 fans were on hand for the 3–0 triumph over Tottenham in the north London derby in December.

TIMELY REMINDER

The famed Highbury Clock was taken down from the old stadium in July 2006. It took a 25-ton crane, four men and nine hours of painstaking manoeuvring to position the massive timepiece at Emirates.

It now sits high up on the outside of the new stadium and symbolically faces towards the Clock End Bridge.

ABOVE: More than one million fans flocked through the 104 turnstiles of Emirates during the 2006–07 season.

▼ BUILDING THE FUTURE

To describe the process of constructing the Club's state-of-the-art new stadium in Islington as a big job would be an architectural understatement. Once the planning permission and the all-important finances were in place, work finally began on the Herculean task in February 2004.

In total, it took 123 weeks and two days, 1,400 construction workers and six million man-hours, 55,000 cubic metres of concrete, 10,000 tons of reinforced steel (3,000 tons in the main roof alone) and 15,000 square metres of glazing to bring Emirates to life in time for the 2006–07 Premier League campaign.

The final cost of the ambitious project was £390 million and 2,500 legal documents had to be signed, sealed and delivered during the construction process of the 60,431-capacity stadium.

The highest point of the ground is 41.4 metres above ground level and the entire site at Ashburton Grove covers 17 acres.

BELOW: The construction of Emirates was a massive operation costing £390 million.

ABOVE: Arsenal's 4–1 win over Sunderland in early 2014 was their 150th victory at the Emirates.

EMIRATES LANDMARK

Ever since relocating to the Emirates, Arsenal have found the stadium very much to their liking and, in February 2014, the team recorded a 150th victory there in all competitions.

The match was a Premier League clash with Sunderland and Arsene Wenger's side ensured they emphatically notched up the milestone 150th win with goals from Olivier Giroud (2), Tomas Rosicky and Laurent Koscielny.

LIQUID REFRESHMENT

There's little danger of going thirsty while watching a match at Emirates. The stadium has 250 food and drink outlets and match day staff can serve up to 2,400 pints of beer per minute across the ground.

SITTING PRETTY

Emirates is invariably full on match days. When the ground is full, 26,646 of the crowd are seated in the upper tier of the stadium. Another 24,425 supporters can watch the game from the lower tier while there are 7,139 more seats available at Club Level.

A lucky 2,222 spectators can feast their eyes on the action from executive boxes, while there is room for 128 guests in the Directors' Box. Arsenal also ensured there were 500 dedicated spaces for disabled supporters in the plans.

CAPTURED IN TIME

Almost two years before the official opening of the new stadium, the Club officially buried a time capsule in the foundations of Emirates to commemorate the Gunners' 93-year stay at Highbury.

Manager Arsene Wenger as well as Patrick Vieira and Thierry Henry were in attendance for the official ceremony in October 2004 as the capsule containing 40 items, 25 of which were chosen by Gunners fans, was lowered into place.

Among the keepsakes was a captain's armband worn by Tony Adams, a shirt worn by the late David Rocastle, marble from the old flooring at Highbury and a lock of Charlie George's hair.

Next to the capsule is the motto: "The deeper the foundations, the stronger the fortress."

▼ FIXTURES AND FITTINGS

Once the shell of the stadium was completed, Arsenal set about installing the trappings of a modern football ground and the Club certainly didn't cut any corners when it came to the finishing touches.

Within Emirates there are 12,000 light fittings, 2,000 doors, 100 flights of stairs, 13 lifts and five escalators. Match days are monitored by 130 separate CCTV cameras and there are also 41 different camera positions to ensure broadcasters don't miss any of the action.

Nine hundred toilets and 370 metres of urinals mean supporters should never be caught short, while the ground's 104 turnstiles guarantee fans won't be late for kick-off.

BELOW: Inside the new state-of-the-art Arsenal dressing room at Emirates.

ARSENAL'S RECORD AT EMIRATES 2006–2015

	P	W	D	L	F	A
League	171	111	41	19	355	138
FA Cup	20	16	3	1	45	10
League Cup	15	11	1	3	36	11
Europe	47	33	8	6	104	34
TOTAL	253	171	53	29	540	193

Other Records – The Derby

The Gunners first faced Spurs in a competitive fixture in December 1900, but it was Arsenal's move to Highbury and north London 13 years later that ignited the rivalry between the two clubs. This section looks at the records produced by one of football's fiercest derby clashes.

ABOVE: Alan Sunderland put Spurs to the sword in the derby in December 1978.

GOALS GALORE

The highest aggregate scoreline in any derby game was Arsenal's dramatic 5–4 victory over Spurs at White Hart Lane in November 2004, a pulsating Premier League clash in which Arsene Wenger's side initially went behind before an unstoppable second-half salvo.

The home side took the lead after 37 minutes with a left-footed volley from Moroccan centre-half Noureddine Naybet, but moments before the break Arsenal equalized against the run of play with a breakaway Thierry Henry goal.

The second 45 minutes produced seven more goals. The Gunners stormed into a 3–1 advantage with a Lauren penalty and Patrick Vieira strike and, although Tottenham pegged them back with a Jermain Defoe goal, Arsenal restored their two-goal advantage when Freddie Ljungberg dissected the home defence on 69 minutes.

Spurs rallied again with a Ledley King header, but Robert Pires made it 5–3 with some nimble footwork. Although Freddie Kanoute reduced the arrears with the ninth goal of the contest two minutes from time, the Gunners held firm for a famous and record-breaking win.

DERBY FIRST

The first-ever competitive match between Arsenal and Tottenham saw the two sides meet in Division One at the Manor Ground in Plumstead in December 1909.

The Gunners won the game 1–0 courtesy of a goal from Walter Lawrence, making the English inside-forward the first Gunner to score against the Club's north London rivals.

▶ O'LEARY'S LEGACY

Legendary centre-half David O'Leary has played in more games against Tottenham than any other Arsenal player, with 35 of his record 722 appearances for the Club coming against the old rivals.

The Irish defender's first taste of the action was in the goalless draw at White Hart Lane in September 1975, while his final involvement in the derby came in the 3–1 loss to the Lilywhites at Highbury in May 1993.

▲ TRIPLE TRIUMPHS

Only two Arsenal players in the history of the derby have registered hat-tricks. Ted Drake was the first, in 1934, and it was to be 44 years before Alan Sunderland emulated his feat with a superb treble in the Gunners' 5–0 triumph at White Hart Lane 48 hours before Christmas Day in 1978.

BELOW: David O'Leary faced Tottenham a record 35 times during his 18-year Arsenal career.

 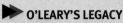

SUPER SUB

The fastest-ever goal scored by an Arsenal substitute against Spurs was recorded in December 2007 when Nicklas Bendtner made an immediate impact for the Gunners from the bench at Emirates.

The derby clash was 74 minutes old and deadlocked at 1–1 when the Danish striker was brought on to replace Emmanuel Eboue – and just 1.8 seconds after his introduction, Bendtner headed Cesc Fabregas' corner past Paul Robinson.

It was the forward's first Premier League goal for Arsenal and enough to secure all three points for Arsene Wenger's side.

BELOW: Cesc Fabregas supplied the corner for the Gunners' quickest ever goal against Tottenham.

EIGHT-GOAL MILESTONE

Three players jointly hold the record for career goals against Spurs, with Alan Sunderland, Robert Pires and Emmanuel Adebayor each finding the net eight times against the Lilywhites.

Togo striker Adebayor also holds the record as the highest individual scorer in the derby, with 10 goals. His first eight came in the red and white of Arsenal but he was on target for Tottenham for his ninth in the Gunners' 5–2 victory at Emirates in February 2012. Nine months later he made it 10 in another 5–2 loss for Spurs at Emirates.

ABOVE: Emmanuel Adebayor has scored for both clubs in the North London derby.

LEAGUE DOUBLE

Arsenal met Tottenham in competitive action for the first time in 1909 but it was not until the 1934–35 season that the Gunners recorded the club's first league double over their north London neighbours.

The first instalment of the historic feat came in October 1934 at Highbury when a goal from Albert Beasley, a Ted Drake hat-trick and an own goal gave George Allison's side a 5–1 success. The result still stands as the Club's biggest home win over Spurs.

Five months later the two teams met at White Hart Lane and Arsenal completed the double with a crushing 6–0 win, the goals coming from Alf Kirchen (2), Ted Drake (2), Peter Dougall and Cliff Bastin from the spot.

The victory also remains the Gunners' most comprehensive in the derby at White Hart Lane.

ARSENAL V TOTTENHAM RECORDS

Biggest Arsenal Home Win
Arsenal 5 Spurs 1 (20 October 1934, First Division)

Biggest Arsenal Away Win
Spurs 0 Arsenal 6 (6 March 1935, First Division

Biggest Arsenal Home Defeat
Arsenal 0 Spurs 3 (14 December 1932, First Division)
Arsenal 0 Spurs 3 (27 February 1954, First Division)

Biggest Arsenal Away Defeat
Spurs 5 Arsenal 0 (25 December 1911, First Division)
Spurs 5 Arsenal 0 (4 April 1983, First Division)

Biggest Arsenal Premier League Win
Arsenal 5 Spurs 2 (26 February 2012)
Arsenal 5 Spurs 2 (17 November 2012)

Biggest Arsenal Premier League Defeat
Arsenal 1 Spurs 3 (11 May 1993)

RECORD UNBEATEN STREAK

The first decade of the 21st century saw Arsenal enjoy a period of unprecedented dominance over their north London rivals. Between 2000 and 2008, Arsene Wenger's side were able to string together a Club-record 21 successive games without defeat to Tottenham.

The incredible run began in March 2000 when an own-goal from Chris Armstrong and a Thierry Henry penalty gave the Gunners a 3–1 victory at Highbury and continued for nearly eight years, climaxing in a 1–1 draw with Spurs at Emirates in January 2008.

The sequence finally came to an end 13 days later when the two sides met in the League Cup semi-final at White Hart Lane – a game the home side won 5–1.

In total Arsenal won 12 of the 21 fixtures during their unbeaten derby streak, scoring 42 goals and conceding just 23.

CROSSING THE DIVIDE

Transfers between Arsenal and Tottenham have remained a real rarity since the formation of the two clubs. The first man to play for both he Gunners and Spurs was a full-back by the name of Lycurgus Burrows.

Signed by Arsenal as an amateur in January 1892, a year before the Club was elected to the old Second Division, Burrows found his first team opportunities limited in the Gunners' new professional era and in October 1894 he signed for the Lilywhites.

The unusual part of the story was that, although Burrows was now a Tottenham player, his amateur status meant he was still registered with Arsenal. He made 10 league appearances for the Gunners during his unique "dual club" status.

▶▶ PULLING AWAY

The Gunners' Division One clash with Spurs at White Hart Lane on Boxing Day in 1983 was a hugely significant contest in the history of the north London derby. Two goals apiece from Charlie Nicholas and Raphael Meade saw Arsenal emerge 4–2 winners and in the process take the lead in the head-to-battle between the two clubs with 40 victories to Tottenham's 39. It is an advantage which the Gunners have not relinquished since.

▶▶ BROWN'S DERBY DOUBLE

A handful of players have featured for both Arsenal and Tottenham in the history of the north London derby, and the first to do so was striker Laurie Brown.

The Gunners signed Brown from Northampton Town in 1961 and in three seasons at Highbury he played in four clashes with the Lilywhites. He headed to White Hart Lane in February 1964 for a fee of £40,000, and in two years at Spurs he turned out against Arsenal three times.

Other players to represent both clubs in the capital's biggest game are David Jenkins, Jimmy Robertson, Pat Jennings, Willie Young, Sol Campbell and Emmanuel Adebayor.

BELOW: Charlie Nicholas (left) scored for Arsenal in the 1983 Boxing Day derby win.

ABOVE: Laurie Brown was the first player to play for both sides in the North London Derby.

DRAMATIC DRAW

The first-ever stalemate between the two north London rivals saw Arsenal register a 1–1 result at White Hart Lane in April 1910. And the highest-scoring draw between the two sides was in the Premier League in October 2008, when they shared the points after an eight-goal thriller.

CUP CONTEST

The first FA Cup derby saw the Gunners face Spurs at Highbury in the third round of the competition in January 1949. Arsenal were the reigning First Division champions while Tottenham were a second-tier side, and the gulf in class told as Tom Whittaker's side emerged 3–0 winners.

Scottish right-wing Ian McPherson made history with the Club's first-ever FA Cup goal against Spurs, the second and third coming Don Roper and Doug Lishman respectively.

The Gunners have played Tottenham five times in FA Cup history and following the latest meeting – the 2–1 victory at Highbury in April 2001 – currently lead the series 3–2.

BELOW: Robert Pires celebrates after scoring at White Hart Lane in 2004 to secure the Premier League title.

Spurs took an early lead at Emirates through former Gunner David Bentley, but goals from Mikael Silvestre, William Gallas and Emmanuel Adebayor saw Arsenal storm into a commanding 3–1 lead.

Darren Bent pulled one back for the visitors but Robin van Persie restored the two-goal advantage just a minute later. The Gunners seemed certain to collect all three points until strikes from Jermaine Jenas and Aaron Lennon earned Tottenham an unlikely, last-gasp 4–4 draw.

BELOW: Frank McLintock is carried off the pitch by delirious Arsenal fans after the Gunners had wrapped up the 1970–71 League Championship with a 1–0 win over Spurs at White Hart Lane; five days later, Arsenal completed the double.

▶ CHAMPIONS AT THE LANE

The Gunners have twice been confirmed as English champions after league games at White Hart Lane.

The first instance was in May 1971 when Bertie Mee's side needed a win or a goalless draw at Spurs in the final match of the season to deny Leeds United the title. The contest was scoreless until the 87th minute when Ray Kennedy headed home a late winner to clinch the silverware at the home of the old rivals.

The second time was in April 2004 when Arsene Wenger's Invincibles needed only a point at White Hart Lane to become champions. Thanks to goals from Patrick Vieira and Robert Pires they came away with a 2–2 draw and the title.

ARSENAL V TOTTENHAM HEAD-TO-HEAD RECORD

	Arsenal Wins	Draws	Spurs Wins
League	66	44	50
League Cup	7	3	3
FA Cup	4	0	2
Other	0	1	0
TOTAL	77	48	55

Other Records – Miscellaneous

The next six pages focus on some of Arsenal's other notable records and milestones, including the Club's first experience of the dreaded penalty shootout, their unique visit to Buckingham Palace and the day Arsene Wenger made Premier League history.

▶ CURSE OF INDISCIPLINE

Arsenal games against Leeds United are invariably fiery encounters and the November 2000 meeting at Elland Road was no exception.

A total of seven Arsenal players – Oleg Luzhny, Tony Adams, Martin Keown, Sylvinho, Ray Parlour, Lauren and Thierry Henry – were booked by referee Dermot Gallagher in a 1–0 defeat, a tally which remains the Gunners' most indisciplined display ever in the Premier League.

NATIONAL VARIETY

Three months after setting a Champions League record with 11 players from 11 nations, Arsenal repeated the trick in the Premier League when they faced Newcastle United at St James' Park.

Arsene Wenger's starting XI for the game on 10 December 2005 featured players from Germany, Ivory Coast, Cameroon, England, Switzerland, Sweden, Spain, Brazil, Belarus, Holland and France.

The Club's worst Premier League season in terms of yellow cards was the 1996–97 campaign when the team received a total of 81 bookings in 38 games. The average cards per team that season was a mere 60.

The Gunners also picked up five red cards during the campaign, with Tony Adams the first to take an early bath after picking up two yellows in just 22 minutes in the game against Newcastle United at St James' Park in November.

LEFT: Edu, from Brazil, was part of the 'foreign' 16-man squad named to play Crystal Palace in 2005.

ABOVE: Oleg Luzhny tackles Alan Smith and was one of seven Gunners to see yellow in the clash with Leeds United in 2000.

◀ GLOBAL GAME

Arsene Wenger is renowned for assembling cosmopolitan squads and in February 2005 the Frenchman broke new ground when he became the first manager in the history of the English game to name a 16-man match squad that featured no British players.

The Gunners boss was without English regulars Sol Campbell and Ashley Cole through injury and illness respectively for the Premier League clash with Crystal Palace, and fielded a team with an unmistakably global, albeit predominantly French, feel.

The Arsenal starting line-up at Selhurst Park was: Jens Lehmann (Germany), Lauren (Cameroon), Gael Clichy (France), Kolo Toure (Ivory Coast), Pascal Cygan (France), Robert Pires (France), Patrick Vieira (France), Edu (Brazil), Jose Antonio Reyes (Spain), Dennis Bergkamp (Holland), Thierry Henry (France).

The bench was warmed by Manuel Almunia (Spain), Philippe Senderos (Switzerland), Cesc Fabregas (Spain), Robin van Persie (Holland) and Mathieu Flamini (France).

Wenger's historic decision paid handsome dividends as his side romped to a 5–1 win over the Eagles.

LEAGUE OF NATIONS

The Gunners made Champions League history in September 2005 when they faced Hamburg in the group stages, becoming the first Club to field a side with players from 11 different countries.

Arsene Wenger initially named a side with two Ivorians (Emmanuel Eboue and Kolo Toure) and nine other nationalities for the match in the Volksparkstadion. But when Toure was forced off after 28 minutes with injury, he was replaced by Englishman Justin Hoyte and Arsenal became a side with 11 players hailing from 11 different countries.

That team was: Jens Lehmann (Germany), Emmanuel Eboue (Ivory Coast), Justin Hoyte (England), Johan Djourou (Switzerland), William Gallas (France), Alexander Hleb (Belarus), Cesc Fabregas (Spain), Gilberto Silva (Brazil), Tomas Rosicky (Czech Republic), Robin van Persie (Holland), Emmanuel Adebayor (Togo).

The introduction of Brazilian Julio Baptista for van Persie on 69 minutes disrupted the dynamic but history had still been made.

► EUROPEAN TRIUMPHS

The Gunners have enjoyed some famous nights in Europe over the years, but what must be two of their greatest results both came in the Champions League – against Real Madrid in 2006 and AC Milan two years later.

Arsene Wenger's side faced Real in the Bernabeu in the last 16 of the competition, and a superb solo goal from Thierry Henry earned Arsenal a brilliant 1–0 victory, the first time any English side had ever beaten the Spain heavyweights in Madrid.

In March 2008, they tackled Milan in the San Siro in the second leg of their last-16 fixture following a goalless draw in the first match at Emirates.

The Italians were the defending champions but late goals from Cesc Fabregas and Emmanuel Adebayor sent them crashing out – and in the process Arsenal became the first English club to beat the Serie A giants in the San Siro.

ABOVE: Paul Merson in action at Anfield in 1989 as Arsenal claimed a dramatic title triumph.

▲ TITLE DECIDER

Arsenal were the first club in the history of the old First Division to claim the title courtesy of the number of goals scored, edging out Liverpool in 1988–89 by the smallest of margins.

The Gunners claimed the trophy courtesy of their dramatic 2–0 victory at Anfield in the final match of the season, leaving the two clubs level on 76 points and both boasting a goal difference of plus 37.

George Graham's side, however, had scored 73 league goals compared to Liverpool's 65, which was enough to see Arsenal crowned champions.

THE ENGLISH ERA

Modern football is an increasingly global affair and the last time Arsenal fielded an entirely English XI was in April 1994 for the Premier League clash with Wimbledon at Highbury.

The Gunners team named by George Graham was: David Seaman, Lee Dixon, Martin Keown, Paul Davis, Steve Bould, Tony Adams, Kevin Campbell, Ian Wright, Alan Smith, Ray Parlour and Ian Selley.

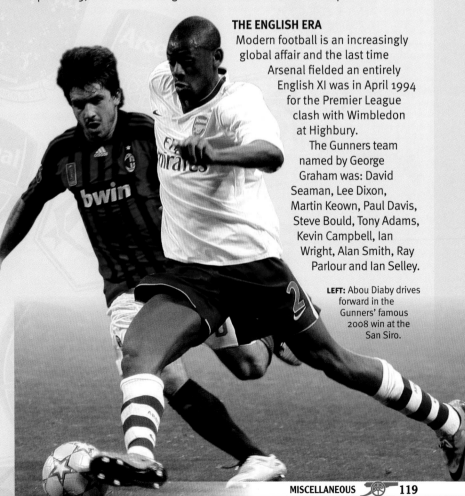

LEFT: Abou Diaby drives forward in the Gunners' famous 2008 win at the San Siro.

WONDERFUL WEMBLEY

Arsenal's 4–0 victory over Aston Villa in the FA Cup final in May 2015 was the 15th time the Gunners had played at Wembley since Arsene Wenger became the club's manager in October 1996.

The Club's first appearance at the home of football under Wenger came in May 1998, when the Gunners beat Newcastle United 2–0 in the FA Cup final thanks to goals from Marc Overmars and Nicolas Anelka.

They have won 13 of those 15 matches, their only defeats coming against Chelsea in the 2009 FA Cup semi-final (2–1) and against Birmingham in the 2011 League Cup final (2–1).

ABOVE: Theo Walcott scored the first of Arsenal's four goals in the 2015 FA Cup final.

TELEVISION PIONEERS

The Gunners have proven to be trailblazers in football on the box over the decades and the Club is in the history books as the very first to have been involved in a televised match.

In fact, Arsenal supplied both sides – the first team and the reserves – for a friendly at Highbury in September 1937 which was organized at the request of the BBC, eager to test new technology and their ability to broadcast sporting events.

No record of the result remains but clips of the start of the programme have survived, showing manager Herbert Chapman and his assistant Tom Whittaker introducing the first team before kick-off.

Twenty-seven years later Arsenal again broke new ground when their Division One clash with Liverpool became the first-ever game to be shown on the BBC's highlights programme *Match of the Day*. Unfortunately for Gunners fans, the show didn't make for happy viewing as Billy Wright's team were beaten 3–2 at Anfield.

On 31 January 2010, the Club made it a hat-trick of television firsts when its Premier League meeting with Manchester United became the first match in the world to be broadcast live in 3D.

Supporters at nine pubs in London, Manchester, Cardiff, Edinburgh and Dublin were the first to experience football in the new format as former Gunners striker Alan Smith provided the commentary.

BELOW: The Gunners' 3–1 home defeat against Manchester United in January 2010 was broadcast in 3D.

EMIRATES CELEBRATES MILESTONE

Chelsea's visit to the Emirates in April 2015 was a special occasion for the Gunners: it marked the 250th competitive match the club had played at their new stadium.

The Premier League clash with the Blues ended goalless, meaning that Arsenal had won 170, drawn 52 and lost only 28 of the games in all competitions at Ashburton Grove since the move from Highbury nine years earlier, scoring 536 goals at the ground and conceding just 191.

The Gunners amassed 370 Premier League points in their 168 games at the ground during the same period, while Arsenal's most familiar opponents at the Emirates in the first 250 fixtures were Tottenham Hotspur and Liverpool, with 12 visits apiece.

The record for the most games for the club at the stadium belonged to Theo Walcott with 157 appearances, while Robin van Persie stood as the most prolific Emirates marksman with 64 goals.

ABOVE: Arsenal's players acknowledge the fans before kick-off against Chelsea in April 2015. The match was the 250th competitive game played at the Emirates Stadium.

ROYAL VISIT

The Queen was scheduled to officially open Emirates in October 2006 but a back injury prevented her from giving the Club's new stadium her royal seal of approval. The Duke of Edinburgh did the honours instead – but four months later Her Majesty invited Arsene Wenger and his players to Buckingham Palace in lieu of her cancelled appearance, making Arsenal the first football club to visit the palace.

RADIO WAVES

Arsenal hold the distinction as the first club to stage a game broadcast live on radio, playing host to the BBC World Service in January 1927 for the Division One meeting with Sheffield United at Highbury.

The BBC had already trialled outside broadcasts for a rugby match at Twickenham, but the match against the Blades saw the use of two commentators for the first time, one providing a running commentary on the game while the other called out grid references to help listeners locate the action areas.

Gunners skipper Charlie Buchan opened the scoring at Highbury but Herbert Chapman's side were denied victory live on the airwaves when United equalized.

BELOW: Arsene Wenger and Peter Hill-Wood meet The Queen at Buckingham Palace.

ABOVE: The Gunners tackled Valencia in Brussels in the final of the 1980 Cup Winners' Cup.

ON THE SPOT

The dreaded penalty shootout is a dramatic but frequently cruel way to settle a match. The Gunners' first experience of the lottery of spot-kicks was in May 1980 when they faced Valencia in the final of the Cup Winners' Cup.

The two teams could not muster a goal between them in 90 minutes or extra-time in the Heysel Stadium in Brussels, and so the final had to be decided from the spot. Mario Kempes and Liam Brady both had their opening efforts saved but the next eight were all converted, leaving the score level at 4–4. Ricardo Arias held his nerve to stroke home Valencia's sixth penalty and it was the unlucky Graham Rix who had his subsequent shot saved – to hand the trophy to the Spanish.

Twelve years later, however, the Gunners won their first penalty shootout, beating Millwall 3–1 from the spot in a League Cup second-round, second-leg clash. The game in October 1992 finished 1–1 but George Graham's side prevailed 3–1 in the shootout.

SUBSTITUTED SUBSTITUTE

Australian international John Kosmina made just four appearances for the Gunners in the 1970s. In three of those four games he came from the bench – and the Kangaroos striker holds the dubious distinction of being the first Arsenal substitute to be substituted in a competitive match.

The game was the Gunners' UEFA Cup second-round clash with Hadjuk Split at Highbury in November 1978. Kosmina was introduced to the action by manager Terry Neill in place of winger Mark Heeley. The Australian didn't last long, however, after picking up a knock and Neill duly replaced him with centre-forward Paul Vaessen.

LEAGUE TREBLE

The Gunners are one of only four clubs to have claimed the top-flight title for three successive years. Huddersfield Town were the first to achieve the championship hat-trick between 1924 and 1926 while Arsenal joined the elite club in 1935 with their third Division One title on the bounce. Liverpool were equally dominant in 1983, 1984 and 1985 while Manchester United emulated the feat in 2001 with their third successive Premier League triumph.

CARDIFF DRAMA

Arsenal were involved in the first-ever FA Cup final to be decided on penalties, overcoming Manchester United from the spot in the Millennium Stadium in May 2005.

Despite the two sides boasting the attacking talents of Dennis Bergkamp and Wayne Rooney, Robert Pires and Ruud van Nistelrooy, neither side scored in normal or extra-time and the game headed to a shootout.

Cameroon defender Lauren, Freddie Ljungberg, substitute Robin van Persie and Ashley Cole were all on target, while Jens Lehmann saved Paul Scholes' second Manchester United effort.

It meant captain Patrick Vieira had to convert the Gunners' fifth penalty for glory, and he calmly beat Roy Carroll to seal the silverware.

LEFT: Patrick Vieria steps up to hit the winning penalty in the 2005 FA Cup final in the Millennnium Stadium.

THE NEWCOMERS

Since the advent of the Premier League, the 1993–94 season is the one in which Arsenal have handed league debuts to the smallest number of players, with winger Eddie McGoldrick the only newcomer to the first team during the course of the campaign.

In contrast, the 1999–2000 season saw Arsene Wenger introduce 11 new players to the side, the Club's highest number of debutants in Premier League history.

Arsenal's three Premier League title-winning campaigns resulted in a total of 20 players breaking into the first team. There were 10 debutants in 1997–98, six in 2001–02 and a mere four as Wenger's Invincibles completed an unbeaten league season in 2003–04.

HAT-TRICK HERO

Only one Arsenal player has ever scored hat-tricks in three successive home games – English centre-forward Doug Lishman.

Lishman's prolific streak came in the 1951–52 season and began with a treble in a 4–3 win over Fulham at Highbury in October. Two weeks later he hit another hat-trick in the 6–3 demolition of West Bromwich Albion, and he completed his amazing sequence at the end of November in a 4–2 victory against Bolton. In total, the striker hit 23 First Division goals for the Gunners in 38 appearances over the campaign.

RIGHT: Doug Lishman was in devastating form for the Club during the 1951–52 season.

BELOW: Eddie McGoldrick broke into the Arsenal side during the 1993–94 Premier League campaign.

ARSENAL'S RECORD IN PENALTY SHOOTOUTS

European Cup Winners' Cup Final (May 1980)
Valencia 0 Arsenal 0 – Lost 5–4 on penalties

League Cup, Second Round Second Leg (October 1992)
Millwall 1 Arsenal 1 – Won 3–1 on penalties

Charity Shield (August 1993)
Arsenal 1 Manchester United 1 – Lost 5–4 on penalties

European Cup Winners' Cup Semi-Final Second Leg (April 1995)
Sampdoria 3 Arsenal 2 (5–5 on aggregate) – Won 3–2 on penalties

FA Cup Third Round Replay (January 1998)
Port Vale 1 Arsenal 1 – Won 4–3 on penalties

FA Cup Quarter-Final Replay (March 1998)
West Ham 1 Arsenal 1 – Won 4–3 on penalties

League Cup Fourth Round (November 1999)
Middlesbrough 2 Arsenal 2 – Lost 3–1 on penalties

FA Cup Fourth Round Replay (January 2000)
Leicester 0 Arsenal 0 – Lost 6–5 on penalties

UEFA Cup Final (May 2000)
Galatasaray 0 Arsenal 0 – Lost 4–1 on penalties

Community Shield (August 2003)
Arsenal 1 Manchester United 1 – Lost 4–3 on penalties

League Cup Third Round (October 2003)
Arsenal 1 Rotherham United 1 – Won 9–8 on penalties

FA Cup Fifth Round Replay (March 2005)
Sheffield United 0 Arsenal 0 – Won 4–2 on penalties

FA Cup Final (May 2005)
Arsenal 0 Manchester United 0 – Won 5–4 on penalties

League Cup Quarter-Final (December 2005)
Doncaster Rovers 2 Arsenal 2 – Won 3–1 on penalties

League Cup Quarter-Finals (December 2012)
Bradford City 1 Arsenal 1 – Lost 3–2 on penalties

League Cup Third Round (September 2013)
West Bromwich Albion 1 Arsenal 1 – Won 4–3 on penalties

FA Cup Semi-Final (April 2014)
Arsenal 1 Wigan Athletic 1 – Won 4–2 on penalties

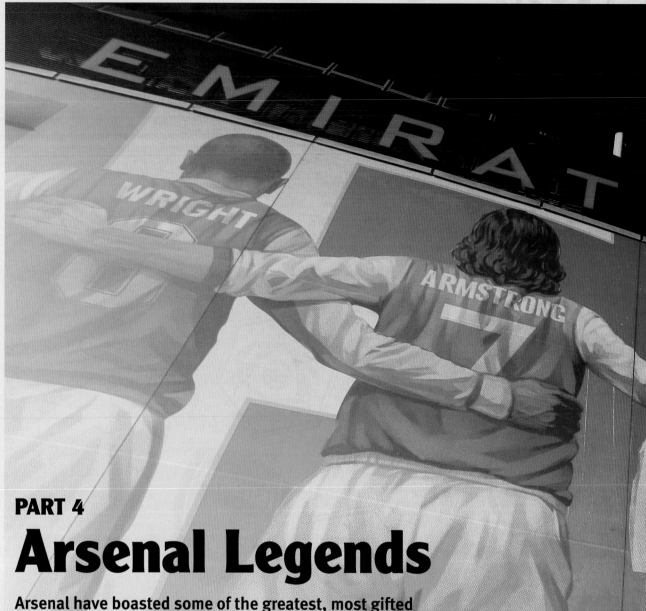

PART 4
Arsenal Legends

Arsenal have boasted some of the greatest, most gifted and most decorated players in the history of the game and this chapter celebrates 12 of the stars who have enthralled Highbury and entertained Emirates over the years.

The dozen legends played in different eras but share a common bond as players whose dazzling displays, years of loyal service and affinity with the Club made them firm favourites with the Gunners faithful.

The 1930s saw Cliff Bastin and Ted Drake both emerge as two of the Club's first true superstars, as the Gunners dominated English football for a decade, while Frank McLintock and Liam Brady are the men from the 1970s and 1980s respectively to feature on the list.

Four players synonymous with the George Graham era – Tony Adams, Ian Wright, David O'Leary and David Seaman – are also included while a trio of French players recruited by Arsene Wenger – Thierry Henry, Patrick Vieira and Robert Pires – and the dazzling Dutchman, Dennis Bergkamp, complete the famous dozen.

ABOVE: Emirates is adorned with striking images of some of the Club's greatest and most iconic players.

Tony Adams

The greatest captain in the Club's long and illustrious history, the lionhearted Adams bestrode Highbury like a colossus for 19 glorious years.

RIGHT: The Gunners skipper strikes a pose which became reassuringly familiar during his time with the Club.

BELOW: Tony Adams won 10 major trophies during his magnificent Arsenal career.

Although it was within the intimate surroundings of Highbury rather than the more expansive setting of the Club's new home in Ashburton Grove that Tony Adams forged his reputation as the Gunners' greatest-ever captain, it is outside Emirates that he is immortalized in bronze.

The striking statue of the former captain was unveiled in 2011 and when Arsenal deliberated on which three legendary servants to honour as part of the Club's 125th anniversary celebrations, Adams' inclusion was a foregone conclusion. He was joined by statues of Herbert Chapman and Thierry Henry but even their magnificent contributions to the Club's illustrious history cannot rival the impact Adams made over 19 remarkable seasons in north London.

Few modern players graduate from the youth ranks to top-flight fame and fortune. Fewer still spend their entire careers with the same club. Adams did both and, despite his well-documented problems off the pitch, he did so with a unique blend of sheer stubbornness, fearless physicality and a sublime reading of the game.

His Arsenal odyssey began in 1980 when he signed schoolboy forms. Three years later he made his first team debut as a 17-year-old against Sunderland and in 1988 he became the Club's youngest-ever captain at the age of 21. He would not relinquish the armband for the remainder of his Highbury career, and under his leadership the Gunners blossomed and the trophy cabinet bulged.

Before George Graham appointed

him captain, Adams had already been part of the side which lifted the League Cup in 1987. Kenny Sansom had led the team out at Wembley that day but once the young centre-half assumed full-time command, the Gunners quickly graduated to even bigger and better things.

The first silverware of the Adams era was the 1988–89 Division One title, clinched in the most dramatic denouement to a season in living memory as his side beat Liverpool 2–0 at Anfield. Michael Thomas will live forever in Gunners folklore as the man who scored the decisive injury-time goal but it was the Arsenal rearguard, stoically led by Adams, that was equally instrumental in the Club's first title triumph in 18 years.

He was still just 22 years old on that famous night on Merseyside but the success was to prove far from transient and, as Adams' influence increased, the Gunners grew stronger.

The 1990–91 First Division title, the 1993 FA and League Cup double and the 1994 UEFA Cup Winners' Cup followed, but it was during the 1997–98 season that the skipper truly scaled the football summit as he led Arsenal to the elusive league and cup double.

Graham had given way to Arsene Wenger since the Club's last trophy.

Some believed the sophisticated Frenchman would struggle to find common ground with Arsenal's archetypal English central defender. But the captain found an added dimension to his game under the new manager and once the 1997–98 Premier League title was in the bag, edging out Manchester United by a solitary but priceless point, Adams guided the team to a 2–0 victory over Newcastle at Wembley.

Injury blighted him in the autumn of his Arsenal career but he underlined his enduring greatness in his swansong season, the 2001–02 campaign, leading his team to a superb second double. Adams' ageing legs could muster just 10 games in the league but he was a typically reassuring and abrasive presence for all 90 minutes of the FA Cup final victory over Chelsea in the Millennium Stadium in Cardiff.

The Gunners faithful did not know it then but it was to be his 669th and last appearance for the Club, leaving him 53 games shy of David O'Leary's record total. He announced his retirement three months after the final and, 19 years after his debut, he was no longer an Arsenal player.

The appearance milestone of O'Leary was one even Adams could

not quite eclipse but it mattered little compared to his other incredible accomplishments, not least his status as the Club's longest-serving and most successful leader, the first player to win top-flight titles in three different decades and the captain of two separate double-winning sides. Leading the side to its major piece of European silverware, not to mention the 66 caps for England, were merely the icing on the cake.

In 2004, he was inducted into the English Football Hall Of Fame but his statue outside Emirates remains a more fitting and more immediate tribute to the man known simply as "Mr Arsenal".

BELOW: The bronze statue of Adams which now proudly stands outside Emirates.

BOTTOM: Tony Adams was a cult figure with the Highbury faithful throughout his career.

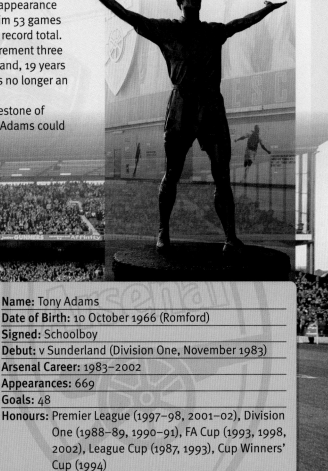

Name:	Tony Adams
Date of Birth:	10 October 1966 (Romford)
Signed:	Schoolboy
Debut:	v Sunderland (Division One, November 1983)
Arsenal Career:	1983–2002
Appearances:	669
Goals:	48
Honours:	Premier League (1997–98, 2001–02), Division One (1988–89, 1990–91), FA Cup (1993, 1998, 2002), League Cup (1987, 1993), Cup Winners' Cup (1994)

Cliff Bastin

A deadly goalscorer, Cliff Bastin spearheaded Arsenal's pre-War rise to First Division superpower status and the Club's successful quest for major silverware.

The unassuming, understated star of the first golden era in Arsenal's history, Cliff Bastin proudly held the record as the Club's greatest goalscorer for 58 years. His prolific exploits at Highbury in the 1930s are inextricably interwoven with the Gunners' emergence as an undisputed giant of the English game.

Bastin was football's original teenage sensation. By the age of 19, he had already won the Division One title and the FA Cup, and been capped for England. Although his glittering club career was prematurely curtailed by the Second World War, he still enjoyed a dazzling decade at Highbury in which he claimed five

Championship winner's medals and two FA Cups. His five titles remains a feat no subsequent Arsenal player has been able to surpass.

In fact, though, his Gunners career began purely by chance. Herbert Chapman spotted him playing for Exeter City against Watford in 1929 but the Arsenal manager was in reality at the game to scout a Hornets player called Tommy Barnett. A 17-year-old Bastin was not on his radar but Chapman's head was quickly turned. Despite Bastin having made just 17 appearances for the Grecians, Chapman decided he was worth the £2,000 it took to bring him to north London.

A stocky and powerful player, Bastin was a remarkably cool and clinical finisher for one so young and was equally comfortable shooting with either foot. These were attributes that served him well at Highbury and his debut season in 1929–30 culminated in a 2–0 victory over Huddersfield Town in the FA Cup final. At the time the fresh-faced Gunner affectionately known as "Boy Bastin" was the youngest player ever to feature in a final.

The following season Arsenal were crowned Division One champions for the first time. Chapman's side edged out Aston Villa for the title and Bastin played all 42 games, scoring 28 times.

Further Championship successes followed in 1932–33, 1933–34, 1934–35 and finally in 1937–38, and in each campaign he made at least 36 league appearances and in each season he reached double figures for goals scored.

His most prolific season was 1932–33 with 33 goals in 42 league games and, although the advent of Ted Drake in March 1934 saw the

LEFT: Cliff Bastin's dazzling skills made him an undisputed star of the English game during the 1930s.

new arrival supersede Bastin as the Gunners' focal attacking point, he remained a key ingredient in Arsenal's potent mix.

What was stunning about Bastin's record in front of goal was the fact that he was an inside-left rather than striker. It was an era when Bastin should have diligently hugged the touchline, dutifully supplying his front man with juicy morsels, but Chapman and subsequently George Allison urged him to cut in and he needed no further encouragement.

His record goals tally is also unusual because for much of his Highbury career he was surrounded by other prolific scorers. In the early days it was Jack Lambert and latterly Drake, and yet Bastin was still able to amass his own record-breaking haul of 178 in 396 appearances. Lambert and then Drake more regularly topped the scoring but neither man was

such an influential figure as Bastin throughout the Club's dominance of the decade.

His final full season in north London in 1938–39 was sadly disrupted by injury, restricting him to a modest 24 appearances in all competitions, and then the war came. He was still only 27 but his increasing deafness meant he was deemed unfit to fight and he spent the hostilities serving as an air raid warden.

He played a plethora of friendlies during the conflict but when the Football League returned for the 1946–47 season he was aged 34 and played just six times. His last appearance came in September against Manchester United at Old Trafford and at the end of the season he hung up his boots.

It was in 1997, nearly 60 years later, that Ian Wright finally went past his milestone. It was a bitter-sweet moment but did at least provide an opportunity for different generations of Arsenal supporters to collectively remember the amazing achievements of the Club's first superstar.

Whether Wright and subsequently Thierry Henry would have been able to topple Bastin as the Gunners' greatest goalscorer had it not been for the war years is a moot point but, while he was cruelly robbed of the autumn of his career, he achieved so much so young that it's difficult to imagine he was unduly aggrieved.

LEFT: Capped 21 times for England, Bastin cost the Gunners just £2,000 in 1929.

Name:	Cliff Bastin
Date of Birth:	14 March 1912 (Exeter)
Signed:	May 1929 (£2,000, Exeter City)
Debut:	v Everton (Division One, October 1929)
Arsenal Career:	1929–46
Appearances:	396
Goals:	178
Honours:	Division One (1930–31, 1932–33, 1933–34, 1934–35, 1937–38), FA Cup (1930, 1936)

Dennis Bergkamp

A goalscorer, a playmaker and a visionary – the striker was one of the most stylish players ever to represent the Club.

The history of Arsenal will forever remember the revolution that engulfed the Club in the wake of Arsene Wenger's arrival, as a flood of world-class players followed him to north London and the Gunners were reborn as the epitome of style and entertainment.

Dennis Bergkamp was perhaps the greatest of this new generation, a peerless combination of dazzling technique and natural vision. But for all his achievements as a manager, Wenger cannot claim the credit for bringing the Dutchman to Highbury and the 11 years of breathtaking artistry that followed.

That accolade goes to his predecessor, Bruce Rioch, who smashed the Club's transfer record to prise Bergkamp away from Inter Milan in June 1995. It cost £7.5 million to convince the Italians to part with him.

Whatever the failings of Rioch's brief reign as manager, the Dutchman was undoubtedly not one of them.

At times, it felt like Bergkamp was playing a different, altogether more cerebral game to everyone else on the pitch, such was his masterly ball control and unerring ability to think three or four passes ahead of other players. If Wenger was the Professor, Bergkamp was his star pupil.

All of the Dutchman's genius was encapsulated by the goal he scored at Newcastle United in early 2002, an effort so glorious that Arsenal supporters voted it the greatest goal in the Club's history. It is of course difficult to do it full justice but all those who witnessed his regal flick past Nikos Dabizas, his sublime spin behind the back of the bemused Magpies defender and his faultless side-footed finish past Shay Given will

LEFT AND BELOW: The Dutchman never failed to entertain with his sublime blend of instinct and skill.

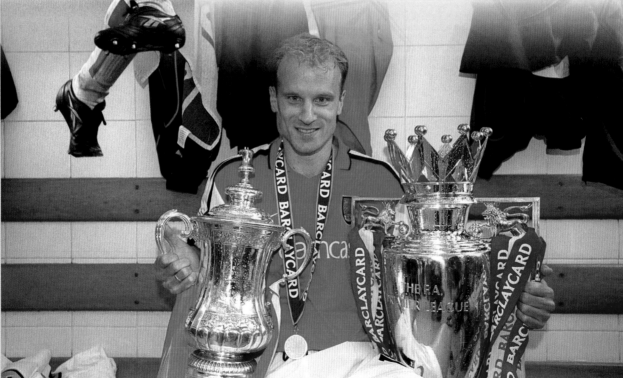

never forget his touch, his movement and his vision.

There were many more similarly spectacular strikes during his Gunners career and his name remains a byword for elegance and style.

Bergkamp was educated at the Ajax Academy in "Total Football" in the Netherlands. He was handed his first team debut by the great Johan Cruyff in 1986, and after his two-year sojourn in Serie A with Inter he became a Gunner.

The frenetic pace of the English game in contrast to the more sedate philosophy he had encountered in Holland or Italy may have been a shock to the system but Bergkamp's speed of thought eased his transition, and in his first season under Rioch he scored 16 times.

Under Wenger, however, he became the heartbeat of the side and, although the goals continued, it was his wider contribution, his plentiful assists and his superb link-up play that defined him and made him a hero at Highbury.

Bergkamp's first silverware at Arsenal was the 1997–98 Premier League trophy, contributing 16 goals in 28 appearances. A hamstring injury ruled him out of the FA Cup final victory over Newcastle United as the Gunners completed the double but his goal in the fifth-round replay win at Crystal Palace

was pivotal in keeping the team in the competition.

His show-stealing displays throughout the campaign earned him the PFA Players' Player of the Year Award. He became only the second foreign player to claim the prize after Eric Cantona in 1993–94, cementing Bergkamp's reputation as one of the Premier League's true stars.

The Dutchman stayed at Highbury for eight more years and, as the Arsenal side evolved and matured, he became more influential. Thierry Henry enjoyed the lion's share of the headlines in terms of goals but it was Bergkamp, sitting behind the Frenchman, pulling the strings and knitting together the Gunners' increasingly expansive play, who frequently dictated the pace and direction of the attack.

The Club's second double in 2001–02 saw the striker miss just five Premier League games and he was on target three times, including the winner in the fourth round against Liverpool, as Arsenal marched to the

FA Cup final to face and beat Chelsea at Wembley.

Now in his 30s, Bergkamp's finely-honed technique defied the passing of time and he played 24 times in the league during the Invincibles season, collecting his third Premier League winner's medal.

The 2005–06 campaign was to be his last and it was fitting, for a player who had enriched Highbury for more than a decade, that he made a cameo appearance in the last-ever match at the old stadium, coming on for Jose Antonio Reyes with 10 minutes left on the clock as the Gunners despatched Wigan 4–2 on a emotional afternoon in north London.

Three days later Bergkamp celebrated his 37th birthday and the time had finally come to call time on his glittering career. Arsenal began a new era at Emirates a few months later without him but the memories of his 11 years in the red and white will never fade.

LEFT: Dennis Bergkamp was one of the most technically gifted players to grace the Premier League.

BELOW: Winning silverware became a habit during Bergkamp's 11-year stay in England.

Name:	Dennis Bergkamp
Date of Birth:	10 May 1969 (Amsterdam, Holland)
Signed:	June 1995 (£7.5m, Inter Milan)
Debut:	v Middlesbrough (Premier League, August 1995)
Arsenal Career:	1995–2006
Appearances:	423
Goals:	120
Honours:	Premier League (1997–98, 2001–02, 2003–04), FA Cup (1998, 2002, 2003, 2005)

Liam Brady

An elegant Republic of Ireland midfielder, Brady lit up Highbury during the 1970s with an intoxicating mixture of artistry and ambition.

RIGHT: The Irishman's technique and raw talent were second to none.

The beautiful game has always reserved a special place in its affections for an educated left foot. The sheer rarity of truly top-class left-footed players has always elevated such individuals above football's also-rans – and in Liam Brady, Arsenal boasted arguably the most mercurial, mesmerizing and magnificent of them all.

That the Dubliner was a Gunner during one of the leaner eras in the Club's history was irrelevant. When Brady was on song, Highbury was spellbound and he wielded

his legendary left boot as if it were the baton conducting the Arsenal orchestra.

His seven years in north London were certainly too brief; the lure of Italy eventually proved irresistible and he signed for Juventus in 1980. But while others played more games, scored more goals and served more seasons with Arsenal, Brady left as indelible a mark as anyone to wear the famous red and white shirt.

Like many of his countrymen before him, Brady left Ireland as a teenager to pursue his dreams of a professional career. His older brothers Pat and Ray had already crossed the Irish Sea to play for English clubs and on his 17th birthday, in 1973, Brady accepted the

BELOW: Liam Brady, on one of his trademark midfield surges, the ball seemingly glued to his feet.

Gunners' offer of a first professional contract.

Just eight months later he was thrust into first-team action, coming on as a substitute in the Division One game against Birmingham City at Highbury. A week later he was in the starting XI for the north London derby against Spurs at White Hart Lane. Despite his age and inexperience, he was rapidly becoming an integral part of Bertie Mee's team.

Slightly built but deceptively strong, Brady always seemed to have more time on the ball than those crashing around him. His beautiful balance, faultless close control and vision were the source of countless assists – and although his left foot was without equal, his right was far from a weakness. Brady almost glided over the grass at Highbury, and through the 1970s he was the player the fans yearned to watch.

It was in the latter years of the decade that Arsenal awoke from its slumbers and the Dubliner was at the heart of the revival. The 1978 FA Cup final may have ended in disappointment and a 1–0 defeat to Ipswich at Wembley, but the following season was arguably Brady's finest as the Gunners ended their eight-year wait for a trophy.

His brace of goals in the First Division season opener against Leeds United signalled the Irishman's intent, and in December 1978 he was famously on target with a sumptuous effort from outside the box, with the outside of that left boot, in a 5–0 rout of Spurs at Highbury.

The 1979 FA Cup final, however, was perhaps his finest 90 minutes for the Gunners. Manchester United were the opponents at Wembley and an inspired performance from Brady saw Terry Neill's team race into a 2–0 half-time lead courtesy of his deft assists for goals from Brian Talbot and Frank Stapleton... only to be dramatically dragged back to 2–2 in the dying minutes.

Extra-time seemed inevitable but Brady had other ideas and it was his surging run that was the catalyst for Alan Sunderland's late winner. The identity of the Man of the Match was the worst-kept secret in football.

The 1979–80 season was to be his last in north London. He was voted the PFA Player of the Year for 1979 (the first man from outside the United Kingdom to win the accolade) and his reputation now went before him. After two typically elegant displays in the two legs of Arsenal's Cup Winners' Cup semi-final win over Juventus, the Turin giants decided the Irishman

ABOVE: Brady proudly holds aloft the 1979 FA Cup which he did so much to win at Wembley.

belonged in Italy. It took £500,000 to convince Arsenal to sell in the summer of 1980 but the deal was eventually done and Brady quietly took his leave of Highbury.

After his two seasons at the Stadio delle Alpi his footballing journey took him to Sampdoria, Inter Milan, Ascoli and West Ham before he hung up the boots in 1990. Six years later he returned "home" when he was appointed as the new head of Arsenal's Youth Academy.

His 17 years nurturing future generations of Arsenal stars were widely regarded as an unqualified success – but, whatever his achievements as a coach and mentor, it was his seven seasons caressing the ball across Highbury's turf that most supporters remember. Brady in his pomp was a joy to behold and few players in the English game before or since have even come close to paralleling his instinctive elegance.

LEFT: Brady didn't play in the 1972 FA Cup final, but he did represent the Club in the competition's centenary parade before the game.

Name:	Liam Brady
Date of Birth:	13 February 1956 (Dublin)
Signed:	Schoolboy
Debut:	v Birmingham (Division One, October 1973)
Arsenal Career:	1971–80
Appearances:	307
Goals:	59
Honours:	FA Cup (1979)

Ted Drake

Lethal in front of goal, Ted Drake was a prolific and powerful centre-forward who left an indelible mark on the early history of the Gunners.

The legendary Herbert Chapman was Arsenal's first great manager. His untimely death in January 1934 robbed the game of one of its finest tactical innovators, but he left an enduring legacy and will forever be remembered as the man who guided the Gunners to the Division One title for the first time in the Club's history.

His reign, however, did have its disappointments and perhaps none greater than his failure to sign Ted Drake. Chapman tried to lure the centre-forward to Highbury in 1933 but Drake rebuffed his advances to remain with home-town club Southampton. It fell to Chapman's successor George Allison to seal the deal, and he eventually signed the prolific Saints striker for £6,500 in March the following year.

It's not hard to understand why both Arsenal managers were so eager to recruit Drake. His 47 goals in 72 league appearances for Southampton may have come in the Second Division but the forward was clearly destined for top-flight football. A goal on his Gunners debut against Wolves conclusively confirmed his credentials.

His arrival at Highbury saw him leading the line alongside Cliff Bastin – and while Bastin was the epitome of grace and guile, Drake's strengths were his pace, power and thunderbolt shot. Bastin supplied the artistry while Drake provided a physical cutting edge and their partnership reaped huge rewards.

In his first full season, the 1934–35 campaign, Drake was simply unstoppable in the First Division and his 42 goals in 41 games propelled Arsenal to the title. He was also on target in the FA Cup and the Charity Shield, and his overall haul of 44 remains a Club record for a single season that no Arsenal player has yet surpassed.

More records were to follow and in December 1935 Drake was at his

LEFT: Drake boasted a phenomenal strike rate of a goal in every 1.3 games for the Gunners.

BELOW: Ted Drake terrorised opposition defences with his physicality, fearlessness and devastating shooting.

destructive best when the Gunners faced Aston Villa, scoring all seven goals in a 7–1 victory at Villa Park. His incredible performance is still a record for goals in a competitive game.

Arsenal surrendered the title to Sunderland in 1935–36 despite Drake's 24 league goals but consolation came in the form of victory over Sheffield United in the final of the FA Cup at Wembley. The contest was settled by a single goal and unsurprisingly it was Drake who provided it, lashing Bastin's 74th-minute cross past Blades goalkeeper Jack Smith with his left foot to win the match.

Drake's physical and fearless approach, though, did not come without a price. For the remainder of his days as a Gunner he had to contend with a series of injuries which limited his appearances. Despite the knocks he was to finish as the Club's top scorer in all five of his full seasons in north London.

The 1937–38 campaign saw Arsenal crowned champions once again and although Drake featured in just over half of the league fixtures, his 17 goals were to prove priceless as Allison's side beat Wolves to the title by just one point.

The outbreak of the Second World War brought Drake's Highbury career to an abrupt and ultimately premature end. Aged just 27 at the start of the conflict, he regularly played in the Club's wartime fixtures but a back injury sustained in 1945 forced him to

retire and sadly he never featured in another league game.

Many more games and goals would surely have come had it not been for the War, but his goalscoring record remains an incredible testament to his talents. No Arsenal player before or since has found the back of the net as rapidly as Drake.

In total he scored 139 times for the Club in just 184 appearances. It took him a mere 108 games to record his century of goals – quicker than anyone in the Club's history – and while Thierry Henry, Ian Wright, Bastin and John Radford sit above him in the all-time list of Arsenal marksmen, his goals per game ratio is superior to them all.

After his playing days were cruelly cut short, Drake turned to management, and after spells with Hendon and Reading he was appointed Chelsea boss in 1952. Within three years the Blues were the Division One champions and Drake became the first man to win the title as both player and manager.

Chapman never had the chance to work with him but Drake's prolific if all-too-brief time with the Club certainly proved the iconic Arsenal manager knew a star when he saw one.

ABOVE: Sadly Drake's record-breaking Arsenal career was cut prematurely short by the Second World War.

BELOW: The striker is still the fastest player to register a century of goals for Arsenal.

Name:	Ted Drake
Date of Birth:	16 August 1912 (Southampton)
Signed:	March 1934 (£6,500, Southampton)
Debut:	v Wolverhampton Wanderers (Division One, March 1934)
Arsenal Career:	1934–45
Appearances:	184
Goals:	139
Honours:	Division One (1934–35, 1937–78), FA Cup (1936)

Thierry Henry

An irresistible force for eight incredible seasons, he rewrote the Club's scoring records as he ripped apart Premier League defences.

Elegant, explosive and extravagantly gifted, Thierry Henry was a match winner *par excellence* and even his phenomenal Club record of 228 goals in 337 appearances fails to tell the full story of the Frenchman's impact on both Arsenal and the Premier League.

Henry was two weeks short of his 22nd birthday when Arsene Wenger, his former manager at Monaco, signed him in August 1999 as a replacement for compatriot Nicolas Anelka. The £11 million fee seemed steep after a lacklustre season in Italy with Juventus and when his first eight appearances in the famous red and white failed to yield a goal, the cynics suggested the youngster was no more than an ill-advised import unable to adapt to the notoriously physical rigours of the English game.

On 18 September 1999, however, the story changed when Henry came off the bench in the 71st minute of a Premier League clash with Southampton at the Dell. Eight short minutes later, he collected a Nigel Winterburn pass, turned his marker and curled a glorious right-footed effort into the goal for the winner. A passionate love affair between player and Club had begun in earnest and, once he had ended his initial drought, Henry never looked back.

He finished the 1999–2000 campaign as the Gunners' top scorer with 26 in all competitions and for seven consecutive seasons he led the way for Arsenal in front of goal. It's a feat of prolific consistency that not even the great Ted Drake or iconic

LEFT: Thierry Henry was top scorer in both seasons in which he lifted the Premier League trophy.

BELOW: The Frenchman was as acrobatic as he was destructive during his remarkable Arsenal career.

Ian Wright could match, both players finishing six seasons each as the top scorer.

In 2001–02 Henry was on target 32 times in 49 games in all competitions as the Gunners completed the fabled league and cup double for the third time. Any lingering doubts about Henry's genius evaporated almost as rapidly as the hopes of the opposition defenders deployed to stop him.

The Frenchman's emergence as arguably the most feared striker in Europe coincided with one of the greatest eras in Arsenal's history. His deluge of goals, searing pace and dazzling dribbling were the catalyst for two Premier League and three FA Cup triumphs during his eight-year fairytale stay in north London.

Arsenal's success led inevitably to individual recognition and awards. A two-time PFA Player of the Year and three-time Football Writers' Association Footballer of the Year, Henry also won the Premier League Golden Boot four times and the European Golden Shoe twice.

At his imperious best, he was virtually unplayable and made a mockery of the old adage that some strikers score great goals while others are great goalscorers. The majority of Henry's 228 strikes for Arsenal were both beautiful and pivotal and, while he was ruthless from close range, he was also an artist outside the box.

His most prolific Premier League season for the Club inevitably came in 2003–04 as Wenger's unbeaten Invincibles majestically swept all before them. Henry scored 30 in 37 league appearances as the Gunners claimed the title, cementing his place in the pantheon of the Club's true greats.

When Henry was appointed Club captain in the wake of Patrick Vieira's departure in the summer of 2005, the burden of leadership did not dim his natural instincts in front of goal. In October 2005 his brace against Sparta Prague in the Champions League took him past Wright's record tally of 185. Set just eight years earlier, Wright's milestone seemed to many as if it would never be eclipsed – but Henry was evidently not reading the same script.

His final full season with the Gunners was 2006–07 and, although injury plagued what was to be his farewell campaign, he once again reached double figures in the league despite featuring just 17 times.

The sense of loss around Emirates when Henry signed for Barcelona in June 2007 was palpable. A year after he left for Spain, Arsenal fans still voted him the Gunners' greatest-ever player in an online poll conducted on the Club's official website.

The striker made an emotional if brief return to London in January 2012 when he rejoined on loan from New York Red Bulls. He made just seven fleeting appearances before returning to America but it surprised no-one when he scored a dramatic winner in the FA Cup against Leeds United in his first game back at his undisputed spiritual home.

Henry's individual records – the Club's all-time top scorer, leading Premier League and Champions League marksman – speak for themselves but his balletic displays on the pitch remain as memorable as the pure statistics.

RIGHT: Henry's record haul of 228 goals is a milestone which may never be eclipsed.

LEFT: A young Henry signs for the Gunners in 1999 and a new era for the Club begins.

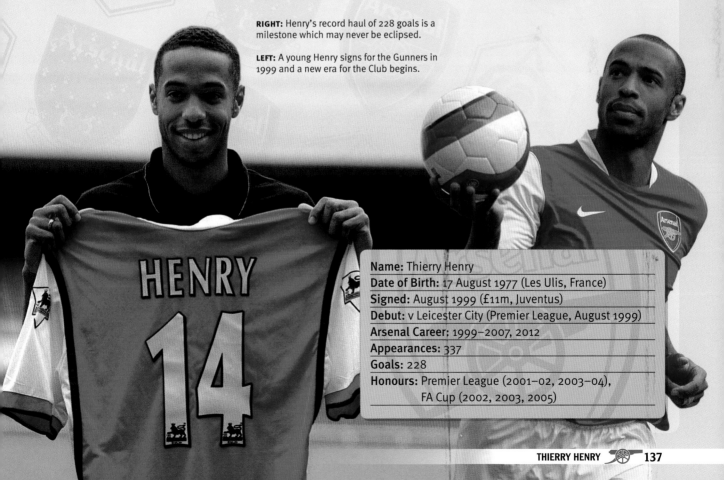

Name: Thierry Henry
Date of Birth: 17 August 1977 (Les Ulis, France)
Signed: August 1999 (£11m, Juventus)
Debut: v Leicester City (Premier League, August 1999)
Arsenal Career: 1999–2007, 2012
Appearances: 337
Goals: 228
Honours: Premier League (2001–02, 2003–04),
FA Cup (2002, 2003, 2005)

Frank McLintock

Frank McLintock galvanized the Gunners for nearly a decade, and never took a backwards step in the Club's battle for trophies.

It was Billy Wright who brought Frank McLintock to Highbury, signing the Scottish international from Leicester City for a Club-record £80,000 in October 1964, but it was his successor Bertie Mee who was to harness the Glaswegian's abrasive talents and transform him into one of the greatest captains in the Club's history.

McLintock was just two months short of his 25th birthday when he arrived in north London. A wing-half by trade, the Scot was the epitome of youthful enthusiasm and aggression, and after making his debut in a defeat against Nottingham Forest, he quickly established himself as a key component in Wright's line-up.

The change of manager in the summer of 1966 saw McLintock's status as a first-team regular unaffected under Mee. But with Arsenal consistently finishing in mid-table, the side's prospects of silverware seemed frustratingly remote and the memories of the Club's 1952–53 title triumph were fading fast.

The 1969–70 season changed everything. A defensive injury crisis forced Mee's hand and he made the bold decision to switch McLintock to centre-half. It was to prove an inspired move and, with the Scot now

LEFT: Frank McLintock celebrates after captaining the side to a 2-1 win over Liverpool in the 1971 FA Cup final.

BELOW: McLintock's switch from wing half to the heart of the Arsenal defence transformed his career.

also wearing the captain's armband, the Gunners' fortunes began to improve dramatically.

Defeats to Leeds United and Swindon Town in the League Cup finals of 1968 and 1969 had at least hinted at progress but the first tangible evidence of McLintock's growing influence came in the 1969–70 Inter-Cities Fairs Cup campaign. With the Scotsman masterfully marshalling the back four, Arsenal conceded just three goals in 10 games en route to the final. Although they were beaten 3–1 by Anderlecht in Belgium in the first leg of the final, McLintock refused to be bowed and a 3–0 triumph in the return match at Highbury six days later saw the Scot lift the trophy.

The Club's first-ever European silverware was to be the hors d'oeuvres rather than the main course and in 1970–71 McLintock was ever-present as the Gunners famously completed the fabled League and Cup double.

By rights, Mee's team had no business claiming the Division One title. The team had finished a distant 12th in the table the previous season, 24 points

adrift of winners Everton, but Arsenal were now an altogether different proposition under the new skipper. They lost just six times as they narrowly edged out Leeds United to become champions.

McLintock was in imperious form throughout. He started all 42 league matches and his immaculate reading of the game, physical presence and forthright leadership saw the team concede only 29 times in a glorious campaign.

Five days after the climax of the league season, it was time for the FA Cup final against Liverpool and a possible place in the history books. McLintock led the side out at Wembley in front of 100,000 supporters and the stage was set for a day of real drama.

The 90 minutes of normal time failed to produce a goal but the Gunners went behind to a Steve Heighway goal early in extra-time and the double dream was dangling by a thread – until McLintock exhorted one last effort from his weary team.

His rallying cry did not go unheeded. Substitute Eddie Kelly equalized in the 101st minute, and when Charlie George beat Liverpool goalkeeper Ray Clemence with a thunderous 20-yard drive 10 minutes later the trophy and the double belonged to Arsenal.

The Football Writers' Association recognized McLintock's contribution to the Club's all-conquering season when they named him Footballer of the Year for 1971. The following year he was awarded the MBE and the Scot was confirmed as one of the Gunners' true greats.

He was to remain the king of Highbury for two more years. The team's 1–0 defeat in the 1972 FA Cup final against Leeds was painful but it could not tarnish the lustre of the previous season's achievements. When McLintock finally parted company with the Club, signing for QPR in the summer of 1973, Arsenal lost one of its finest and most feared leaders.

He was 38 when he finally hung up his boots. His brief forays into management with Leicester and latterly Brentford did not bring great success but that did little to detract from his reputation within Highbury and beyond.

In total, McLintock made 403 appearances for the Club, scoring 32 goals, and in 2009 he was inducted into the English Football Hall of Fame, a fitting tribute to a player who led the Gunners out of the Club's 17-year-long trophy drought.

BELOW: The former skipper was one of the greatest-ever Arsenal players.

LEFT: The Scottish international joined the Gunners from Leicester City in 1964 for a Club record £80,000.

Name:	Frank McLintock
Date of Birth:	28 December 1939 (Glasgow)
Signed:	October 1964 (£80,000, Leicester City)
Debut:	v Nottingham Forest (Division One, October 1964)
Arsenal Career:	1964–73
Appearances:	403
Goals:	32
Honours:	Inter-Cities Fairs Cup (1970), Division One (1970–71), FA Cup (1971)

David O'Leary

The epitome of class and staggering consistency, O'Leary's career spanned three separate decades and a record-breaking 722 first team appearances for the Club.

By his own admission, David O'Leary was far from a typical specimen in the abrasive world of centre-halves. Standing a modest six foot and built like a middle-distance runner rather than an archetypal rugged central defender, the adopted Irishman initially appeared ill-equipped for the physical rigours of his chosen profession.

But what O'Leary may have lacked in height or raw power, he more than made up for with his other attributes. Deceptively quick despite his unmistakable loping gait, unflappable, brave and composed, he oozed class while his Club-record 722 career appearances speaks volumes about his mental and physical durability.

Born in Hackney, O'Leary moved with his family to Dublin when he was just three but returned to England in 1973 when he signed apprentice forms with the Gunners. Two years later he was thrust into Bertie Mee's side just three months after his 17th birthday.

Arsenal were struggling. The previous season the side had finished a lowly 16th, just four points clear of relegated Luton Town, and when O'Leary ran out for his first team debut against Burnley at Turf Moor in August even the most ardent supporters were apprehensively bracing themselves for another difficult campaign.

LEFT: A mainstay of the Gunners' defence for 18 years, the Irishman was a fans' favourite.

BELOW: O'Leary broke into the first team at the age of 17 and never looked back.

The Gunners came away from Burnley with a goalless draw but the fans' fears were confirmed as the season unfolded and once again the side limped home, finishing 17th in the table.

The one bright spot, however, was O'Leary. Partnering either Terry Mancini or Terry Powling in the heart of the defence, the teenager equipped himself with a maturity he had no right to display and made 27 appearances in the first of 17 seasons of loyal service for the Club.

The first silverware of his career came in 1979 when Arsenal faced Manchester United at Wembley in the FA Cup final. It was a pulsating encounter that Terry Neill's side won 3–2 courtesy of Alan Sunderland's last-gasp goal and O'Leary collected his first winner's medal. He was subsequently named in the PFA First Division Team of the Year and his reputation as one of the most accomplished centre-halves in the country continued to grow.

By now the Irishman was part of the furniture at Arsenal and his elegant distribution from the back, his beautifully-timed tackles and aura of calm confidence in even the most frenetic of situations were all reassuringly familiar to the Highbury faithful.

Part of the side that lifted the 1987 League Cup, O'Leary was yet to win the Championship but the arrival of George Graham in 1986 had seen the Gunners emerge as serious contenders and in 1988–89 they ended the Club's 18-year wait for the title. O'Leary played 26 times during the campaign and was part of the team that famously beat Liverpool 2–0 at Anfield in the final, winner-

takes-all match of the season.

Although he was now in his 30s and vying with both Tony Adams and Steve Bould for selection, he continued to play regularly, albeit at right-back, and he clocked up another 21 games during the 1990–91 season as Graham's Gunners were crowned champions for a second time.

The 1992–93 campaign and the advent of the Premier League was to be his last in Arsenal colours and, although he made a modest 11 league appearances, O'Leary ensured he signed off in suitable style with two triumphant appearances at Wembley and two more winner's medals for his collection.

The first instalment of the farewell came at Wembley in April in the shape of the League Cup final against Sheffield Wednesday. O'Leary started in the 2–1 victory over the Owls and he was back at Wembley a month later for the FA Cup final against the same opposition.

This time he was named among the substitutes but came on for extra-time of the 1–1 draw and five days later he was again on the bench for the replay, coming on for Ian Wright after 81 minutes as the Gunners were taken into extra-time before clinching a 2–1 win.

The replay was the 35-year-old's 722nd and final game for the Club and in August he headed north when he signed for Leeds United. Not even team-mate Tony Adams was subsequently able to surpass his record number of appearances and many believe his phenomenal tally will never be eclipsed.

ABOVE: David O'Leary enjoyed the most successful period of his Highbury career under George Graham's management.

BELOW: The defender's elegant efforts earned him six major trophies in Arsenal colours.

Name: David O'Leary
Date of Birth: 2 May 1958 (London)
Signed: Apprentice
Debut: v Burnley (Division One, August 1975)
Arsenal Career: 1975–93
Appearances: 722
Goals: 14
Honours: Division One (1988–89, 1990–91), FA Cup (1979, 1993), League Cup (1987, 1993)

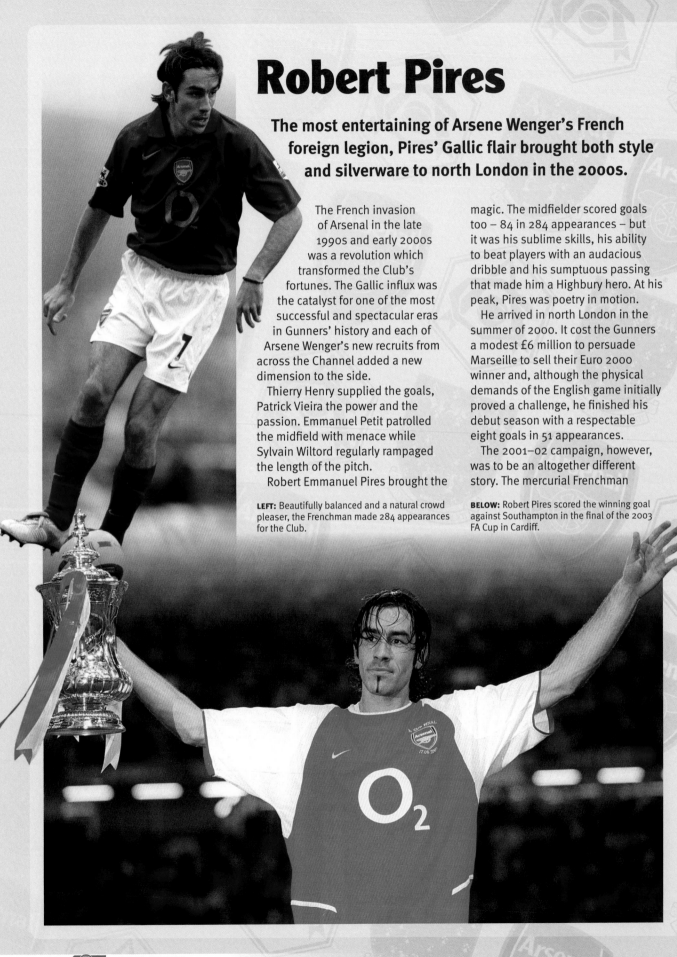

Robert Pires

The most entertaining of Arsene Wenger's French foreign legion, Pires' Gallic flair brought both style and silverware to north London in the 2000s.

The French invasion of Arsenal in the late 1990s and early 2000s was a revolution which transformed the Club's fortunes. The Gallic influx was the catalyst for one of the most successful and spectacular eras in Gunners' history and each of Arsene Wenger's new recruits from across the Channel added a new dimension to the side.

Thierry Henry supplied the goals, Patrick Vieira the power and the passion. Emmanuel Petit patrolled the midfield with menace while Sylvain Wiltord regularly rampaged the length of the pitch.

Robert Emmanuel Pires brought the magic. The midfielder scored goals too – 84 in 284 appearances – but it was his sublime skills, his ability to beat players with an audacious dribble and his sumptuous passing that made him a Highbury hero. At his peak, Pires was poetry in motion.

He arrived in north London in the summer of 2000. It cost the Gunners a modest £6 million to persuade Marseille to sell their Euro 2000 winner and, although the physical demands of the English game initially proved a challenge, he finished his debut season with a respectable eight goals in 51 appearances.

The 2001–02 campaign, however, was to be an altogether different story. The mercurial Frenchman

LEFT: Beautifully balanced and a natural crowd pleaser, the Frenchman made 284 appearances for the Club.

BELOW: Robert Pires scored the winning goal against Southampton in the final of the 2003 FA Cup in Cardiff.

unleashed his full array of attacking talents and he was to be a key figure as Arsenal famously completed a league and cup double.

Pires signalled his intent with a goal in the 4–0 mauling of Middlesbrough at the Riverside on the opening day of the season and never looked back as Wenger's side gathered momentum. The side lost just three times en route to the Premier League title and, while a cruciate ligament injury ruled Pires out of the Gunners' 2–0 win over Chelsea in the FA Cup final, it was his second-minute goal in the quarter-final replay against Newcastle that inspired the team's 3–0 triumph.

The double-winning side of course was brimming with stars, but it was Pires' cultured contribution to the cause that caught the imagination within Highbury and beyond. In 2002 he was named both the Arsenal Supporters' Club Player of the Year and the Football Writers' Association Footballer of the Year.

Pires, however, had unfinished business and 12 months after missing the FA Cup win against Chelsea he was to the fore as Arsenal retained the trophy, scoring the only goal in the final at the Millennium Stadium as Southampton were despatched 1–0.

His role in the Invincibles' breathtaking 2003–04 campaign was even more significant – he hit the winning goals in the league clashes with Everton in August, Liverpool the following month and Southampton in December before scoring the second against Tottenham at White Hart Lane in April to earn the side a 2–2 draw and confirm Arsenal as champions. In total, he scored 19 times from midfield in all competitions in 2003–04, as well as providing 15

assists, and his reputation as one of the English game's most dazzling but deadly performers was cemented.

His rich vein of form continued through the 2004–05 campaign. For the third consecutive season he scored 14 Premier League goals to finish as the division's third most prolific player and, although the title was to elude Wenger's team, there was more silverware in the shape of another FA Cup success. The trophy headed to Highbury for the third time in four years after Manchester United were beaten in a penalty shootout in Cardiff – but the Gunners might not have even reached the final had it not been for Pires' strike in the 1–1 draw with Sheffield United in the fifth round.

The final chapter of Pires' Gunners story was written in 2005–06 – but the climax to his glittering Arsenal career, the Champions League final against Barcelona in Paris, was not the fairy-tale ending he richly deserved.

The eagerly anticipated clash in the Stade de France saw goalkeeper Jens Lehmann sent off after just 18 minutes. Wenger was forced to bring on Manuel Almunia to wear the gloves for the remaining 72 minutes and the manager reluctantly sacrificed Pires as he reorganized his depleted line-up. Arsenal eventually suffered a 2–1 defeat in the French capital and Pires never played for the Club again.

The popular Frenchman headed to Spain the following month when he signed for Villarreal on a free transfer. His six years at Highbury had come to an end but the bitter disappointment of defeat to Barcelona would not overshadow his other magnificent achievements and in 2008 supporters voted Pires as the sixth-greatest player in Arsenal history.

ABOVE: Robert Pires was an integral part of the Gunners' famed Invincibles throughout the 2003–04 season.

BELOW: Despite playing in midfield, Pires still scored 84 goals in six seasons for Arsenal.

Name: Robert Pires
Date of Birth: 29 October 1973 (Reims, France)
Signed: July 2000 (£6m, Marseille)
Debut: v Sunderland (Premier League, August 2000)
Arsenal Career: 2000–06
Appearances: 284
Goals: 84
Honours: Premier League (2001–02, 2003–04), FA Cup (2002, 2003, 2005)

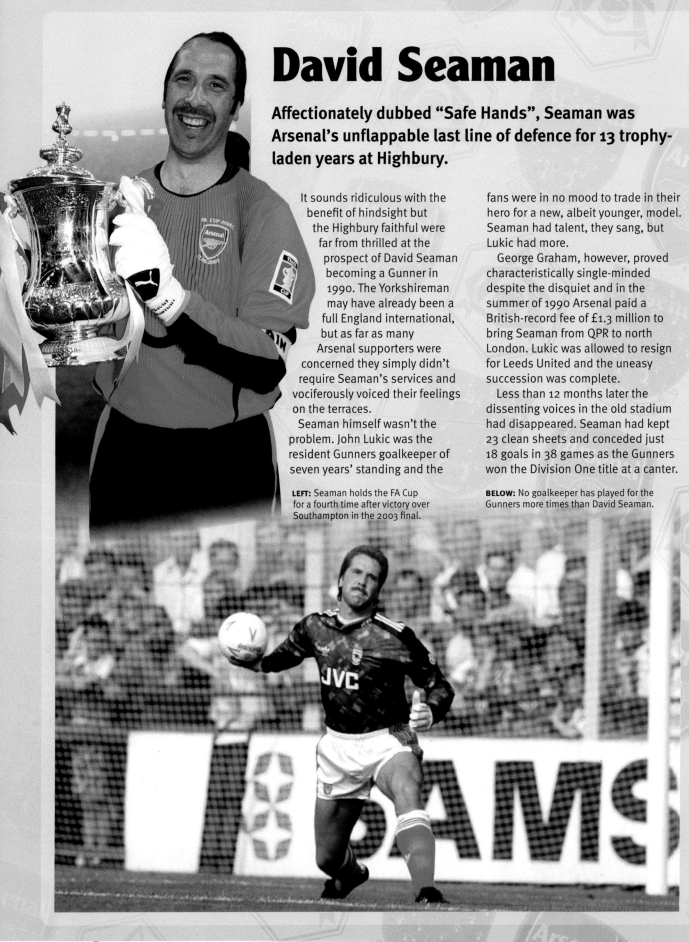

David Seaman

Affectionately dubbed "Safe Hands", Seaman was Arsenal's unflappable last line of defence for 13 trophy-laden years at Highbury.

It sounds ridiculous with the benefit of hindsight but the Highbury faithful were far from thrilled at the prospect of David Seaman becoming a Gunner in 1990. The Yorkshireman may have already been a full England international, but as far as many Arsenal supporters were concerned they simply didn't require Seaman's services and vociferously voiced their feelings on the terraces.

Seaman himself wasn't the problem. John Lukic was the resident Gunners goalkeeper of seven years' standing and the fans were in no mood to trade in their hero for a new, albeit younger, model. Seaman had talent, they sang, but Lukic had more.

George Graham, however, proved characteristically single-minded despite the disquiet and in the summer of 1990 Arsenal paid a British-record fee of £1.3 million to bring Seaman from QPR to north London. Lukic was allowed to resign for Leeds United and the uneasy succession was complete.

Less than 12 months later the dissenting voices in the old stadium had disappeared. Seaman had kept 23 clean sheets and conceded just 18 goals in 38 games as the Gunners won the Division One title at a canter.

LEFT: Seaman holds the FA Cup for a fourth time after victory over Southampton in the 2003 final.

BELOW: No goalkeeper has played for the Gunners more times than David Seaman.

Highbury had a new hero and for the next 12 seasons the adulation showed no signs of waning.

Physically Seaman was the embodiment of a perfect keeper. Six-foot-three and athletic, he was blessed with sharp reflexes and innate bravery while technically he was faultless and read the game like a natural sweeper. Some keepers are famed for their shot-stopping prowess, others for their reliability under the high ball and crosses. Seaman could do it all.

His dazzling debut season was no one-off. The 1993 FA Cup, the first of the four in his career, and the League Cup earlier in the year added to his burgeoning reputation while his bravery was in evidence in the 1994 Cup Winners' Cup final against Parma, playing through the discomfort of a broken rib with a combination of pain-killers and archetypal Yorkshire grit as the Gunners completed a famous 1–0 victory that owed much to a stoical rearguard from Seaman and the

back four as the Italians searched insistently for the equalizer.

But as for so many of his Highbury contemporaries, he was yet to truly scale the heights and it was his typically uncomplicated contribution to the double-winning campaigns of 1997–98 and 2001–02 that cemented his legacy as the greatest keeper in the Club's history.

The 1997–98 season saw Seaman play 31 of the 38 Premier League fixtures en route to the title. He was preferred to Alex Manninger for the FA Cup final against Newcastle and, while the inevitable dimming of the light saw him sharing custodial duties in 2001–02 with Manninger and Richard Wright, he once again played in the Cup final as Chelsea were despatched 2–0 and yet another clean sheet was chalked up on his miserly CV.

The 2002–03 season proved a prolonged goodbye to the Club but there was time yet for both one more magnificent save and one emotional moment of celebratory farewell.

The save came in the FA Cup semi-final against Sheffield United. The Gunners were 1–0 up but seemed destined to be pegged back in the dying minutes when Paul Peschisolido's header flew towards goal – only for Seaman, just five months shy of his 40th birthday, to spectacularly claw his effort towards safety.

In the absence of the injured Patrick Vieira, Seaman captained the side in the final against Southampton in Cardiff. One last clean sheet and a Robert Pires goal were enough to see the veteran lift the famous trophy in his final act in an Arsenal shirt.

A little over two weeks later he was a Manchester City player, although his last hurrah in Manchester was cut short by a shoulder injury. In January 2004, he packed away the gloves and announced his retirement.

His Highbury career encompassed 564 appearances and eight major trophies. In the Premier League he played 344 times and kept 141 clean sheets. He also amassed 72 England caps while he was an Arsenal player. Like all goalkeepers, he made mistakes but they were notable for their rarity.

His trademark pony-tail and moustache were legendary but it is his nickname – "Safe Hands" – that encapsulates his 13 years with the Gunners and how he will always be remembered.

ABOVE: David Seaman kept a remarkable 141 clean sheets in 344 Premier League appearances.

LEFT: The goalkeeper was a pivotal player as Arsenal claimed the double in both 1997–98 and 2001–02.

Name:	David Seaman
Date of Birth:	19 September 1963 (Rotherham)
Signed:	June 1990 (£1.3m, QPR)
Debut:	v Wimbledon (Division One, August 1990)
Arsenal Career:	1990–2003
Appearances:	564
Goals:	0
Honours:	Premier League (1997–98, 2001–02), Division One (1990–91), FA Cup (1993, 1998, 2002, 2003), League Cup (1993), Cup Winners' Cup (1994)

Patrick Vieira

The indomitable heartbeat of the Arsenal side from 1996 to 2005, the French midfielder was both warrior and poet in a Gunners shirt.

When Arsene Wenger agreed to become the new Arsenal manager, he insisted on one condition before officially agreeing to take the Highbury job. It was neither a demand for a generous transfer budget nor a hefty performance-related bonus. The Frenchman simply insisted the Gunners hierarchy sign Patrick Vieira.

Wisely, the Club agreed. It cost £3.5 million to prise the 20-year-old away from AC Milan and, in the summer of 1996, the first recruit of the Wenger revolution arrived in London. The Arsenal faithful may have been unsure what to expect from their new,

unheralded midfielder but their new manager knew exactly what the future held for his new signing.

From the very start, it was utterly impossible to ignore Vieira. His six-foot-four frame made him an intimidating physical presence but his raw power belied his artistry and intelligence and he quickly found the pace, aggression and passion of the English game fitted him like a glove. The Frenchman was a natural football Anglophile and, as he began to exercise a vicelike grip on the Arsenal midfield, the Gunners grew in confidence.

The side finished his debut season seven points adrift of champions Manchester United but 12 months

LEFT: Lifting trophies was a regular event during the Frenchman's nine-year career at Highbury.

BELOW: Patrick Vieira soon became the team's talisman after signing from AC Milan in the summer of 1996.

later, driven relentlessly and robustly on by Vieira, they were Premier League champions for the first time. The midfielder missed just five games and the best was yet to come as Arsenal despatched Newcastle 2–0 in the FA Cup final at Wembley to complete the double.

As the Gunners under Wenger continued to evolve, Vieira's influence increased. The likes of Marc Overmars, Thierry Henry, Freddie Ljungberg and Dennis Bergkamp were all brought in to provide the pyrotechnics but, without Vieira providing the cement, the new-look Arsenal would have been little more than a house built on sand.

The 2001–02 season saw the Frenchman once more integral to the Club's success, playing in 36 of 38 Premier League games as Arsenal once again claimed the title, before nullifying the threat of the Chelsea midfield as Wenger's side beat the Blues 2–0 in the final of the FA Cup to register a second double.

By now Vieira's reputation was almost as fearsome as his performances on the pitch. His angry spats with Manchester United's Roy Keane solidified his public image as a muscular midfield enforcer but he continued to be an infinitely more three-dimensional player who relished galloping forward with the ball at his feet as much as a physical confrontation. Arsenal scored a deluge of goals during his nine-season sojourn in the capital and, although he contributed a relatively modest 33 to that total, he never lacked a genuine goal threat.

In 2002 he assumed the Club captaincy. At any other time, Tony Adams' retirement could have left a dangerous vacuum but Vieira was hewn from the same rock and, in his first season wearing the armband, the team claimed the 2003 FA Cup despite the new skipper missing the final through injury.

The pinnacle of his Highbury career, however, came in 2003–04 as the unbeatable Invincibles ripped up the record books to claim a third Premier League crown. A hamstring injury limited Vieira's games early on in the historic campaign but 22 appearances in the closing 23 matches, scoring pivotal goals in the 2–1 win over Chelsea at Stamford Bridge in February and the 2–2 draw with Spurs at White Hart Lane in April, powered the Gunners to glory.

The 2004–05 campaign was to be his last but the football gods contrived to send him off in the most dramatic style.

The scene was the FA Cup final against Manchester United at the Millennium Stadium and, with neither side able to conjure a goal in 90 minutes or extra-time, the contest headed to a shootout.

After four penalties apiece, the score stood at 4–3 to the Gunners but it soon became 4–4 when Vieira's old sparring partner Keane converted.

The Frenchman only had to score to lift the trophy and in a fitting farewell to the team and the Club, to Wenger and the fans, he beat Roy Carroll and the party began.

A little less than two months later the Gunners accepted a £13.75 million bid from Juventus for the skipper. He was on his way back to Italy and an Arsenal adventure that encompassed 406 appearances was finished.

His departure, though, failed to arouse the ire of the Highbury faithful. They were undoubtedly sad to see him go but the memories of his majestic midfield displays, his rampaging runs and his brooding physical presence were still too fresh and too fond.

ABOVE: Patrick Vieira is one of an exclusive group of Arsenal players to have made more than 400 appearances for the Club.

LEFT: The midfielder succeeded Tony Adams as Arsenal captain in 2002.

Name:	Patrick Vieira
Date of Birth:	23 June 1976 (Dakar, Senegal)
Signed:	September 1996 (£3.5m, AC Milan)
Debut:	v Sheffield Wednesday (Premier League, September 1996)
Arsenal Career:	1996–2005
Appearances:	406
Goals:	33
Honours:	Premier League (1997–98, 2001–02, 2003–04), FA Cup (1998, 2002, 2003, 2005)

Ian Wright

A predatory, tireless and hugely popular marksman, Ian Wright was the man who finally broke Cliff Bastin's long-standing Arsenal scoring record.

There was always an irresistible, irrepressible sense of urgency to Ian Wright's Arsenal career. Perhaps it was the fact that the striker only arrived at Highbury two months short of his 28th birthday, or maybe it was merely his natural hunger for goals, but whenever Wright played, he was invariably in a hurry.

The striker's need for speed reaped phenomenal rewards. For six consecutive seasons he finished as the Gunners' top scorer and in September 1997 he famously broke Cliff Bastin's long-standing record of 178 goals for the Club with

a hat-trick against Bolton Wanderers. Bastin took 396 games to set his milestone, Wright eclipsed it in just 266 appearances for the Club.

Wright scored a dazzling array of goals. A predator at close range inside the box, he also had the ability to produce the spectacular from long range and his explosive pace, energy and perpetual movement made him a constant thorn in the side of every team he faced.

George Graham brought the striker to Highbury in September 1991. Despite an impressive 117 goals in 253 starts for Crystal Palace, some still questioned the wisdom of

LEFT: Ian Wright's appetite for goals was as inexhaustible as the energy and desire he displayed on the pitch.

BELOW: Wright broke Cliff Bastin's Club goalscoring record in 1997 with a hat-trick against Bolton Wanderers.

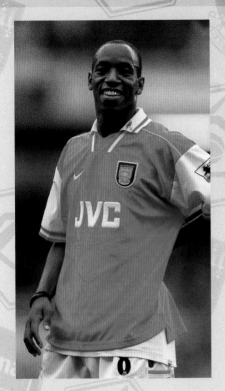

ABOVE: The striker claimed a Premier League winner's medal at the end of the 1997–98 campaign.

investing a then Club-record £2.5 million to persuade the Eagles to sell their prized centre-forward.

The sceptics also pointed out that Alan Smith was still scoring with reassuring regularity and a young Kevin Campbell was maturing into a proven marksman. The new signing, they feared, was an expensive luxury for the reigning First Division champions.

The doubts, however, were immediately dispelled when Wright scored a dazzling hat-trick on his league debut in a Division One clash with Southampton at the Dell. Twenty-three more goals followed during the 1991–92 campaign – including another hat-trick against the Saints on the final day of the season to snatch the Golden Boot from Tottenham's Gary Lineker – and Highbury had a new idol.

The first silverware of his Arsenal career came in 1993 as Graham's side completed a fabulous FA and League Cup double. Wright scored 15 goals in 15 cup appearances as the Gunners beat Sheffield Wednesday in the final of both competitions, including strikes in both the first Wembley match and the replay as they claimed

the FA Cup for the sixth time in the Club's history.

Suspension ruled him out of the team's 1–0 win over Parma in the 1994 Cup Winners' Cup final but the goals continued to flow and his youthful exuberance continued to counter his advancing years. Wright's appetite for the game was his hallmark and, even when he was not on target, his work rate and commitment were beyond question.

The arrival of Arsene Wenger in north London in September 1996 initially cast a shadow over Wright's future. The striker was just two months short of his 33rd birthday when the Frenchman was appointed – but rather than accept a changing of the guard under the new manager, Wright was spurred to even greater heights and under Wenger's watchful eye he responded with 23 goals in 35 Premier League games.

A Premier League winner's medal had so far eluded the centre-forward but there was still enough gas in the tank to complete his collection. Injury and the emergence of Nicolas Anelka limited Wright's appearances in 1997–98 but he characteristically refused to remain in the shadows and his winning goals against Coventry in August and Newcastle in December secured six points that ultimately proved pivotal as Arsenal narrowly edged out Manchester United for the title.

His Highbury farewell came in early May in a 4–0 romp over Everton. Surprisingly, Wright did not help himself to yet another Gunners goal but it was no more than a minor irritation as he said an emotional goodbye to the supporters who had witnessed him find the back of the net an incredible 185 times for the Club

over seven record-breaking seasons.

His last-ever Arsenal appearance came at Aston Villa a week later. Wright was booked, testament to the combative spirit that so naturally complemented his unerring eye for goal, and in the summer of 1998 the 34-year-old was sold to West Ham United.

His career with the Gunners may have been relatively short compared to longer-serving legends but Wright ensured he made the most of every minute of his time. The subsequent exploits of Thierry Henry may have rewritten many of the Club's goalscoring records but, in terms of goals per game for the Gunners, Wright remains the undisputed king.

RIGHT: Wright was the Gunners' leading goalscorer for six consecutive seasons.

Name:	Ian Wright
Date of Birth:	3 November 1963 (London)
Signed:	September 1991 (£2.5m, Crystal Palace)
Debut:	v Southampton (Division One, September 1991)
Arsenal Career:	1991–98
Appearances:	288
Goals:	185
Honours:	Premier League (1997–98), FA Cup (1993, 1998), League Cup (1993), Cup Winners' Cup (1994)

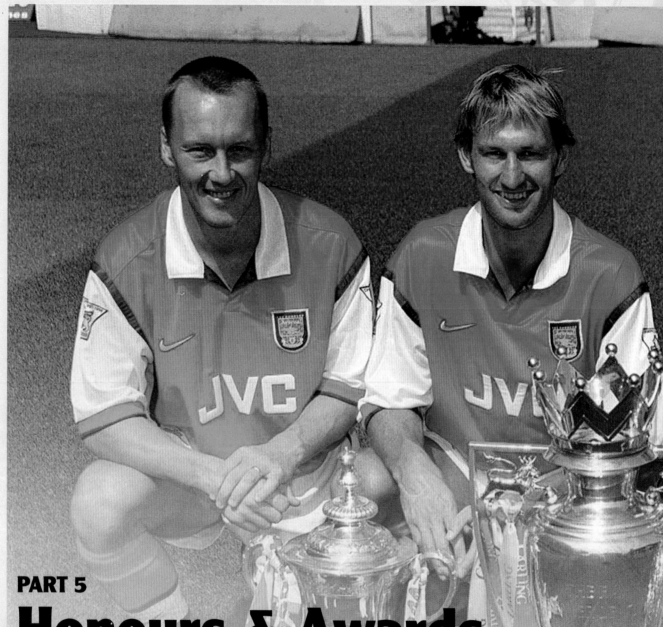

PART 5
Honours & Awards

The late, great Joe Mercer became the first-ever Gunner to win a major individual award when he was named the Football Writers' Association Footballer of the Year in 1949–50 – and ever since, Arsenal players and managers have been winning recognition from the wider football family.

From Liam Brady's breakthrough PFA Player of the Year success in 1978–79 to Thierry Henry's unprecedented double European Golden Shoe triumph, this chapter details the Arsenal players whose performances have earned them personal accolades and awards. There are also details of all of the winners of the coveted Arsenal Football Supporters' Player of the Year, as well as the Club's inductees into the prestigious English Football Hall of Fame.

ABOVE: Arsenal players over the decades have been no strangers to either team trophies or individual accolades.

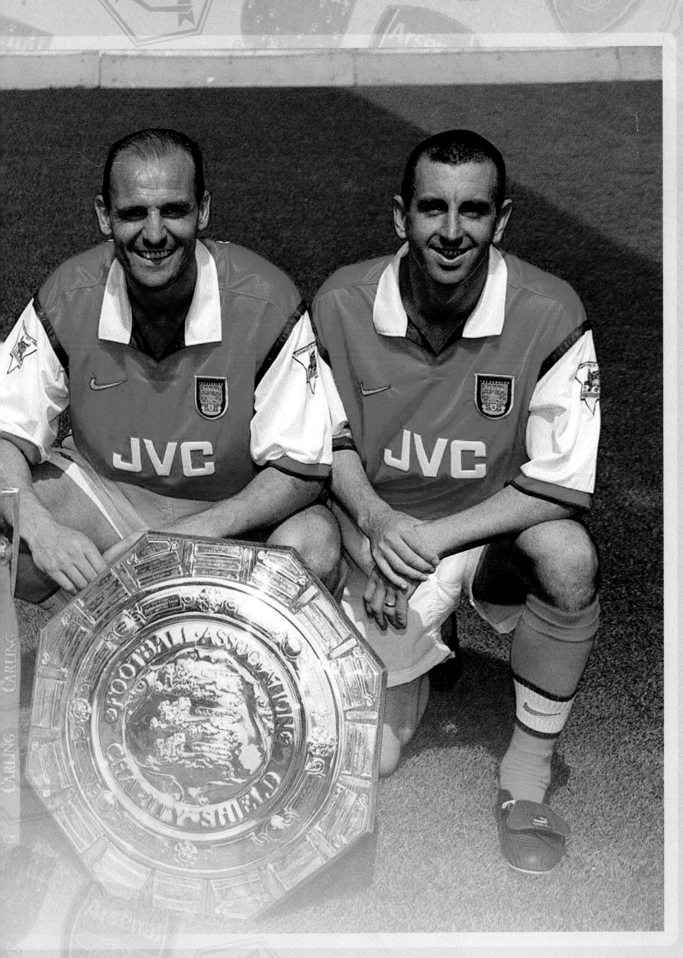

Honours & Awards – Individual

DAZZLING DECADE

The 2000s were one of the finest eras in Arsenal's history and in 2011 Arsene Wenger's role in the Gunners' achievements was recognized when he was named as the decade's greatest manager by the International Football Federation of History & Statistics.

The Frenchman was honoured after the IFFHS devised a points-based system based on results and managerial awards over the past 10 years which saw Wenger beat runner-up Alex Ferguson and third-placed Jose Mourinho to the prize.

FOOTBALL'S FINEST

The English Football Hall of Fame was created in 2002 to honour the game's most iconic players and managers and the first Arsenal inductees to the exclusive club in 2003 were Alan Ball, Pat Jennings and Herbert Chapman.

Tony Adams and Viv Anderson joined them 12 months later while Ian Wright's name was added to the Hall of Fame in 2005.

In 2006 both Liam Brady and Arsene Wenger were recognized by the selection panel and the following year Dennis Bergkamp was also included after a supporters' poll was conducted by the BBC's *Football Focus* programme.

Thierry Henry joined the growing Arsenal contingent in 2008, as did former manager Bertie Mee, while Cliff Bastin, Frank McLintock and Joe Mercer were honoured in 2009.

Former centre-forward and co-founder of the Football Writers' Association Charlie Buchan was inducted in 2010, the most recent Gunner to be nominated for the Hall of Fame which is now housed in the National Football Museum in Manchester.

BRADY HONOURED

The Professional Football Association's Player of the Year Award is one of the most prestigious accolades in the game and the first Arsenal player to earn the recognition of his fellow players was Liam Brady after his stunning contribution during the 1978–79 season.

The Republic of Ireland midfielder was in vintage form with 13 goals in 37 appearances in the old First Division but it was his dazzling displays in the FA Cup, including a Man of the Match performance in the Gunners' 3–2 win in the final at Wembley against Manchester United, that ultimately clinched the playmaker the coveted PFA award.

YOUNG TALENT

The PFA Young Player of the Year Award is presented annually to the most promising and exciting youngster in the top-flight and five Gunners players have received the accolade since its inaugural season in 1973–74.

Tony Adams was the first Arsenal recipient in 1986–87 and two seasons later he was followed by Paul Merson as a PFA winner. Nicolas Anelka won the award in 1998–99 while Cesc Fabregas was honoured in 2007–08.

The most recent young Gunner to be recognized was Jack Wilshere, who collected his award in 2010–11.

LEFT: Arsene Wenger was named Manager of the Decade in 2011 after two league and three FA Cup triumphs.

BELOW: Jack Wilshere's breakthrough in the 2010–11 season was rewarded with the PFA Young Player of the Year award.

FANS' CHOICE

The Arsenal Football Supporters' Club have been voting for their Player of the Year since 1967 and Thierry Henry is the only player to date to have won the award four times. The Frenchman first won the fans' vote in 2000 and after repeating the success in 2003 and 2004, he made it a hat-trick of awards in 2005.

The first recipient of the award was Frank McLintock, while the first player to win it twice was John Radford, who attracted the lion's share of the vote in 1968 and then again in 1973.

The first player from outside Great Britain and Ireland to be honoured was Dennis Bergkamp, who was confirmed as the Gunners' Player of the Year in 1997.

LEFT: Thierry Henry recorded a brace of PFA awards during his Arsenal career.

▲ HENRY'S DOUBLE

Only five players – Mark Hughes, Alan Shearer, Thierry Henry, Cristiano Ronaldo and Gareth Bale – have ever won the PFA Player of the Year Award twice but Henry is the only one to have lifted the trophy in successive seasons.

The legendary French striker was first voted the winner after scoring 33 goals in 55 appearances for Arsenal in the 2002–03 season but was in even more prolific form during the Gunners' famed Invincibles campaign of 2003–04, hitting the back of the net 39 times in just 51 games to help the Club claim another Premier League title and himself back-to-back PFA awards.

▶ MERSON MAKES HIS MARK

The Alan Hardaker Trophy has been presented to the Man of the Match of the League Cup final since 1990 and to date the only Arsenal player to win the trophy is Paul Merson.

The midfielder won the prize in 1993 after the Gunners' 2–1 victory over Sheffield Wednesday at Wembley in recognition of his equalizing goal for George Graham's side and his subsequent assist for Steve Morrow's winner.

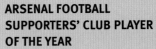

ARSENAL FOOTBALL SUPPORTERS' CLUB PLAYER OF THE YEAR

1967	Frank McLintock
1968	John Radford
1969	Peter Simpson
1970	George Armstrong
1971	Bob Wilson
1972	Pat Rice
1973	John Radford
1974	Alan Ball
1975	Jimmy Rimmer
1976	Liam Brady
1977	Frank Stapleton
1978	Liam Brady
1979	Liam Brady
1980	Frank Stapleton
1981	Kenny Sansom
1982	John Hollins
1983	Tony Woodcock
1984	Charlie Nicholas
1985	Stewart Robson
1986	David Rocastle
1987	Tony Adams
1988	Michael Thomas
1989	Alan Smith
1990	Tony Adams
1991	Steve Bould
1992	Ian Wright
1993	Ian Wright
1994	Tony Adams
1995	David Seaman
1996	Martin Keown
1997	Dennis Bergkamp
1998	Ray Parlour
1999	Nigel Winterburn
2000	Thierry Henry
2001	Patrick Vieira
2002	Robert Pires
2003	Thierry Henry
2004	Thierry Henry
2005	Thierry Henry
2006	Jens Lehmann
2007	Cesc Fabregas
2008	Cesc Fabregas
2009	Robin van Persie
2010	Cesc Fabregas
2011	Jack Wilshere
2012	Robin van Persie
2013	Santi Cazorla
2014	Aaron Ramsey
2015	Alexis Sanchez

LEFT: Paul Merson was in magnificent form as the Gunners beat Sheffield Wednesday in the 1993 League Cup final

Honours & Awards – Combined Team

The Professional Footballers' Association Team of the Year was first unveiled in 1973–74 but it was not until the 1977–78 season that an Arsenal player was included in the end-of-season XI when Liam Brady was named in a side that also featured Manchester United's Gordon McQueen, Martin Buchan, Steve Coppell and Joe Jordan, Nottingham Forest duo Peter Shilton and John Robertson, Aston Villa's John Gidman, West Bromwich Albion's Derek Statham, West Ham's Trevor Brooking and Birmingham's Trevor Francis.

The Gunners' largest contingent in the prestigious PFA team came 26 years after Brady's breakthrough on the back of the Invincibles' exploits during the 2003–04 campaign when six Arsenal players were named in the side.

The full line up was: Tim Howard (Manchester United), Lauren (Arsenal), Sol Campbell (Arsenal), John Terry (Chelsea), Ashley Cole (Arsenal), Steven Gerrard (Liverpool), Frank Lampard (Chelsea), Patrick Vieira (Arsenal), Robert Pires (Arsenal), Thierry Henry (Arsenal), Ruud van Nistelrooy (Manchester United).

ABOVE: Liam Brady was the first Gunner to be included in the PFA Team of the Year.

GOALS GALORE

The European Golden Shoe has been awarded to the leading goalscorer in matches from the top division of each European league since 1967–68 and Arsenal have twice boasted the Continent's most prolific marksman.

On both occasions it was Thierry Henry who collected the award, courtesy of his 30 Premier League goals in 2003–04 and his 25 strikes during the 2004–05 season.

MEDIA EXPOSURE

The Football Writers' Association Player of the Year award has been won eight times by six different Arsenal players since Blackpool's Stanley Matthews first received the accolade in the 1947–48 season.

The first Gunner to be recognized by the football scribes was left-half Joe Mercer in 1949–50, while centre-half Frank McLintock won the award 21 years later.

Dutch striker Dennis Bergkamp was honoured in 1997–98 and Robert Pires in 2001–02. Thierry Henry won his first FWA title in 2002–03 and completed his hat-trick, the only player in the award's history to be named the winner three times, in 2005–06.

The Club's most recent recipient was Robin van Persie in 2011–12, who was honoured after scoring 37 times in 48 Arsenal appearances.

RIGHT: Joe Mercer made history in 1950 when he was named the FWA Player of the Year.

▶ WENGER'S TRIUMPH

The League Managers Association has been naming a Manager of the Year since 1994 and Arsene Wenger is one of only four men to have received the accolade twice in his career.

The Frenchman was first recognized by his peers in 2002 after masterminding Arsenal's Premier League title triumph, and two years later he collected the award for a second time after his side famously went the entire league campaign unbeaten.

▶ GREATEST GOALS

The BBC's *Match of the Day* has organized its "Goal of the Season" competition since the 1970–71 season and on four occasions an Arsenal player has scored the winning effort.

Dennis Bergkamp was the first to be recognized for his spectacular score against Leicester City at Filbert Street during the 1997–98 campaign, a breathtaking example of first-time control and vision. The mercurial Dutchman made it a BBC double in the 2001–02 season with a sublime flick, turn and finish against Newcastle United at St James' Park.

The following season it was Thierry Henry who was the winner after a superb, long-range solo effort in the north London derby against Tottenham at Highbury,

while Emmanuel Adebayor was the 2007–08 recipient of the award after another clash with Spurs, beating Paul Robinson at White Hart Lane with a stunning volley from the edge of the area.

ABOVE: Arsene Wenger was honoured by his managerial peers in 2002 and again in 2004.

BELOW: Emmanuel Adebayor's spectacular strike against Spurs earned him the 2007–08 "Goal of the Season" accolade.

SANSOM'S RECORD

The player with the record number of appearances in a PFA Team of the Year is Kenny Sansom, with 11 separate nominations in the combined side.

The former Arsenal full-back was first included in the old Third Division Team of the Year in 1976–77 when he was a Crystal Palace player and subsequently made the First Division Team of the Year for 1980–81 after his summer switch from Selhurst Park to Highbury.

His 11th and final nomination came in 1986–87, featuring alongside fellow Gunners Viv Anderson, Tony Adams and David Rocastle.

ARSENAL'S FWA PLAYER OF THE YEAR AWARDS

1949–50	Joe Mercer
1970–71	Frank McLintock
1997–98	Dennis Bergkamp
2001–02	Robert Pires
2002–03	Thierry Henry
2003–04	Thierry Henry
2005–06	Thierry Henry
2011–12	Robin van Persie

Index

Picture Credits

The publishers would like to thank the following sources for their kind permission to reproduce the pictures in this book.

Photography © Arsenal Football Club with the following exceptions:

Colorsport: 5L, 13TR, 14, 15, 16TR, 18BR, 19L, 38, 39TR, 39B, 40BL, 40BR, 49TR, 50TL, 52R, 55TR, 57TR, 61, 64BL, 64TR, 65R, 66TR, 68TR, 70TR, 72TL, 74BL, 76T, 79BL, 80BR, 82BL, 84B, 85TR, 87TL, 88TR, 88B, 91B, 96C, 102TR, 103, 104BL, 104R, 105TL, 105BR, 108, 109, 116TR, 122TL, 123BL, 123TR, 128, 129, 132TL, 132B, 133BL, 133TR, 134L, 137BL, 138L, 138BR, 139BL, 140TL, 140B, 141TR, 144B, 154T, 154BR; /Darren Blackman: 92B; /Andrew Cowie: 10-11, 12TR, 34L, 42TR, 45BL, 47, 53BL, 69B, 71T, 75TR, 81BL, 83, 86BR, 92TR, 114BR, 119TR, 148TL, 153TL; /Colin Elsey: 9; /Stewart Fraser: 75BL; /Matthew Impey: 126L; /Stuart MacFarlane: 4R, 25R, 26B, 33TR, 46, 58B, 80TR, 82BR, 126B, 145TR, 150-151; /Tomikoshi: 90BL; / Mike Wall: 117R; /Wilkes: 69T, 73R, 86TL, 93BR, 102L

Getty Images: /Bentley Archive/Popperfoto: 8R; /Bongarts: 90TR; /Shaun Botterill: 51TR, 59T; /Clive Brunskill: 56T, 118R; /Central Press: 134BR; /Phil Cole: 55BR; /H F Davis/ Topical Press Agency: 36B, 68BL; /Paul Ellis/AFP: 87B; /Evening Standard: 62TR; /Evening Standard/Hulton Archive: 98B; /Stu Forster: 49BL; /Fox Photos: 135B; / George Freston/Fox Photos: 84TR; /S R Gaiger/Topical Press Agency: 20TR; /Fiona Hanson/AFP: 121B; /Mike Hewitt: 111B; /Hulton Archive: 12BL; /Kirby/Topical Press Agency: 21L; /Alex Livesey: 91T; /Dennis Oulds/Central Press: 114TR; /Popperfoto: 63TR, 89TR, 99TR, 101B, 135TR; /Ben Radford: 26TR, 93TL; /Michael Regan: 152TL; /Bob Thomas: 8BR, 17BL, 19R, 37TR, 53R, 99BL, 116BR; /Bob Thomas/ Popperfoto: 13C, 17BR, 18L, 45BR, 85BL; /Topical Press Agency: 110TL; /Topical Press Agency/Hulton Archive: 60

Press Association Images: 54B, 101TR, 152BR; /AP: 110T; /S&G and Barratts: 52B, 97B, 111TL; /SMG: 89BL

Every effort has been made to acknowledge correctly and contact the source and/or copyright holder of each picture and Carlton Books Limited apologises for any unintentional errors or omissions that will be corrected in future editions of this book.